A cultural and transformative guide to thrive abroad

GLOBAL
Citizen

TOYI RODRÍGUEZ

ISBN: 979-8-9920836-0-6 (Hardcover)
ISBN: 979-8-9920836-1-3 (Paperback)
ISBN: 979-8-9920836-2-0 (Kindle)

LIBRARY OF CONGRESS CATALOGING-IN PUBLICATION DATA
Name: Rodriguez, Toyi (author)
Title: Global Citizen: A Cultural and Transformative Journey / by Toyi Rodriguez
Description: Carmel, IN (2025)
p. cm.
Includes bibliographical references.
Library of Congress Control Number: 2024926693
1. Self-help
2. Memoir
3. Travel / Immigration
First Edition: March, 2025
For more information, visit: toyirodriguez.com
Cover design by Toyi Rodriguez.
Cover Adaptation by Monica Chavez & Adam Hay
Edited by: Toyi Rodriguez
Proofreading Assistance by William Johnson and Francisco Olguin.
Picture by: Karina Roe

To Jose Luis, Andrea, and Luis
I love you with my whole heart.

CONTENTS

A cultural and transformative guide to thrive abroad

GLOBAL
Citizen

TOYI RODRÍGUEZ

INTRODUCTION

"You are only free when you realize you belong no place–you belong every place–no place at all."
— *Maya Angelou*

The pandemic brought unexpected challenges and transformations for all of us, but it was particularly poignant for two of my closest friends. After living in the U.S. with their families for corporate assignments, they returned to their home countries, each with unique experiences. Their journeys reflected the highs and lows of expat life—moments of triumph and resilience alongside the struggles of adapting to new languages, cultures, and professional landscapes.

As a Destination and Intercultural Consultant, I had spent years guiding expats through these challenges, equipping them with tools to survive and thrive in their new environments. Yet, during the global shutdown, my career was put on hold as borders closed and relocations halted. This rare pause allowed me to reflect deeply on the core question that defined my work: Why do some individuals flourish in these transitions while others struggle to find their footing? This period of introspection allowed me to gather insights from both personal and professional perspectives, enriching my understanding of the challenges of cultural adaptation and the essential factors that contribute to a successful, fulfilling experience.

Global Citizen is the result of that introspection—a blend of practical advice, heartfelt empathy, and the wisdom gained from years of navigating the intricate dance of cultural adaptation. It's written for anyone standing at the crossroads of change, ready to embark on a journey of growth, resilience, and discovery.

My friend inspired this book—the one who faced the greatest challenges while living abroad. It points towards the advice I shared with her during her time in the U.S. and the guidance I wish I had been able to provide before her return home. Initially, I set out to compile a few practical tips to support my clients once borders reopened, helping them navigate their transitions with confidence and ease. What started as a modest advice collection became a comprehensive guide, eventually evolving into this book.

As you turn these pages, I hope you feel the presence of a trusted friend—someone who truly understands your journey and is here to listen, encourage, and support you every step of the way. You are not alone in this adventure! Let me help you uncover the opportunities and growth this incredible experience offers and make it as rewarding and fulfilling as possible.

WHAT YOU CAN FIND IN THIS BOOK

As a passionate advocate for diversity and inclusion, my mission is to inspire a mindset of empathy, curiosity, and respect when approaching cultural differences. Through this book, I aim to foster meaningful emotional and intellectual connections by providing a roadmap for understanding and embracing diverse perspectives. *Global Citizen* reflects my commitment to this vision, combining practical insights from my professional experience as an Intercultural Consultant—where I've supported dozens of families from 28 different nationalities in adapting to new environments—with a wealth of knowledge gained through personal interactions with individuals from over 100 nationalities.

This book is also deeply personal. It draws from my 25-year journey living abroad in Belgium, the United States, and Mexico and traveling to 48 countries in Asia, Europe, Africa, and the Americas. Each chapter is infused with lessons learned, stories shared, and a profound belief in the transformative power of cultural exploration.

Global Citizen is a self-help book that combines elements of a memoir, motivational tips, quotations, research, and common-sense Expat talk. Its prevailing message revolves around successfully interacting and communicating with people from diverse cultures and embracing the experience of living abroad. It's aimed at anyone looking for new experiences in a foreign country or curious about diversity.

This book is designed to be flexible. You can read it cover to cover or jump to the chapters most relevant to you. Chapter 1 lays the foundation for understanding cultural differences by reflecting on your values, beliefs, and biases. From there, feel free to explore topics that resonate with your needs and experiences, culminating in Chapter 16, which invites you to reflect on your journey and discover your most authentic self.

The book unfolds in two distinct parts, each designed to equip you with the tools to thrive in a globalized world. The **first part** takes you on a deep dive into understanding diverse cultures, empowering you to learn and communicate across cultural boundaries with ease and empathy. Bridging cultural gaps fosters mutual respect and lays the foundation for more harmonious relationships.

Too often, well-meaning interactions lead to conflict, missed opportunities, or diminished trust simply because we struggle to grasp different cultural perspectives. I aim to reduce this confusion by promoting cultural sensitivity and offering insights into diverse traditions and values, ultimately fostering a world where differences are embraced rather than misunderstood.

This section spans eight thought-provoking chapters and weaves the wisdom of cultural theorists, sociologists, anthropologists, and psychologists, blending these insights with my observations and the latest research—chapters three through seven focus on exploring specific cultural dimensions, spotlighting their contrasting extremes. Packed with relatable examples and actionable strategies, these chapters serve as a practical roadmap to help you navigate cultural differences confidently.

The book's **second part** also contains eight chapters, each filled with practical tips and guidance on adapting to a new environment. From deciding whether to move to mastering a new language and making friends, these chapters draw on insights from psychology, philosophy, and sociology. The content is rooted in personal experience and thorough research, with real-life examples and valuable advice. Finally, the book concludes with Chapter 16, inviting you to discover your most authentic self.

I aim to empower you to embrace a new culture, learn from diverse experiences, and ultimately find a deeper understanding of yourself. This is more than just a guide; it's an invitation to transform and fulfill your potential. You will discover that every interaction and cultural adaptation compels you to rethink who you are at your core, challenging your perceptions and pushing you to grow. Ultimately, true freedom lies not in tying yourself to one place or identity but in finding authenticity and connection wherever you are, transcending societal labels and social norms, and allowing yourself to exist authentically anywhere.

In essence, the heart of this book is to help you:

- Gain a deeper understanding of other cultures and perspectives.
- Promote global human connection and collaboration.
- Overcome obstacles and difficult situations when moving to a new environment.
- Make a new place feel like home.
- Celebrate individual uniqueness.

Whether you're an expat, a traveler, or simply someone curious about the world, I hope this book inspires you to reflect on why you and others think, act, and believe as you do. This book is crafted to guide you toward a more authentic life while encouraging you to cultivate empathy and curiosity toward others. As you journey through these pages, you may find the inspiration to live with an open heart and a readiness to learn from the world around you.

WHY THIS BOOK?

I wanted to write a book that would help people successfully adapt to a new country, break down biases and stereotypes, foster genuine relationships, and develop a profound appreciation for the diverse ways people experience the world to make the journey as rewarding as possible.

Living abroad isn't just about changing your address—it's about transforming your perspective. It's an invitation to step beyond the familiar and immerse yourself in a world brimming with new ideas, people, and ways of life. It's about discovering who you are when faced with the unfamiliar and how you grow when you embrace the unexpected. It comes with challenges but also incredible rewards. The obstacles you encounter are opportunities for growth, resilience, and a broader perspective on the world.

Living abroad has been one of the most transformative experiences of my life. It has broadened my horizons, strengthened my adaptability, and reshaped my understanding of the world. I've seen how it has profoundly impacted others, too—challenging preconceived notions, cultivating independence, and forging deep bonds with people from vastly different backgrounds.

As you embark on your journey, I hope this book becomes a trusted companion. To help you navigate the challenges, celebrate the joys, and embrace the adventure of becoming part of a global community. As you explore these pages, you'll uncover strategies for thriving in new environments, insights to help you question your assumptions, and stories to inspire you to dive wholeheartedly into the experience.

Living abroad is about discovering yourself. It accelerates personal growth in ways staying home never could. With this book by your side, I hope you'll find the courage to push past your comfort zones, the wisdom to appreciate diversity, and the joy of creating a sense of belonging wherever you are. Open yourself to a world of growth and transformation that can enrich every facet of your life.

WHAT IS CROSS-CULTURAL AWARENESS?

The intercultural field emerged as a response to the growing need to understand and navigate cultural differences, gaining momentum after World War II. Concerns about hate and violence among religious, ethnic, and cultural groups, coupled with increasing global interactions in diplomacy, business, and military contexts, highlighted the importance of fostering cross-cultural understanding. Rooted in anthropology, sociology, psychology, and linguistics, the field aims to bridge divides and reduce misunderstandings by promoting empathy, cultural intelligence, and mutual respect.

Various factors, including personal experiences, social norms, stereotypes, biases, and emotional responses, shape our perceptions and opinions about others. Stereotypical categorization, or the "least effort principle," often leads us to make assumptions based on superficial traits like appearance, body language, or tone of voice.

While stereotypes are a natural part of cognition, and these mental shortcuts help us process information quickly, they are frequently unfounded and result in inaccurate judgments, fueling prejudice, division, and discrimination. Prejudice typically stems from fear, ignorance, and misunderstanding rather than reason, creating barriers to meaningful connection.

Misunderstandings often arise from invisible cultural boundaries and unspoken norms, causing well-intentioned individuals to misinterpret each other's actions or intentions. By recognizing these influences and questioning our assumptions, we can form fairer, more empathetic perceptions, improve our ability to interact across cultures, and create a more harmonious world.

A PERSONAL NOTE ON THE CONTENT

This book fosters mutual understanding and appreciation across cultures, encouraging unity, respect, and empathy for everyone regardless of color, race, gender, language, or beliefs. I hope that learning about our differences will help bridge divides, overcome misunderstandings, and create a more harmonious and inclusive world.

I have worked to remain sensitive, respectful, and mindful when addressing cultural differences, but I recognize that culture is a sensitive topic and that some comments may be interpreted differently. If any part of this book unintentionally offends, please know that was never my intention. This book is not intended to point fingers, judge, generalize, or reinforce stereotypes. Instead, my goal is to highlight the beauty of cultural diversity to foster understanding and respect, not division, and to help you navigate the misunderstandings and misinterpretations that can arise from these differences.

Everyone is unique; some come from diverse, multifaceted backgrounds that blend elements from multiple cultures. Even within the same country, significant sub-differences are shaped by factors such as geography, religion, race, urban or rural settings, economic status, immigration's influence, and the length of time someone has lived in a particular place. It's important not to make assumptions about a person's traits based solely on their place of origin. While I have done my best to avoid generalizations, some were necessary to provide practical guidance. Please consider the ideas presented as broad principles rather than absolute rules—exceptions will always exist, and no single perspective can encompass the full range of human experiences.

I write from my perspective as an intercultural consultant, drawing on personal observations and professional insights. Therefore, some of my observations may differ from your own experiences. I am also fully aware of my privileges and recognize that not everyone shares them. However, I believe the principles in this book are relevant to most people, regardless of their circumstances.

I recognize the biases inherent in my background. While biases are a natural part of being human, I consciously try to remain aware of them. I aim to approach each interaction with openness, respect, and a genuine desire to understand.

I believe that most people are inherently good, have kind intentions, and genuinely wish to understand and connect with one another. Misunderstandings often arise from ignorance rather than malice, situations we've all found ourselves in at some point. We can't appreciate something that we do not understand. Our differences should never divide us; instead, we can learn from them and see them as opportunities for growth and self-discovery.

I hope this book serves as a small step toward easing conflicts, resolving misunderstandings, and promoting empathy and respect, which would lead to deeper relationships and a more harmonious world.

With gratitude,
Toyi Rodriguez

PART I

Getting to know each other

*Cultural Differences and Unspoken
Languages of The World*

Cultural differences have long shaped human history, defining communities while uniting us through shared humanity. At the heart of these differences lies an intricate web of unspoken languages—gestures, customs, rituals, and silent cues that convey meaning far beyond words. These subtle yet profound forms of communication reveal the essence of who we are, shaping our identities and interactions.

In this section, we'll explore the fascinating world of cultural differences, unspoken languages, and cultural nuances that define societies around the globe. From the subtle art of nonverbal communication to the traditions that anchor identities, we'll uncover how these elements shape relationships, foster understanding, and sometimes spark confusion. Understanding these hidden codes will empower you with a deeper insight into the world.

Together, we'll uncover the implicit rules that govern behavior across cultures. You'll discover how body language transforms across regions, how a simple gesture in one culture can carry an entirely different meaning in another, and how silence can speak volumes depending on the context. We'll also explore the rituals and unwritten etiquette that define social interactions, revealing the depth of cultural expression.

Understanding and respecting cultural differences can facilitate meaningful and effective communication in business, diplomacy, or everyday encounters. Beyond practical benefits, this journey into cultural awareness is also a path toward greater empathy. Learning about the customs and nonverbal communications of others offers profound insight into their values and perspectives, fostering a sense of connection that transcends superficial differences.

As we dive into this rich world of cultural dynamics, I encourage you to approach it with curiosity and openness. Embrace how humanity expresses itself and celebrate the diversity that makes our world extraordinary. In doing so, you'll deepen your understanding of others and enrich your appreciation for the complexity and beauty of human culture.

CHAPTER 1

Beneath the cultural surface

"A nation's culture resides in its people's hearts and soul."
— *Mahatma Gandhi*

DISCOVERING THE DEPTHS OF CULTURAL DIFFERENCES

Before I lived in the US, I believed I had a solid understanding of American culture. I had traveled to the country several times, interacted with some Americans, learned about its geography and history, watched numerous movies and TV shows, and memorized the lyrics to dozens of songs. I knew I needed to work on my English, but I assumed that was the only cultural aspect I was missing.

I was so wrong!

I quickly realized that cultural differences extend beyond language, architecture, weather, clothing, food, or art. The more I interacted with Americans, the more I uncovered the non-universal aspects of cultures that shaped our interactions and worldviews. Here are some of the assumptions I initially made:

- **Humor:** I thought we all laughed at the same jokes and found the same things funny.
- **Values**: I assumed values were universal and everyone prioritized the same things in life.
- **Privacy**: I believed we all shared similar levels of openness and expected the exact boundaries in sharing information and spending time with friends or family.

- **Respect and Power**: I thought respect and admiration were shown for the same traits everywhere, and I assumed people understood which behaviors were respectful and appropriate in different situations.
- **Etiquette**: I assumed that dress codes, concepts of modesty, and rules of etiquette were consistent worldwide.
- **Body Language**: I considered everyone interpreted hand gestures, signs, physical touch, and personal space similarly.
- **Conversation Topics**: I thought we all knew which topics were appropriate for specific situations and conversations.
- **Voice Volume**: I assumed we all adjusted our voice levels similarly according to our emotions and the context.
- **Justice, Fairness, and Ethics**: I believed that concepts of right and wrong were as universally clear-cut as black and white.
- **Communication**: I assumed everyone could "read between the lines" and grasp contextual clues in conversations.
- **Work**: I thought we all understood the roles of bosses, subordinates, and co-workers the same way, along with how to show respect and make a good impression at work.

My notions of a one-size-fits-all culture were entirely mistaken. While some similarities do exist, there are notorious differences, too. Each of these areas held unique cultural distinctions that I had overlooked, and this realization reshaped my understanding of what it truly means to connect across cultures. For instance, in Mexico, we make fun of ourselves and laugh at our mistakes or misfortunes. Sometimes, our jokes might seem cruel to outsiders, but it's our way of relaxing, staying happy, and not taking life too seriously when we have little or no control over a situation.

Mexican humor is rich and diverse. We enjoy clever wordplay and puns, often using double meanings to create humorous and sometimes risqué jokes. This type of humor, known as "album," is a verbal art form that involves quick thinking and cultural knowledge. Making fun of oneself or our shortcomings, dark humor, cultural and social satire, and irony are commonly used in Mexico.

We make jokes and memes about everything: earthquakes, fires, politics, presidents (both good and bad), divorce, death, birth, women, men, doctors, lawyers, everyday life, pets, school, work, physical attributes, and ourselves. We laugh and aren't easily offended, even if someone makes fun of us. We often respond with another joke and laugh again.

However, what is considered teasing in Mexico may be perceived as bullying in another country. If these kinds of jokes were told openly in the US or many other countries, they could be highly offensive, prohibited, or illegal. Nevertheless, not all Mexican jokes are mean-spirited; many are universally funny and easy to understand. The same goes for humor around the world. Each country has a unique style of humor and inside jokes that outsiders may not understand, at least not initially.

Each type of humor reflects the unique cultural landscape from which it arises, providing insight into what different societies find amusing and why. Understanding humor offers a glimpse into the intricate layers of cultural identity, but it's just one piece of a much larger puzzle. To fully appreciate the complexities of human interaction, we must step back and explore the broader concept of culture itself.

WHAT IS CULTURE?

Culture is a complex and broad concept encompassing the social behavior, norms, knowledge, beliefs, arts, laws, customs, capabilities, and habits of individuals within a group. It includes how people do things, why, and the meanings they assign to these activities.[1]

Elements of a culture:

- **Values and Beliefs**: The core principles and ideologies that guide behavior and provide a sense of right and wrong.
- **Social Norms and Customs**: These are the rules and expectations by which a society guides the behavior of its members. These can be explicit laws, or implicit social rules passed down through generations.
- **Language**: The spoken words, written symbols, and nonverbal signals used to communicate, all of which carry cultural meanings.
- **Art and Symbols**: Visual arts, literature, music, and cultural symbols that convey a culture's aesthetic values and shared history.
- **Rituals, Traditions, and Ceremonies**: Regularly practiced activities that reinforce the values and norms of the culture, including religious ceremonies and community celebrations.
- **Technology and Tools**: The products and techniques a culture develops, reflecting its values and priorities in solving problems and making life easier.
- **Education and Knowledge**: How a culture transmits knowledge and skills to its members, including formal and informal education.
- **Social Institutions**: Organized structures within a society that meet the needs of its members and maintain social order.

- **Economic Systems:** The methods and principles by which a culture produces, distributes, and consumes goods and services.

CULTURAL ICEBERG

In 1976, inspired by the icebergs, Edward T. Hall developed the Cultural Iceberg Model as an analogy for culture. The concept is that we can only see a small portion of the iceberg above the surface while the much more prominent part remains hidden below. This hidden part represents culture's intangible and profound aspects, such as values and beliefs. The Cultural Iceberg Model explores and explains the complexities of culture—what is seen and what remains hidden.[2]

Visible elements of culture

Some of these components are easy to observe and tangible, like music, dance, food, language, architecture, clothing, art, and cultural symbols like flags, religious icons, or national emblems. These cultural components can be experienced with our senses; we can taste, hear, see, touch, or smell. They represent a small part of their culture.

Invisible elements of culture

The larger and more complex part of any culture is more challenging to see. This is the deeper part, which includes preferences, opinions, values, and beliefs. Attitudes toward marriage, gender, elders, authority, foreigners, and death. Their non-verbal communication includes facial expressions, eye contact, personal space, greetings, signs, tone of voice, and silence. Rules of etiquette, manners, and sense of humor. Roles related to gender, age, hierarchies, and class. Perceptions of morality, beauty, leadership, modesty, time, formality, and justice. These hidden aspects are often more challenging to understand and articulate.

For example, in a *business meeting*, the visible aspects would be the dress code, formal language, and meeting protocols. The hidden elements would be attitudes toward hierarchy, the importance of relationships, and approaches to decision-making. In social interactions, the visible elements would be greetings, body language, and social rituals. The hidden elements include personal space, emotional expressiveness, and informal vs. formal behavior.

Understanding the cultural iceberg model is crucial for effective cross-cultural communication and interaction. Misinterpretations often arise when we judge a culture based only on its visible aspects without recognizing the deeper elements that influence behavior.

In the following chapters, we will delve deeper into specific cultural elements, focusing on the intangible aspects of deep culture—the often unseen and most challenging parts to understand. Yet, it is precisely these elements that allow us to form deep connections with others.

Surface Culture
Language
Music   Food
Gestures & Greetings
Architecture   Literature
Art   Clothing   Holidays
Traditions & Festivals
Society Roles & Expectations Concept of Time
Definition of Right and Wrong
Biases Values Beliefs Concept of Justice
Notion of Modesty   Personal Space
Notions of Respect & Politeness
Attitudes Toward Work & Success
Body Language   Family Values
Hierarchy & Authority Perception
Communication Styles
Pride and Honor
Concept of Beauty
Deep Culture   Gender Roles
Work Ethic
Manners

Figure 1: The Cultural Iceberg

YOUR CULTURAL ICEBERG

Understanding your cultural iceberg is essential to becoming more self-aware and improving your interactions with people from different cultures. Just as we use the cultural iceberg model to understand others, we can also use it to explore and analyze our cultural background, values, and behaviors. This chapter will guide you through uncovering your culture's visible and hidden aspects and understanding how it shapes your identity and worldview.

To understand another culture, you must first understand your internal culture and identify your beliefs, biases, thoughts, drives, and values. These will help you to discover your most authentic selves and grow personally, emotionally, and spiritually. In this chapter, I want to encourage you to look within.

Who are you?

A person's identity is multifaceted, combining both tangible and intangible elements. Try to answer this question without mentioning your name, role, profession, or physical attributes. You are defined by your values, beliefs, dreams, goals, achievements, aspirations, passions, skills, behaviors, biases, what you stand for, and what matters to you.

Identity encompasses how one perceives oneself and how others recognize them across different contexts. It integrates various aspects of an individual's life, encompassing a range of personal, social, and cultural components. Understanding the diverse elements of an identity can facilitate deeper self-awareness and more meaningful interactions with others. This holistic approach acknowledges the richness of individual and collective human experiences by recognizing and understanding the depth of personal identities. It reflects the complexity of human life and the diverse influences that shape our perceptions of ourselves and others.

In 1902, sociologist Charles Horton Cooley presented his perspective: "I am not who I think I am; I am not who you think I am; I am who I think you think I am."[3] This quote underscores the complexity of identity, highlighting how others' opinions influence our perception of ourselves and, inevitably, our perception of others.

We all face external pressures throughout our lives. Our family, friends, religion, society, and media dictate what we should be and do. When we tailor our identities to meet others' expectations, we often feel unhappy, depressed, unworthy, or dissatisfied.

We are typically surrounded by others who behave similarly to us. When we move to another place, the exposure to new cultural norms and values drives us to reflect on our values and beliefs. This process leads to either the reinforcement or abandonment of those beliefs.

Living in another country can profoundly affect your identity, influencing and reshaping how you see yourself and others perceive you. This experience impacts various dimensions of your identity, exposing you to diverse experiences, values, and belief systems that can help you better understand yourself. How can you know if you like or dislike something if you have never tried or experienced it?

EMBRACING SELF-DISCOVERY TO NAVIGATE A DIVERSE WORLD

Our needs, wants, desires, values, and beliefs influence our emotions, actions, and behaviors. In other words, they drive our lives. Embarking on a journey of self-discovery can be profoundly rewarding. It can help you understand your true self, align your life with your innermost desires and values, and improve your interactions with others. This is the crucial first step and the foundation for ensuring a fulfilling and enriching experience while living abroad. Here are five simple steps to guide you through this transformative process:

1. Reflect
2. Identify your core values
3. Discover your beliefs
4. Recognize your biases
5. Examine social norms and expectations

Self-discovery also involves understanding your strengths and weaknesses, identifying your passions, and recognizing your emotional patterns, but I won't delve into these here.

1. Reflect

Dedicate time regularly for deep thinking or journaling about your experiences, what you feel passionate about, and where you find meaning. Silence the outside voices and external influences, listen to your own, and don't lose sight of your true self.

Analyze and question your fears, thoughts, behaviors, emotions, beliefs, motives, and doubts. They are good indicators for discovering your authenticity. What is underneath them? Why do you continue to hold on to them?

2. Identify your core values

Values help us navigate through life wisely. They are more than just personal preferences; they are deep-rooted assumptions that guide our behaviors and influence our social interactions and emotional responses. Understanding and reflecting on your values can lead to greater self-awareness, better relationships, and behaviors that align with your goals.

Being aware of your values and beliefs requires deep self-awareness. Interestingly, while most people can quickly identify their favorite color, song, or food, they often lack insight into their core values. They tend to follow the expected societal norms without much reflection. This can become particularly challenging when moving to a new country, where cultural differences lead to shock as the societal norms shift in unfamiliar ways. Understanding and clarifying your values provides a compass, helping you navigate these unfamiliar cultural currents more quickly and confidently.

I recommend making a long list of the values that are important to you. Then, brainstorm and ask reflective questions that help you dig deeper into your beliefs and motivations to identify your core values.

What were the most rewarding moments of your life? Why did these moments feel so fulfilling—what values were you honoring?

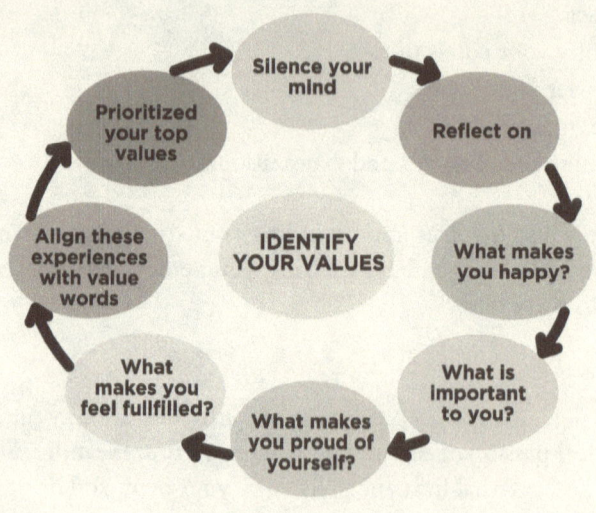

Figure 2: Identify Your Values

Here are some thought-provoking questions to help you discover and define your core values:

- When have you felt the happiest, more content, or fulfilled? Analyze what was happening at these times and what values were being met.
- What was a time when you were at your best, and why? Which values did you honor?
- Think about times you were upset or frustrated. What values were being challenged or ignored in these situations?

- What are your most significant accomplishments?
- Who do you admire most and why? What qualities do you admire in your friends and why?
- How have your upbringing and background influenced your values?
- Are there any qualities in others that you can't tolerate?
- What legacy do you want to leave behind? How would you spend your time if money were no object?
- What activities make you lose track of time?
- What are deal-breakers for you in relationships? Knowing what you cannot tolerate can often highlight your values.
- What does success mean to you?
- What injustices or problems do you feel most passionate about?

These questions provoke deep thinking and reflection about what truly matters to you. It's an excellent way to determine whether your values are genuinely your own or imposed by society. This process can be complex but essential in the journey of self-discovery.

Now, review your list with your previous answers in mind. Prioritize your values by importance and narrow them down to the top three to five. These core values will offer you a clearer sense of direction and purpose.

The Impact of Values When Living Abroad

Values are beliefs, opinions, or ideals that shape our perceptions and actions. While some values may evolve with circumstances, core values are deeply ingrained and form a vital part of our identity. These intrinsic principles are essential to recognize and uphold, mainly when living abroad.

Relocating to a foreign country can leave you feeling vulnerable and distanced from familiar surroundings such as family, friends, and your usual environment. Some individuals may compromise their core values to adapt to a new culture and fulfill the innate need for connection. This compromise, however, can lead to frustration, sadness, resentment, or even depression, as it may feel like a betrayal of one's authentic self.

Encountering a different culture exposes you to diverse experiences, values, and belief systems, offering an opportunity for self-reflection and insight. Growth and personal enrichment emerge when this process aligns with your core values, allowing you to remain true to yourself. Also, when our values align with moral virtues, embracing them with discretion—free from fanaticism—enhances our character and fosters genuine acceptance.

Approach the experience with openness and a willingness to adapt, flexibly embracing new perspectives and values. Strive for personal growth and self-improvement, but prioritize honoring and protecting your core values. Treat yourself with compassion and take pride in the principles that define you. Those who remain rooted in their values while embracing cultural differences tend to have a clearer sense of purpose, make thoughtful decisions, and lead more fulfilling lives.

3. Discover your beliefs

What are your fundamental beliefs? Those that influence significant life decisions or your perspective on controversial issues? These include assumptions about politics, religion, morality, relationships, career, and personal capabilities.

For each belief, try to trace its origin. How did you come to hold this belief? Is it based on personal experiences, influences from others (family, friends, mentors), cultural background, or education?

Evaluate the evidence that supports your beliefs. Consider: is my belief based on factual, reliable information or assumptions? Have I actively sought out information that both supports and contradicts this belief?

Actively challenge or question your beliefs by exposing yourself to different perspectives. Challenging your assumptions is not about proving yourself wrong but ensuring your beliefs are as accurate and constructive as possible. It's a courageous and enlightening process that not only strengthens your convictions but also makes you more open and empathetic towards the views of others.

Expand your horizons by reading a variety of books and articles, exploring different perspectives, and watching news from diverse sources. Engage in meaningful conversations with people with opposing viewpoints, approaching these discussions respectfully and open-mindedly. Doing so will challenge your thinking, foster greater understanding, and develop a broader worldview. This practice sharpens your critical thinking and deepens your empathy for others' experiences and beliefs.

Emotional solid attachments can often cloud our judgment. Are you holding onto this belief because it makes you feel safe, comforted, or justified? Would you come to the same conclusion if you set aside emotions (fear, anger, safety, confusion)?

Prepare yourself to change your beliefs if evidence and reason suggest you should. Changing a belief doesn't mean you were wrong; it signifies intellectual maturity and critical thinking skills.

4. Recognize your biases

The Oxford Dictionary defines bias as *"a prejudice in favor of or against one thing, person, or group compared with another, usually in a way considered unfair."* [4]Biases can affect our perceptions, decisions, and interactions subtly but significantly.

188 known cognitive biases that impact our thinking and actions. [5]These biases arise from various factors, including information processing shortcuts, emotional motivations, and social influence. We all have biases, but by becoming aware of them, we can make more informed decisions and foster greater understanding and equity in our interactions.

Despite often having a negative connotation, biases can also be helpful in specific contexts. Their impact depends on the context and how they are applied. While they can lead to errors and prejudices, they also serve essential functions that can enhance decision-making, social cohesion, and personal well-being. Recognizing the dual nature of biases can help us leverage their benefits while mitigating their potential downsides.

The biases are sorted into smaller groups, including cognitive, social, memory, perception, decision-making, and specific context biases. Here are some tips to identify your bias:[6]

Identifying your bias begins with self-awareness and critical reflection on your thought processes. Actively seek out information that challenges your beliefs. For instance, when researching or forming an opinion, deliberately look for opposing evidence or perspectives and evaluate them with an open mind. This approach can help prevent the tendency to only focus on data that supports your preconceptions.

Practice mindfulness and deliberately expand your focus beyond immediate thoughts or emotions. When you notice that you're concentrating on specific details, ask whether there might be other relevant factors you are ignoring. Question whether your beliefs or actions are driven by independent thought or the influence of others around you. Being aware of social pressures can help you maintain objectivity.

For social biases like ingroup bias and outgroup homogeneity bias, reflect on your assumptions about people from different social groups. Challenge your natural tendency to view your group as more diverse and outsiders as more homogeneous. This bias can be reduced by interacting with people from diverse backgrounds and avoiding overgeneralization. Regarding stereotyping and prejudice, be conscious of the assumptions you make based on someone's appearance, race, or background, and try to treat everyone as a unique person rather than as a group representative.

For decision-making biases, like *status quo* bias and loss aversion, consider how fear of change or loss influences your decisions; recognizing when you cling to the familiar simply because it's comfortable or when you avoid risks due to potential loss can help you make more balanced and rational choices.

Understanding these biases can help develop strategies to counteract their influence, promoting more rational decision-making and fairer, inclusive social interactions. Each type of bias provides a specific challenge to objective thinking and impartial judgment, revealing the importance of awareness and corrective measures in our thinking patterns.

Be mindful of your language and reactions in various situations, particularly when interacting with individuals from different racial, gender, sexual, or socio-economic backgrounds. The words you use and how you respond to people from diverse groups can reveal subtle, underlying biases you might not be aware of. Regularly reflecting on these interactions can help you identify patterns indicating prejudiced assumptions or stereotypes.

Diversify your environment. Actively seek out and engage with people, cultures, and ideas different from yours. Exposing yourself to various perspectives can challenge and ultimately reduce your biases. Become more aware of your immediate reactions and the thoughts behind them. Commit to ongoing education on issues of prejudice and discrimination. This can include reading books, watching documentaries, and attending workshops.

When you assume, please step back and ask why you think that way and whether the evidence supports it. Recognizing and addressing your biases contributes to fairer interactions and decisions in your personal and professional life.

5. Examine social norms and expectations

Consider the social norms and behaviors that are common in your culture. How do people interact? What are the unspoken rules about respect, communication, and relationships? What is considered wrong and right, moral and immoral? What's the concept of beauty, success, and love? What are the gender, status, or rank roles?

Pay attention to behaviors, practices, and beliefs commonly accepted in your society. Note any patterns in how people act and what they consider "normal." Question norms and think critically. Reflect on your behavior and assumptions. Consider which norms you follow and why.

- Why does the norm exist? Who established it, and for what purpose? Who benefits from it? Who might be disadvantaged or harmed by it? Does it promote equity and justice? Is it based on logic, tradition, or both?

- Here are some questions that can help you explore and learn more about a more profound culture:
- What are the roles and responsibilities of different family members? How are elderly people treated and regarded in your culture?
- What are the cultural norms around marriage and relationships? How are children raised and educated in your culture? What is the importance of extended family and community in your culture?
- What are the major cultural or religious holidays, and how are they celebrated? What are some important life-cycle rituals (birth, coming of age, marriage, death)?
- How are traditional stories and myths passed down through generations?
- What are the core values that your culture emphasizes? How does your culture view honor, respect, and duty? What are the primary religious or spiritual beliefs in your culture?
- How do people communicate respect or disrespect? What role does non-verbal communication (gestures, body language) play? How are stories, proverbs, and folklore used in communication?
- Are there any food-related customs or taboos? How do cultural practices influence food choices and eating habits? What role do communal meals play in your culture?
- What are the cultural norms around modesty and appearance? What are the traditional clothing styles and their meanings? How do people dress for different occasions (festivals, ceremonies, daily life)?
- What are the expectations for behavior in public and private settings? How is the hospitality shown to guests and strangers? What are the norms for greeting and addressing others?
- What are the customs around gift-giving and receiving?
- How is conflict typically resolved within the community?
- What are some significant historical events that shaped your culture? How is cultural heritage preserved and celebrated? What are the stories of major cultural heroes or figures? How has your culture evolved? How do colonization, migration, or globalization influence your culture?
- What are the attitudes towards gender roles and equality in your culture? How are traditional values and practices being maintained or adapted today?
- How is your culture represented in the media, and how does this impact cultural identity?

These questions can initiate a profound and meaningful exploration of culture, revealing the intricate layers that shape its essence. To truly grasp the power of tradition and cultural norms, it helps to see how they manifest in real-life decisions, often intertwining with deeply personal moments. One such example from my life is the story of my wedding dress.

MY WEDDING DRESS

Choosing what to wear on a significant day like your wedding isn't just about personal style; cultural norms, family traditions, and societal expectations deeply influence it. Here's a relatable example highlighting the significant influence in shaping a person's decision (and life): my wedding dress.

For many women, the most important dress in their lives is often considered to be their wedding dress. While the significance of a dress may differ depending on personal experiences and cultural backgrounds, the wedding dress is typically seen as the most meaningful due to its profound emotional, symbolic, and aesthetic importance. It represents a pivotal moment and serves as a lasting reminder of the day a woman celebrated her love and commitment to her partner.

If it's the most important dress in a woman's life, wouldn't it be chosen in our favorite color and in a pattern and style that represents our unique personality? We usually choose the design and style, but what about the color? If you live in a Western culture like me, would you consider using a red, green, black, or any bold color for your wedding dress?

My wedding dress was... you guessed it—white! Or ivory, if I wanted to make it sound more unique. It was white, just like my mother, grandmother, and all the women in my family for generations. I remember asking why white since I would have chosen many other colors. The answer was unanimous: white symbolizes purity, virginity, and new beginnings in Western culture. I wasn't convinced, though—after all, women marrying for the second or third time still wear white. For me, the color didn't carry any deep symbolic meaning; it was simply about tradition.

The values of purity and virginity for women have been deeply ingrained in my culture for generations. While newer generations may approach these concepts differently, the tradition of wearing white wedding dresses remains strong, and its cultural meaning has not significantly changed.

Although I appreciate the elegance and beauty of white, my favorite colors are red and blue. If I chose a wedding dress based on symbolism, I would undoubtedly opt for red, which represents love, passion, desire, energy, joy, and excitement—qualities I value more than the traditional notions of virginity and purity.

Still, the thought of departing from the tradition of wearing white never occurred to me. The custom was so embedded in my upbringing that I always imagined myself in a beautiful white gown on my wedding day.

Years passed, and one day, while living in Belgium and waiting for my massage appointment to start, I read a wedding article in a magazine. Something caught my eye: a gorgeous wedding dress. It was elegant, sexy, super feminine, and it was RED! Until then, I had wrongly assumed all wedding dresses were white.

Red is traditionally the color worn by brides during Indian weddings. It symbolizes prosperity, fertility, and marital bliss. The red bridal sari or lehenga is regarded as fortunate and thought to attract good luck to the marriage. Red is also believed to have protective qualities.

To my surprise, red is a traditional (though not exclusive) wedding dress color in several countries and cultures worldwide, including China, India, Vietnam, Nepal, Pakistan, Bangladesh, South Korea, Turkey, and Japan. In these cultures, red carries various symbolic meanings, such as good luck, joy, prosperity, purity, love, commitment, happiness, spirituality, and protection. Additionally, in many other countries, brides often wear colorful dresses adorned with floral patterns or geometric designs, showcasing the rich diversity in wedding traditions around the globe.

Curious about the history of our white wedding dresses, I discovered that wearing a white wedding dress is relatively recent in marriage customs. From Biblical times through the early 19th century, brides in Western culture did not traditionally wear white. Not only was a white dress seen as impractical,[7] but it was also not financially wise for brides to purchase a dress to wear only once.

In 1840, Queen Victoria of the United Kingdom wore a white gown for her wedding to Prince Albert. Their wedding was one of the first heavily photographed royal weddings. She chose to wear a white dress in Honiton lace to help the struggling factory where the fabric was created. She accessorized her white gown with a flower crown instead of a tiara to show she would be a more down-to-earth monarch[8]. Her choice was highly publicized and widely admired, setting a trend that would be followed by many brides after that.

In the past, white clothing was difficult to maintain and clean and could be worn only by the wealthy. Wearing a white wedding dress signified affluence and high social status, implying that the bride and her family could afford a dress that might be worn only once and required careful upkeep.

The bridal industry and popular media have continued reinforcing the tradition of white wedding dresses. Bridal magazines, movies, and advertisements frequently depict brides in white gowns, perpetuating the idea that a white dress is the standard for weddings. So, it was not necessarily the symbol of purity and innocence commonly thought. According to the history of white wedding dresses, white was seen as a color for the rich, more about showing off one's affluence rather than purity.

However, traditions and their significance also change and adapt through the years. Today, many brides choose white simply because it represents a timeless aesthetic or reflects their personal style or cultural heritage. The meaning of a white wedding dress has evolved, shifting from a symbol of wealth to a varied and unique one, as the brides who wear it.

This is a clear example of the power of traditions. Brides have been wearing white dresses for their weddings worldwide for years without questioning or trying to change the tradition. Even as modern society has evolved, challenging and redefining notions of purity and virtue, the tradition of the white wedding dress has remained largely unaltered.

In every corner of the globe, weddings have long been a mix of traditions, cultural values, and societal expectations passed down through generations. The white dress has become more than just a garment; it symbolizes conformity to a cultural norm and societal expectations that have stood the test of time. This dynamic reveals a fascinating aspect of human behavior: the willingness to adhere to traditions, even when they no longer align with contemporary values. It reminds us how deeply rooted customs, societal values, traditions, and expectations can influence our thinking, beliefs, and actions.

I'm not suggesting that customs or traditions are inherently wrong. They serve an essential purpose by helping individuals stay connected to their cultural roots and fostering a sense of identity and continuity. Traditions often honor history and keep us linked to the past, reminding us of the values and collective experiences passed down through generations. They create a sense of belonging and help strengthen relationships within communities. Moreover, traditions bring structure and meaning to key life events, offering comfort and stability, especially during times of change, while reinforcing important cultural and moral principles.

I do not regret wearing a white dress at my wedding. It was a beautiful reflection of tradition and my vision for the day. However, it also serves as a powerful reminder of how deeply ingrained customs and societal expectations can be and how they influence our personal choices—often without us realizing it. While traditions can offer comfort, identity, and unity, it's important to reflect on whether they align with our values and desires or if we are following them out of habit or social pressure. Ultimately, recognizing this balance allows us to honor the past while creating space for individual expression.

KEY TAKEAWAYS

- Cultural differences extended far beyond surface elements like language and food.
- Culture encompasses social behavior, norms, knowledge, beliefs, arts, laws, customs, capabilities, and habits, shaping how people do things and the meanings they assign to activities.
- The Cultural Iceberg Model by Edward T. Hall's model illustrates those visible cultural elements (e.g., music and food) are just the tip of the iceberg, while deeper, invisible elements (e.g., values and beliefs) lie beneath the surface.
- To understand another culture, one must first explore their internal culture, values, beliefs, biases, and social norms. This self-awareness fosters personal, emotional, and spiritual growth.
- Identifying and honoring core values is crucial, especially when living abroad, to maintain a sense of identity and navigate new cultural environments without sacrificing essential personal values.
- Traditions shape and reflect societal values. Despite changing values, traditions persist due to social pressure and collective cultural memory.

CHAPTER 2

Right, wrong, or different

"It is not our differences that divide us. It is our inability to recognize, accept, and celebrate those differences."
— *Audre Lorde*

When we learn to view things from various angles and shift our perspectives, we often discover that there can be multiple correct answers or ways of doing things. We tend to believe that our experiences and beliefs define what is accurate, and anything that deviates from them must be wrong. However, this isn't always the case. Embracing diverse perspectives reveals the richness of alternative approaches and reminds us that truth and rightness are not always absolute.

From birth, we are taught how to behave, dress, act, eat, and distinguish right from wrong according to society's expectations. Religion, culture, and traditions are key in shaping who we are and how we think. We grow up with norms, rules, and standards that guide our behavior within social groups, passed down through generations, and reinforced by family, friends, teachers, and religious figures to help us adapt.

We are taught appropriate behaviors for various contexts, such as dressing for church, work, or dinner, greeting others, showing respect, and practicing politeness. Yet, these concepts are relative, varying widely between families, individuals, or places. What one person considers proper conduct might be entirely the opposite for someone else. Despite our good intentions, actions can sometimes be misinterpreted by those from different backgrounds.

So, what happens when you find yourself in an unfamiliar environment with norms and traditions that differ from yours? What if their conduct— perfectly acceptable in their society—feels impolite or disrespectful in yours?

Do you feel left out, misunderstood, or even discriminated against? Do you avoid interaction out of confusion or self-protection?

Are they wrong? Are you right? Or are we simply different?

In the following pages, I will share examples from my experiences with various cultures and traditions. I'll explore how to navigate these nuances with understanding and how to find common ground.

MATERNITY WARD

I grew up in Mexico, where family, friends, and social interactions form the foundation of our core values. When a baby is born, it's customary for family and a large group of friends to visit the hospital to meet the newborn and congratulate the parents. While hospitals often feel tense with concerns about a loved one's health, the maternity area is a vibrant and joyous place.

In Mexico, the maternity ward is filled with flowers, presents, balloons, and people eager to share on the special day. The new parents often prepare small souvenirs, usually chocolates in beautifully decorated boxes, as gestures of gratitude for everyone who comes by. Not visiting the new baby within the first few days might be seen as a lack of friendship or indifference, so we prioritize and make time to visit.

A few months after moving to Memphis, we received an email from our American friends, Bonnie and David, announcing the birth of their first child. As we would have done in Mexico, we left work, stopped by a store for flowers and a gift, and headed to the hospital to meet the new family member. But when we arrived, we were surprised to find an empty hallway with no signs of visitors, flowers, or vibrant decorations (except for some signs at the door: "It's a boy or a girl"). When we knocked, David opened the door, surprisedly greeted us, and asked if we wanted to come in. Inside were only the couple and their newborn— no bustling crowd, just they and us, the two unexpected intruders.

Awkward!

We were at a loss for what to do, as it was immediately evident that they hadn't anticipated any visitors. Despite their surprise, they welcomed us warmly, and we shared a brief, precious time with their newborn before leaving. We couldn't help but wonder why no one else had come. In Mexico, a new baby would typically attract a crowd. The absence of visitors might have suggested some labor complications, poor health, or strained social ties.

The explanation had nothing to do with health concerns or social dynamics. It was straightforward: cultural differences—ones we hadn't recognized or understood.

In the U.S., only close family members and a few best friends typically visit parents in the hospital. In contrast, in Mexico, I've seen hospital rooms filled with more than ten people inside, with even more waiting outside for their turn to enter.

Years later, my husband and I moved to Columbus, Indiana, where Bonnie and David had also relocated, coincidentally. Shortly after, I became pregnant with our daughter, Andrea. Our friends threw baby showers for her, and when Andrea was born, my parents flew in from Mexico to be there and help the inexperienced new parents.

Andrea was born at 4 a.m. after 16 hours of labor. My parents, who had been in the waiting room the whole time, came immediately to our room to meet and hold their granddaughter in their arms. We took pictures and shared the news with loved ones, who responded with heartfelt congratulations.

Around 7 a.m., I finally managed to close my eyes, hoping for a bit of rest, but the nurse arrived shortly after to ensure I had fed the baby. By 8 a.m., the pediatrician was there to check on Andrea. Around 9 a.m., the hospital photographer came by not long after to take family photos—an offer I promptly declined. I wasn't up for looking like a zombie holding a baby and didn't have the energy to get dressed for the occasion. Just as I was settling back in, around 9:30 a.m., the gynecologist appeared to check on me, followed by the nurse again. And so it continued—an endless parade of doctors and nurses, each with their tasks.

By 5 p.m., I hadn't slept in over 40 hours and was utterly exhausted. At that moment, I finally understood why some people prefer not to have visitors right after giving birth. Yet, just an hour later, my Latin friends arrived with presents and flowers, just as I had anticipated. Somehow, my Latin spirit kicked in, and the pride and excitement of introducing our daughter to them gave me a surge of energy, allowing me to stay awake and savor those precious hours together. Following our Mexican tradition, we handed out boxes of chocolates with Andrea's name as a thank-you to each friend who visited us.

Unlike in Mexico, though, none of my American friends visited us at the hospital. Only Bonnie and David, who had experienced our Mexican customs during their years there, showed up. Instead, our American friends visited after we had returned home. They didn't come for a social call; they came bearing meals—three- and four-course home-cooked dishes that they dropped off without expecting to stay or see us. I didn't have to cook a single meal for nearly two months. This gesture of kindness and practicality was a beautiful gift that allowed me to rest and spend time with my newborn. This was a tradition I hadn't encountered in Mexico, but it quickly became one I sincerely appreciated and adopted.

When we returned home, we placed a pink "it's a girl" balloon on our front door—a gesture we'd seen others use to announce that the baby had arrived home. Soon after, some neighbors quietly left presents and cards on our porch, not ringing the bell to avoid disturbing us or risking waking the baby.

Fast-forward to 2009, when my son Luis was born, and the hospital had changed its policies—limiting visitors and setting strict visiting hours. Maybe they'd had enough of us foreigners turning the maternity ward into a fiesta! While it did weaken our usual celebrations, we adapted and moved the party back home. It's worth mentioning that all of this happened pre-pandemic. Since then, hospitals worldwide may have also implemented new rules regarding gatherings and visitors.

This experience taught me a valuable lesson: people offer what they value most to those they care about. For some, it's presence and physical connection; for others, it's time and practical support. I felt loved and appreciated by both groups. My Latin friends gave me the laughter, hugs, and companionship I craved. In contrast, my American friends offered time and thoughtful support that eased my transition into motherhood and allowed me to spend precious time with my newborn.

So, who did it the "right" way? Was it my friends who came to the hospital or those who waited to meet the baby and brought meals? In the U.S., showing up unannounced might be seen as intrusive, whereas in Mexico, not visiting immediately could be perceived as indifference. What is considered correct in the U.S. could be seen as wrong in Mexico, and vice versa.

Fortunately, my friends, Bonnie and David, understood we arrived with the best intentions, unaware of the customs and nuances at play., just as I refrained from assuming my American friends were distant simply because they didn't follow my Mexican expectations. It's easy to fall into the trap of thinking our way is the only way. We might judge others based on their behavior, dress, or interaction, mistakenly labeling differences as shortcomings.

I felt incredibly blessed and grateful for the beautiful gestures of affection from my Latin and American friends. Each group gave us their time, made an effort, and showed their friendship and love. Both wanted to make us happy, hosted beautiful baby showers for us, and were exceedingly generous—they expressed it uniquely.

These differences often create substantial cultural barriers. The unfamiliar, the unknown, a lack of empathy, and the fear of belonging can hinder our ability to form connections with those different. However, my experiences have shown that understanding the reasons behind these differences helps bridge the gap and builds connections. Rather than labeling, judging, or avoiding others based on these differences, I encourage you to ask questions and approach with empathy.

When adapting to new traditions doesn't contradict our core values, embracing and learning from differences can foster personal growth and stronger relationships. Some of my closest friends are Americans who didn't visit the hospital when I had my babies, who don't party until 3 a.m., or greet me with a kiss as my Latin friends do. Yet, our bond remains strong, and I know they will always be there for me, just as I will be for them.

Let the differences around you inspire greater understanding, compassion, and openness. While connecting across our differences can sometimes be challenging, it's also one of the most rewarding journeys you can undertake. It offers a unique opportunity to embrace the best aspects of multiple worlds.

HOW TO VALUE DIFFERENT PERSPECTIVES

*"People see what they want to see,
and what people want to see isn't always the truth."*
- Roberto Bolaño

Figure 3: Valuing Different Perspectives

We all have a unique and valuable perspective. It's our way of seeing and understanding the world based on our values, beliefs, thoughts, knowledge, and experiences. Therefore, no one can have the same perspective as you. People with similar backgrounds may have similar perspectives, while those with different backgrounds may see things differently.

Understanding that your perspectives and perceptions are just that—perspectives and perceptions, not absolute reality—will allow you to be open to new and different points of view. Valuing different perspectives involves trying to understand another person's point of view with respect, support, and empathy, even if it differs from your own. It's about broadening your outlook. This doesn't require agreement, but it does mean recognizing how their experiences and circumstances have shaped their perspective.

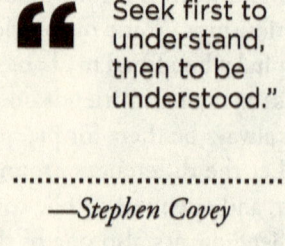

Seek first to understand, then to be understood."

—*Stephen Covey*

To achieve this, first, be aware of your perspective. Reflect on how it was formed: What events or experiences influenced your views? How do your beliefs, values, and biases shape your thinking? By understanding your position, you can better appreciate it while remaining open to others.

Next, listen actively. Seek to understand why someone thinks the way they do. What experiences have shaped their views? Let them share their story, exploring their background with compassion. What are their fears, desires, and motivations? Listening with curiosity rather than judgment fosters deeper connections and understanding.

When sharing your perspective, do so openly and respectfully. Acknowledge your triggers and focus on understanding others rather than reacting. Develop the ability to express your emotions while regulating them, ensuring the conversation remains constructive.

Consider how their perspective differs from yours. You don't have to agree or judge, just to recognize that their experiences and background have led them to a distinct viewpoint. Ask yourself: Can I learn something from this? Does it offer new insights or possibilities? Seeing perspectives as neither inherently good nor bad can help you grow.

Valuing diverse points of view requires being willing to learn and humble enough to recognize that no one has all the answers and that there are countless ways to approach challenges and opportunities.

To cultivate an environment where diverse viewpoints thrive, ensure everyone feels heard, respected, and free to express themselves without fear of judgment or isolation. Focus on strengths rather than weaknesses.

FIRST HALLOWEEN IN THE US

It was September in Collierville, a small suburban city near Memphis, Tennessee. Stores had already begun decorating and stocking Halloween merchandise, with shades of orange and black dominating every display. Skeletons, monsters, ghosts, creepy clowns, witches, superheroes, vampires, and pumpkins filled the aisles. Horror movies played on nearly every channel, and the excitement for the holiday was unmistakable.

In Mexico, we celebrate "El Día de Muertos" (the Day of the Dead), a pre-Hispanic indigenous tradition associated with the Catholic celebrations of All Saints' Day, held on November 1st. It's a holiday to honor life and remember loved ones who have died. Some people confuse the two holidays, perhaps because they are just one day apart or because they both involve skeletons and the dead.

However, the meanings and ways of celebrating them are entirely different. That said, Halloween is not as popular in Mexico. We host a few Halloween parties, and people dress up for the occasion; trick-or-treating is not a significant event like it is in the US.

Even though Halloween is not such a big day in Mexico, it has been one of my favorite celebrations for a long time. I think it's super fun, I love the creativity involved, and I enjoy being a superhero, a witch, a doctor, or anything I want for a day.

In the U.S., we were invited to several Halloween parties, and as I encountered more costumes and decorations, my curiosity about how Halloween was celebrated here grew. I wanted to participate fully, so I asked one of my friends to explain the tradition in detail. She told me, "Kids dress up in costumes and go door to door, ringing the bell and saying 'trick or treat.' It's like they're saying, 'Give us candy, or we'll play a trick on you.' You'll need a lot of candy, especially in your neighborhood."

Our neighborhood was known for its excellent schools, large parks, and sports facilities, which attracted many young families. Nearly every house had school-age children, so a long parade of trick-or-treaters was expected. Taking my friend's advice, I bought a mountain of candy, filled a giant, bright orange plastic pumpkin, and got ready for the big day.

On my way home from work, I noticed some kids had already started trick-or-treating. I hurried home, eager not to miss out. I set up the candy and waited by the door, watching from my living room as kids in fantastic costumes went from one house to the next, skipping mine entirely.

Why weren't they stopping at our house? Maybe they knew we didn't have kids, or perhaps they assumed, as new neighbors and Mexicans, that we didn't celebrate Halloween. I waited twenty or thirty minutes, watching them pass by without ringing the bell until I couldn't resist. I grabbed the pumpkin of candy and went outside, determined to share my treats. I didn't want to keep all those sweets to myself.

Once the kids saw me outside with the massive pumpkin full of candy, they began to stop by. Each child took just one piece before heading off. Only one candy? It felt insufficient for me. Back home, piñatas are all about grabbing as much as you can, so I started handing out handfuls of candy to each child. Word quickly spread; soon, we were the most popular house on the block!

Chatting with a group of kids, I mentioned that I'd been waiting inside, but no one had come. They looked around my house and said, "*Oh, it's because you didn't have your front door light on. We think you might be on vacation, sick, working, or unwilling to participate if it's off. So, we don't ring the bell.*"

It hadn't even occurred to me that the outdoor light was the reason. My friend had forgotten to mention that critical detail. Despite all the lights being on inside, they'd skipped our house because one light was off outside. This simple oversight reminded me of how small adjustments can significantly impact. Even the tiniest detail, like a light switch, can mean the difference between connecting or being passed by.

So, always be curious, ask questions, and remember to turn your lights on!

HOW TO ADAPT TO A NEW CULTURE

Adapting to a new culture requires self-awareness, emotional resilience, active learning, and adaptability. The best approach is to embrace it with curiosity, openness, and flexibility. Curiosity allows you to explore unfamiliar customs, traditions, and values with genuine interest, helping you appreciate the unique aspects of the culture. Keeping an open mind lets you set aside preconceived notions and learn from experiences that challenge your beliefs and habits. Flexibility enables you to adjust to other social norms, try unfamiliar foods, and understand varied communication styles.

This adaptable mindset allows you to navigate new environments more efficiently, show respect for local customs, and enrich your overall experience as you immerse yourself in it.

Life abroad is different, and it's easy to miscommunicate or misinterpret signals. Understanding your new environment's norms and cultural practices and the reasons behind them can significantly aid your adaptation and positively impact your relationships.

Here are some tips to reduce misunderstandings and successfully adapt to a new culture:

- Observe
- Listen
- Ask – Cultivate curiosity with a willingness to learn.
- Maintain an Open Mind
- Be Flexible – Small changes go a long way.
- Find a Mentor
- Imitate (whenever possible without compromising your values or authenticity)

Observe

Observe those around you. What do they do? How do they behave? What conversation topics do they have? How do they spend their free time or weekends? What gifts do they give on different occasions (for a dinner invitation, a birthday, or a wedding)? How much do they usually spend on a present? What's the dining etiquette? What is the dress code?

Pay attention to verbal and nonverbal cues, body language, tone of voice, gestures, and personal space (proxemics). How do they approach elders, women, children, or higher-ranking people? How do they greet each other (between close friends, acquaintances, strangers, family, the same and the opposite sex)? How do they communicate with each other?

Understanding and familiarizing yourself with these behaviors can help demonstrate cultural sensitivity and respect.

Listen

Listen actively to their thoughts and perspectives without judging. Let your biases, expectations, assumptions, and beliefs take a backseat. Be willing to unlearn old ideas, learn new things, and see the world through their eyes.

Engage in the conversation by being fully present without distractions. Ask open-ended questions, pay attention to body language (both theirs and yours), and maintain eye contact (make sure to understand the culturally appropriate length). Paraphrase or summarize to ensure you know what they're communicating. Listen to understand, not just to respond, judge, or offer advice.

Ask, ask, ask

Cultivate a mindset of curiosity by embracing a genuine openness to learn. Curiosity is one of the most effective teachers, driving you to explore, question, and understand the world with a more profound sense of purpose. It encourages you to ask insightful questions and analyze information critically rather than accepting it at face value. By considering multiple perspectives, you gain a richer, more nuanced understanding of the world around you.

Always ask "why," "how," and "what if" to deepen your understanding of the world around you. Don't be afraid to ask even the most basic questions. Engage with people from different backgrounds and fields.

Empathize with different viewpoints by trying to understand cultural practices from the perspective of those who follow them. Consider the historical, social, and emotional contexts that shape these traditions. Asking questions effectively clears doubts, shows genuine interest, and demonstrates involvement in a new culture. However, always ask respectfully and thoughtfully.

I vividly remember back in 2003 when someone asked me if there were cars or TVs in Mexico. I couldn't tell if they were joking, genuinely clueless, or perhaps picturing every Mexican riding a donkey to work. Of course, not everyone in Mexico owns a car, but that question was way off! Around the same time, someone asked a Brazilian friend if people in Brazil dressed like they do during Carnival all year round. Seriously?

These kinds of questions often stem from unconscious biases and assumptions. To avoid making assumptions, asking open-ended questions that allow for a genuine understanding is better. Instead of asking if there are cars or TVs in Mexico, they could have asked, "What are the most common transportation methods in Mexico?" and followed up with, "How accessible is it for people to own a car?" Similarly, rather than assuming Brazilians dress like it's Carnival all year, a better question would be, "What is the typical dress code for work or social events in Brazil?" Open-ended questions like these invite a deeper, more respectful exploration of different cultures.

If you're unsure how to navigate a situation, ask for guidelines from someone familiar with the culture. Some helpful questions could be:

- What is the right thing to do in this situation?
- What should I do in this case?
- What can I bring?
- I'm planning to do this. Would that be fine?
- Are there any food allergies or dietary restrictions I should know? Are there any ingredients or foods I should avoid or include when hosting a party?
- I noticed this _____. Could you explain what it is or is about?
- What am I expected to do or avoid in this country or situation?
- How do you celebrate this special event or holiday?
- Is it acceptable to join in on this event or celebration?

- How can I show respect for your culture? For my boss? For the opposite sex?
- Are there any cultural boundaries I need to be aware of?
- What is the dress code for this event?

The more you prepare and learn about the new culture, the better. However, we all inevitably make mistakes when dealing with unfamiliar situations, which is okay. It's how we learn, and most people won't make a big deal if they know you're a foreigner, not breaking any laws, and acted with good intentions.

If you make a cultural faux pas, apologize, learn from it, and move on—it's all part of the adventure! Don't be too hard on yourself. We've all been there, and honestly, it'll probably make for an excellent story to share later.

Maintain an open mind

Keeping an open mind allows you to view the world through diverse perspectives, enriching your understanding and broadening your horizons. This involves letting go of preconceived notions to embrace new ideas and experiences. Avoid making assumptions based solely on your perceptions.

Approach a new environment with respect and a willingness to learn. Give others the benefit of the doubt and seek to understand their perspective. What may seem rude or unusual in one culture could be entirely acceptable in another. Cultural differences are not about right or wrong—they reflect the diversity of human experiences. By respecting local customs and showing a willingness to adapt, you create opportunities for deeper bonds.

Be flexible

Plans don't always unfold as expected, but embracing change and staying adaptable can transform challenges into opportunities. Flexibility involves being open to new experiences and stepping beyond your comfort zone, whether exploring new hobbies, discovering unfamiliar places, or adjusting to different routines and work cultures. It's about welcoming the chance to adapt to new situations, like weather or local customs, and finding joy in engaging with the community in ways you hadn't initially considered.

Flexibility smooths your transition. Most of the time, it only requires little changes (like turning the light on). Being flexible doesn't mean you have to sacrifice your authenticity. You can find unique ways to contribute while staying true to yourself.

For example, during our first Halloween in the US, I embraced a bit of local tradition by turning on the front door light and handing out candies.

But you did it my way—giving out lots of goodies when no one else in the neighborhood was doing so. Combining a willingness to adapt with a personal touch created a memorable experience, making my first Halloween in the US a big success!

Find a local mentor

Find a local mentor early on to help you adapt quickly to the country's culture, including its unique habits and behaviors. Ideally, choose someone native to the area to gain valuable insights into their perspective and better understand your approach and theirs.

Imitate

After observing how others behave and actively listening, consider mirroring their actions when appropriate while staying authentic. Do they speak softly, avoid eye contact, or maintain a larger personal space? Or are they more likely to hug, kiss, talk loudly, and openly display their emotions? Notice their unique behaviors, and adjust your approach in ways that foster connection, allowing you to adapt without compromising your individuality.

Why imitate? It often shows you care for and respect their culture. For example, if you're invited to a house and see the host family and other guests remove their shoes at the entrance, it's courteous to do the same. If everyone at the table shares dishes, it's nice to join in. If no one starts eating even when the food is served, wait! It may be disrespectful to be the first to dig in. If you notice everyone lining up on the right side of an escalator, follow suit.

Acting differently than locals might be perceived as offensive or disrespectful. When in doubt, ask. If you can't ask and are unsure what to do, the best approach is to imitate those around you unless it conflicts with your values.

However, don't confuse appreciating and imitating some cultural norms with cultural appropriation, which can be rude. Merriam-Webster defines cultural appropriation as "taking something without authority or right" and exploiting, disrespecting, or stereotyping a minority group's cultural elements. Please don't use or display something from another culture without understanding its significance, especially religious objects or traditions. Ask a trusted local if you have questions.

Curiosity, an open mind, and minor adjustments can make a big difference.

KEY TAKEAWAYS

- Approach a new culture with curiosity, flexibility, an open mind, and a willingness to learn.
- Small changes can make a big difference.
- Be compassionate and forgive cultural mistakes, both others' and your own.
- Being right doesn't mean others are wrong. Right, wrong, good, and bad are relative.
- Create an environment where everyone feels heard, supported, respected, and free to express themselves and share their thoughts.

CHAPTER 3

Lost in translation

*"I know you think you understand what you thought I said, but I'm not
sure you realize that what you heard is not what I meant."*
— *Alan Greenspan*

Communication, the lifeblood of human interaction, acts as the bridge
that connects individuals, cultures, and societies. Yet, how we communicate varies significantly worldwide, often leading to misunderstandings and misinterpretations. This challenge is particularly pronounced in the
distinction between direct communication cultures, which value clarity and
straightforwardness, and indirect communication cultures, which prioritize
harmony and subtlety.

MY EXPERIENCE: FROM INDIRECT TO DIRECT COMMUNICATION

I grew up in Mexico, where people generally avoid saying "no" or making
unpleasant comments directly. Instead, we tend to express disagreement or disapproval in subtle, indirect ways to maintain harmony and avoid discomfort.
Negative feedback is often delivered gently, with great care to minimize offense.

One of the things I admire most about Dutch and Germans is their directness. They say exactly what they think, making expectations clear. However, adapting to this straightforward communication style took time for me.
Growing up in a culture where directness is often perceived as rudeness, I
initially found adjusting challenging.

In Mexico, people often prefer a small lie to avoid conflict rather than honesty that might offend. This helps maintain harmony and spares feelings but can also cause misunderstandings and confusion.

When I first encountered the direct communication style in the United States, it was a culture shock. Hearing blunt comments—especially in places like Germany and Belgium, where communication can be even more direct— often caught me off guard. Here are a few instances where my indirect communication style clashed with the more direct approach:

Figure 4: Indirect and Direct Communication

Declining an invitation

In Mexico, when someone receives an invitation to an event, they know they cannot attend, they might respond with, "I'll see if I can make it" or "I'll try my best to be there," even if they are already sure they won't be able to go. Unless a clear and acceptable excuse, such as a prior trip or a more significant commitment, directly declining the invitation is often avoided. This approach helps soften the refusal, minimizing disappointment for the inviter. In Mexican culture, such indirectness is viewed as polite and considerate.

While living in Memphis, I invited an American friend to a party. Her response? "I'm sorry, but I can't attend your event. I already have other plans." And that was it—no further explanation, no excuse, nada! I admit I was a bit taken aback by how brisk it felt. In Latin cultures, we would rarely be so direct. Instead, we'd offer an entire novella of excuses to ensure the person knows we want to be there.

I'd have said, "Thank you so much for considering me! I'm genuinely honored, but I'll be traveling with my family that week. I'm so sorry to miss it, but maybe we can do a rain check?"

Yes, I know—it's a lot of words. But to us, it's not just polite; it's how we show we care! We love a good reason to add some flair, even to say, "No, I can't make it." It's not unnecessary; it's our way of softening the blow and keeping the connection. In Latin culture, a little extra warmth goes a long way.

In the U.S., I quickly discovered that this indirect approach could lead to misunderstandings. For example, when someone responded to an invitation by saying, "I have visitors at home, but I will attend your party for a short time," a Mexican would likely read between the lines and understand that this person probably won't come. However, in the U.S., the host took it as a definite "yes" and felt disappointed when the guest didn't show up. Americans value a clear and direct "yes" or "no" response to invitations. This straightforwardness not only sets expectations but also avoids confusion and ensures that both parties understand the commitment.

In the U.S., being direct is often seen as a sign of respect, showing that you're considering the host's planning. A clear response helps the host know exactly what to expect, which can save them from frustration or disappointment later.

Challenging the professor

Stepping from an indirect communication culture into a direct one can be quite an eye-opener. I experienced this during my first semester studying abroad.

In one of my classes, we were reviewing a complex historical analysis. A German student raised her hand and said, "I don't think this argument is well-supported," right in front of the whole class. She had a valid point and backed it up with strong reasoning, citing inconsistencies in the sources and gaps in the evidence.

What surprised me wasn't just her boldness but the teacher's reaction. Instead of getting upset, they simply nodded and asked, "What would strengthen it?" The discussion continued, with both the teacher and students engaging in a thoughtful exchange. No one took offense, and the conversation remained constructive. Meanwhile, many of the students from indirect communication cultures—Japanese, Mexican, Chinese, and Nepalese—watched in disbelief.

Seeing a student openly challenge a teacher—and be encouraged to do so—was something I wasn't used to. In indirect cultures, this would be entirely out of line. Instead of disagreeing openly, people may ask questions or add veiled comments to guide the conversation in the direction they want. They might present their facts and information in private. In more extreme cases, they may remain silent even when they disagree. Most indirect cultures are hierarchical (chapter 5), and disagreeing with someone with more power or a higher rank is disrespectful and could also affect your position.

Indirect cultures often prefer to hint at issues rather than address them head-on, valuing harmony and saving face over confrontation. This approach works wonderfully in maintaining pleasant interactions but can be challenging when you find yourself in a culture that prizes directness.

While direct communication can be initially uncomfortable for those who aren't used to it, it can lead to more efficient problem-solving and explicit expectations. His comment helped move the project faster and more efficiently.

From then on, I tried to express my concerns and suggestions more openly, understanding that clarity and honesty were strengths rather than rudeness in this culture. I still retained some of my indirect roots, especially when dealing with more sensitive topics, but I found a balance that allowed me to be respectful and straightforward.

THE 50 MEANINGS OF NO

For a direct communicator, "yes" means "yes," and "no" means "no." It's clear, straightforward, and leaves little room for interpretation. You get an honest answer that reflects exactly what they're thinking, with no hidden messages to decode.

In contrast, for an indirect communicator, "yes" can mean a variety of things: it could be a genuine "yes," but it might also mean "yes, but I actually can't," "no," or "I'm not sure." The interpretation depends heavily on the context. Often, they say what they believe you want to hear to avoid conflict or discomfort. However, if you read between the lines, you'll likely find the proper answer within their words or body language.

The same applies to "no," which can have many meanings. It might translate to "maybe," "not right now, but yes later," "ask me again," or "I'm interested, but I'm too shy to say so directly." Indirect communicators often use phrases like "I need to think about it," "perhaps," "I may need to check," or "that could be difficult" as polite ways of saying "no."

In an indirect communication style, honest answers are often wrapped in layers of politeness and subtle hints. Understanding this style requires listening closely, observing, and sometimes reading between the lines to uncover the underlying message. For those accustomed to direct communication, this nuanced approach can feel like navigating a maze of implied meanings—but for the indirect communicator, it's all about maintaining harmony and respect.

Example #1:
Friend Stopping by a Friend's House

Mexican - Mexican Indirect-Indirect	American - American Direct-Direct	Mexican - American Indirect-Direct
Mexican 1: I made Margaritas; would you like one?	American 1: I made Margaritas; would you like one?	Mexican: I made Margaritas; would you like one?
Mexican 2: No, thank you.	American 2: No, thank you.	American: No, thank you.
Mexican 1: Are you sure?		Mexican: Are you sure?
Mexican 2: Yes, they look great, but no thanks.		American: Yes, I'm sure, thanks.
Mexican 1: Just one?		Mexican: Just one?
Mexican 2: Okay, just one.		American: [In his mind] What is wrong with this guy who doesn't understand that I do not want any Margaritas?
Mexican 1: Do you want another one?		
Mexican 2: Sure! Why not?		

In Mexico, as in many cultures, including Japan, Saudi Arabia, Iran, and India, when someone offers you something once—a drink, a thing, or a favor—it's often just a polite gesture. However, if they offer two or more times, that's a sign they genuinely want to take care of you as a guest or friend and sincerely hope you'll accept.

Accepting an offer immediately, on the other hand, can come across as a bit too eager. It might give the impression that you're desperate, overly hungry, or in need, even if you are! The polite approach is to decline once or twice, then accept after they insist a few times. For instance, if someone comments, "The Margaritas look great," it's often a sign: "I'd love to try some, but I'll wait for you to ask again, so I'm sure it's not a hassle to share."

This dance of offers and refusals is part of cultural etiquette, a way to ensure that the host means their offer and that you, as the guest, aren't imposing. It's all about maintaining a balance of generosity and humility, a subtle way of showing that you appreciate the offer but aren't presumptuous enough to take it at face value on the first round.

Example #2:
Going for Lunch When You Are Hungry

Japanese - Japanese Indirect-Indirect	German - German Direct-Direct	German - Japanese Direct-Indirect
Japanese 1: [Notices by body language that his friend is hungry] Would you like to eat something?	German 1: Are you hungry?	German: Are you hungry?
Japanese 2: Only if you want to as well.	German 2: I'm starving. Let's get something to eat	Japanese: Hmm, just a little. [His stomach is rumbling, and he's starving]
Japanese 1: Where do you want to eat?	German 1: Me too. Let's go!	German: Then, let's continue with what we're doing.
Japanese 2: Wherever you want.		Japanese: [Silence, except for his belly rumbling]
Japanese 1: You can choose.		
Japanese 2: What kind of food do you like?		
Japanese 1: Anything you like is fine with me.		
Japanese 2: Do you like sushi?		
Japanese 1: Yes, I do like sushi.		
Japanese 2: Then, we can go to a sushi restaurant.		

Germans are known for their direct communication style. They'll likely express it straightforwardly if they're hungry, angry, excited, or proud, leaving little room for interpretation. They say what they mean and mean what they say.

In Japan, however, indirectness is seen as a hallmark of politeness. Declaring, "Yes, I'm starving," might sound impolite and self-centered. Japanese culture is collectivist, where the group's harmony often takes precedence over individual desires. When deciding on a meal, for instance, a Japanese person might first ensure that others are also hungry and discuss what everyone would like to eat, emphasizing the group's needs over their own.

The phrase "just a little" illustrates this cultural contrast. For a German, "just a little" means precisely that. But for a Japanese person, it could mean "Yes, I'm quite hungry" while downplaying the intensity. They would be taken aback if their German counterpart ignored the subtle cues like a rumbling stomach or body language that hint at true hunger.

Japanese silence also serves as a powerful communication tool. Silence can convey a range of meanings, such as "I'm disappointed," "I don't agree with you," or simply "I'm reflecting on this." It's often used to avoid conflict, giving people space to process without feeling pressured to respond immediately.

In Japanese communication, "yes" may sometimes mean "no." Imagine you're giving a presentation, and afterward, you ask a Japanese colleague if they understood everything. They might respond, "Yes, I did," even if they didn't. Why? Because saying "no" outright might suggest that you didn't explain well enough or could imply criticism, making you lose face. By answering "yes," they aim to protect your feelings and their honor, maintaining social harmony.

Example #3:
Invitation to a Party You Know You Can't Attend

Thai - Iranian Indirect-Indirect	Australian - Dutch Direct-Direct	Dutch - Thai Direct-Indirect
Thai: I'll host a party this Saturday to celebrate my birthday. Could you come?	Australian: I'll host a party this Saturday to celebrate my birthday. Could you come?	Dutch: III host a paty this Saturday to celebrate my birthday. Could you come?
Iranian: I'd like to go, but I'm unsure if I can because I have to visit my grandma. I will let you know.	Dutch: I'm sorry, I cant make it. I already have other plans.	Thai: It's my husband's birthday, but I believe I can stop by your party for a little while
A week after the party:		Saturday:The Dutch are waiting for theThai, who never showed up
Iranian: I'm sorry I missed your party. My grandma needed some help, and I couldn't get away.		

For many Asians, Middle Easterners, and Africans, saying "no" outright can be challenging. In these cultures, nuanced responses provide a way to decline without offending or disappointing the inviter. If the other person is also an indirect communicator, they will likely read between the lines and understand the intended message. However, such responses can feel ambiguous or even misleading for a direct communicator. They might interpret the nuanced reply as a tentative "yes" and feel disappointed when the person doesn't attend.

Conversely, when an indirect communicator receives a straightforward response like, "I can't go; I have other plans," it may be abrupt or inconsiderate. They might perceive it as a lack of appreciation for the invitation or event. For those accustomed to softer refusals, a direct "no" can seem overly blunt, lacking the courtesy and subtlety they expect.

This clash of communication styles highlights differing values: direct communicators prioritize clarity and efficiency, while indirect communicators emphasize harmony and politeness, even if it means the answer is less definitive.

DIRECT AND INDIRECT CULTURES

Mastering the balance between indirect and direct communication styles is crucial for fostering understanding and effective interactions. While indirect communication prioritizes harmony and minimizes confrontation, it can appear ambiguous or evasive to direct communicators who value clarity and efficiency.

Conversely, direct communication, though clear, may feel blunt or offensive to those accustomed to more subtle approaches. Adapting to these styles requires time, awareness, and an appreciation of their underlying values.

DIRECT COMMUNICATION

This communication style emphasizes clarity, honesty, simplicity, and transparency. Its open expression of thoughts and feelings leaves little room for ambiguity. Cultures that value direct communication often prefer straightforward responses, such as "no," "I can't," or "I don't know," over making excuses or avoiding the issue. This approach is seen as a sign of respect, fostering trust and encouraging genuine, effective dialogue.

It is associated with efficiency and assertiveness in many Western countries, including the United States, Germany, Denmark, the Netherlands, and Australia. Speakers express their intentions, needs, and ideas with few words, valuing concise and frank exchanges. Feedback and criticism are given openly and taken less personally, with debates and disagreements seen as standard steps toward resolution. Active listening and the absence of hidden messages create a transparent and solution-focused communication style that prioritizes clarity and mutual understanding.

Here are some tips when communicating with indirect cultures:

- Allow time to build rapport before getting right to the main topic.
- Be patient; understand that unfamiliar styles may take longer to reach the same point.
- Show that the person matters more than the business or transaction.
- Observe body language, gestures, and tone; listen "between the lines." Recognize that phrases like "It may be difficult" or "I'll try" may signal reluctance.
- Use subtle communication and avoid short, direct answers like "No, I can't."
- Understand key phrases that can have different meanings in distinct contexts, such as "It may be difficult," "I would try to…," "I'm not sure," "Tomorrow," and "In a minute."
- Ask a local for clarification if you are confused.
- Provide negative feedback in private and be gentle, with added context or background.
- Avoid pushing for immediacy; indirect communicators may take longer to answer.
- Practice, practice, practice, and have a lot of patience!

INDIRECT COMMUNICATION

These cultures prioritize harmony, subtlety, and context, often relying on non-verbal cues, tone, and situational context to convey meaning. Critique or confrontation is typically avoided, as maintaining social harmony and preventing offense is paramount. Disapproval is often expressed through non-verbal signals, while true intentions may be conveyed using stories, metaphors, body language, or other indirect methods.

To preserve relationships and avoid hurting feelings, communicators may avoid direct or blunt responses, often refraining from saying "no" outright. Instead, they might offer excuses or indirect replies. In these cultures, being diplomatic and "saving face" is more important than giving a straightforward answer, as short or direct responses can be perceived as impolite.

This style is prevalent in many Asian countries, including Japan, China, and Thailand, as well as in Saudi Arabia, India, much of Latin America (e.g., Mexico, Honduras, and Chile), and most African nations. Indirect communication is valued for its ability to show respect and maintain relationships.

Tips when communicating with direct cultures:

- Don't take it personally. Direct speakers make straightforward statements without intending to offend.
- Recognize that short answers, specific requests, or critical comments aren't signs of aggression. They're just expressions of honesty and efficiency.
- Practice saying precisely what you think, feel, or your intentions.
- Use fewer words in written and spoken communication, focusing on the main point.
- Keep them informed of any progress or new developments.
- Remember, direct speakers value short and honest answers over gentle ones. It's a sign of trust and respect.

KEY TAKEAWAYS

- Direct communication: emphasizes clarity, honesty, simplicity, and transparency.
- Indirect communication: value harmony and subtlety, using non-verbal cues, tone, and context to communicate meaning.
- Embracing direct and indirect communication enhances your skills, allowing you to balance honesty and tact.

What time is it?

"The way we spend our time defines who we are."
— Jonathan Estrin

Time, a universal constant, is perceived and valued differently across cultures. While a day universally consists of 24 hours, a week of seven days, and a year of 12 months, how people use, organize, perceive, and value this pacing can vary dramatically from one place to another. This chapter explores attitudes toward time, highlighting key differences and their implications.

Numerous scholars have explored this concept. Edward T. Hall examined the contrast between monochronic (linear) and polychronic (cyclical) time orientations. Geert Hofstede analyzed long-term versus short-term orientation as part of his cultural dimensions theory, emphasizing how societies plan or focus on immediate results. Fons Trompenaars differentiated between sequential and synchronic time orientations. Richard Lewis categorized cultures into **linear-active**, multi-active, and reactive time orientations, offering insights into how various societies approach time management and relationships.

I'll simplify it into three general categories:

- **Flexible-Time Culture:** Time is perceived fluidly, focusing on relationships and flexibility.
- **Sharp-Time Culture:** Time is seen as linear and sequential, strongly emphasizing schedules and punctuality.
- **Recurring-Time Culture:** Time is viewed cyclically, focusing on the natural flow of events.[9]

FLEXIBLE-TIME CULTURES

Mexican time

When I mention "Mexican time," I'm not talking about the time zone—it's more like a whimsical approach to time itself. In Mexico (and other countries like Brazil, Italy, Spain, India, and Bangladesh), time flows slightly differently compared to places like Germany, the UK, Japan, Switzerland, or the U.S.

So, what exactly is "Mexican time"? There's no official dictionary definition, but it generally means showing up 15 to 30 minutes after the planned time. Is this considered late in Mexico? Not really. While punctuality is catching on for work, especially in global companies, social events still thrive on a flexible schedule.

Since I was young, I've loved hosting parties. I threw three to four big ones a year at my parents' house in Mexico, where I lived then. As with anything else, the more you do, the more experience and knowledge you accrue. And with parties, I learned that no one ever shows up on schedule. The early birds were usually 10-15 minutes late. Most guests would typically arrive about half an hour after the stated start, though there were always a few outliers who would appear at some unpredictable moment.

I do not like to sit and wait for the guests to arrive, so I planned my day to the minute, setting up, cleaning, and cooking with a countdown to start the party. The last thing I'd do is shower and get ready so I don't smell like food or worry about my outfit getting messy while cooking; it also makes me feel refreshed and relaxed. So, if the party started at 7 p.m., I'd be out of the shower, finishing up my makeup around 7:15 p.m., ready just before the first guests would arrive. Perfect timing—every time.

For years, this schedule worked E V E R Y T I M E!

Except once. I'd invited someone new, a friend who, I later learned, was a clock-watching anomaly in my city. I was fresh out of the shower, my hair dripping wet, and my body was still covered by a towel when the doorbell rang. My mom opened the door and immediately rushed to my room, warning me that the first punctual guest had arrived. I hurriedly threw on clothes. I didn't have a moment to dry my hair or put on any makeup. I wasn't concerned about the makeup, but my hair was another story. If left alone, it gets incredibly frizzy, and I knew it would be a disaster if I let it air-dry—and it was. Thanks to this punctual guy, I looked like a lion for the whole party.

I went downstairs to welcome the guest, who clearly didn't understand that Mexican girls need at least 15 minutes past the set schedule to finish getting ready. And who was he? Of course, he had to be the guy I had a crush on. He was all dressed up and put together for the party, while I was a freshly showered mess.

This man is now my husband. To this day, I remind him how he ruined my party prep routine that night. He claims he just wanted a little extra time with me before everyone else arrived. Nice try, but I'm not buying it. It's been over 26 years together, and I still don't get a single extra minute with him. He's still on the dot for everything.

And in case you were wondering—yes, he's Mexican. A Mexican with a foreigner's watch—proof that every rule has its exception.

Tick-tocks and tuk-tuks

Figure 5: Sharp and Flexible Timing

Imagine living in the world's second most populous country, where fewer than 5% of households own a car. To get anywhere, you'll likely depend on the second largest and one of the busiest train networks globally—one that carries over 22 million passengers daily and is late more than 20% of the time[10]. Once off the train, you'll face the bustling streets, navigating on foot or by taxi, bus, or tuk-tuk (auto-rickshaw) alongside a seemingly endless stream of pedestrians, bicycles, motorcycles, cars, cows, stray dogs, monkeys, and other animals. Welcome to India, where transportation is an adventure and punctuality is a rare gem.

Accidents, breakdowns, and other unpredictable events may lead to traffic jams and delays. After navigating this labyrinth, can you realistically expect to be on schedule for your appointment? Probably not. In India, as in many similar countries, dealing with infrastructure issues, traffic, and transit woes is part of daily life.

Chances are, you're not the only one who missed the bus or arrived late. Meetings commonly start behind schedule and run late, creating a ripple effect that delays the rest of the day. An accident might block a main road, forcing a lengthy detour and further stretching your journey. And now, you're late for your next appointment, too.

However, transportation hurdles do not alone contribute to unpunctuality. Family obligations, extended meals, doctor's appointments, and spontaneous celebrations also play a role. This relaxed approach to scheduling is generally accepted and rarely regretted, especially outside the workplace. Indians are extremely adaptable to plans, and delays are seen as a natural part of life rather than an inconvenience.

Do people in India expect apologies for tardiness? Not really. If the government, train conductors, bus drivers, or cows don't apologize for delays, why should they? Some Indians don't bother calling to say they're running late because they often have no idea when they'll arrive. Punctuality is more of a suggestion than a rule; most people don't expect it.

Why don't they leave 30–40 minutes early to ensure they arrive promptly? Perhaps because they know others will be running late too—so what's the point of being punctual if you might be the only one there? Sticking to a rigid schedule in a society where most people embrace a relaxed view of time can be stressful. Instead, they go with the flow. Indian Standard Time (IST) is humorously dubbed "Indian Stretchable Time." While "Mexican Time" might mean arriving 10–15 minutes late, IST often means being 45–60 minutes behind schedule.

This laid-back approach to scheduling is also common in government and public sectors. However, in multinationals and private businesses, Indians generally adhere to schedules and deadlines, with punctuality highly valued in professional settings. Yet, when it comes to social events, timing remains flexible.

Ironically, Indians are highly punctual regarding "*Muhurtha*" rituals. *Muhurtha* is a science of timing rooted in Vedic (Hindu) astrology[11], meticulously dictates the most auspicious times for significant life events, such as weddings, purchasing property, or sealing essential deals. In this context, timing is everything.

Specific days and hours are considered inauspicious for business or significant transactions, which can lead to sudden cancellations or unexpected last-minute changes. For example, Tuesdays, Thursdays, and Fridays are particularly favorable days to buy land or a home. The *Abhijit Muhurat*, a highly regarded 48-minute window around midday, is ideal for weddings and other sacred ceremonies[12].

The work culture in India differs significantly from that of the West. Business hours typically start later, often around 9 AM or later, and extend well into the evening. A key rule in many workplaces—especially in hierarchical settings—is to never leave before your boss does.

Retail hours also reflect this late schedule; most malls don't open until 11 AM. If you're looking for food, you'll find that restaurants stay open late—often until 2 AM. This is one reason why many Indians have dinner much later, around 8 or 9 PM, compared to Western norms.

If you're traveling or conducting business in India, it's wise to prepare for long waits, sudden schedule changes, and frequent interruptions. Flexibility is your best ally. Before arranging a critical meeting or appointment, consider the local superstitions and beliefs that could impact the timing. If you're uncertain, consulting a local can offer valuable guidance. Understanding the fluid nature of scheduling in India and other flexible-time cultures will help you adapt to cultural nuances, work more effectively with hardworking, diligent, and remarkably friendly people, and thrive in these vibrant settings.

CHARACTERISTICS OF FLEXIBLE-TIME-CULTURE

In a flexible-time culture, time is seen as fluid, with human relationships taking priority over strict schedules. Personal interactions matter more than punctuality; tardiness is generally accepted as social commitments often come first.

Members of these cultures tend to be more relaxed with schedules and tasks. Unpunctuality is common, but it does not imply a lack of respect for work. Instead, there is a calm approach to completing tasks, prioritizing activities based on their importance, urgency, or personal interest.

People can quickly switch from one task to another and handle multiple tasks simultaneously. They are accustomed to interruptions and changes of plans and adapt quickly without becoming upset. They see them as a natural part of life rather than a disruption. They are excellent improvisers and skilled at handling chaotic situations.

These individuals often feel restricted and limited by strict agendas, schedules, or deadlines. They prefer verbal or in-person communication over written correspondence. Socially, relationships play a crucial role and are central to business efficiency. They invest generously in building and maintaining strong relationships. They are expressive and never cut conversations short or rush through a good meal.

For these cultures, the present moment is more important than adhering to an agenda, schedule, or appointment. They value the significance of each moment and try to make the most of every opportunity. Some countries in this category include India, Saudi Arabia, Mexico, Brazil, Italy, Spain, Kenya, and Nigeria, where there is a more relaxed attitude toward time.

INTERACTING WITH FLEXIBLE-TIME CULTURE

As a Recurring or Sharp-Time-Culture:
Although punctuality is not expected or reciprocated in this culture in most cases, it is appreciated, and it is always a good idea.

When invited to a social event, ask a local guest when it's good to arrive. Aim to arrive 10 minutes earlier, but wait outside until you see other guests ringing the bell. Avoid being the first one there. You don't want to catch the host in their bathrobe!

Always bring a small snack. You never know when food will be served; meal schedules can vary. If you're starving, eat your snack discreetly, avoiding doing so in front of others to prevent disrespect.

Arrive promptly for meetings but anticipate delays. Have something to keep you engaged—whether it's work on your laptop, a podcast, or a book—so waiting feels productive rather than wasted.

> "Patience is a form of wisdom. It demonstrates that we understand and accept the fact that sometimes things must unfold in their own time."
>
> —Jan Kabat-Zinn

Anticipate that deadlines might not be met. Schedule your needs beforehand—if you need something by November, request it for September. Follow up regularly to ensure progress.

Building strong relationships is essential in flexible-time cultures. Prepare to socialize—a lot! These cultures prioritize personal relationships, so plan for unhurried meals by allowing extra time in your schedule (and whatever you do, avoid bringing up work during meals unless they do). Mealtimes are almost sacred and serve as an excellent opportunity to connect personally.

In these cultures, sharing a meal is much more than just eating. It's a chance to build trust, share stories, and form bonds beyond the boardroom. Slow down, savor the moment, and allow the conversation to flow naturally.

By doing so, you'll respect their customs and lay a solid foundation for a successful partnership.

Be prepared for lengthy introductions, social interactions before meetings, and some session interruptions. It requires patience, as schedules may shift. Flexibility will be your greatest strength.

SHARP-TIME CULTURES

Wedding in Germany

We were invited to a friend's wedding in Germany—a Mexican guy marrying a German lady. Several friends and family members from Mexico attended, some unfamiliar with German customs.

During the reception, the groom announced, "Dinner will be served buffet-style, and we'll do it the German way. Beginning from the left and moving right, each table can take turns serving themselves. When table one has finished, table two can follow, and so on."

Everyone followed his instructions to a T. We got our food in a highly functional, efficient, and orderly fashion. Almost no one spoke in the line; we marched straight to the buffet, grabbed our food, and returned to our tables to enjoy it. The whole process was quick, quiet, and astonishingly organized.

Imagine how things might have unfolded if he hadn't requested the German style for the buffet. Chaos? Spontaneity? Probably a bit of both!

The Mexican guests would probably have approached it in their way—whenever they felt like it. If they were hungry, they'd beeline to the buffet right away. They might have waited until the last possible moment if they weren't. Conversations would've continued, undisturbed by any notion of a schedule. Some would've waited for the line to thin out before jumping in, while others would seize the chance to cut in when they spotted a gap. Lines would form and dissolve as guests casually strolled over, grabbing food whenever they felt like it rather than waiting for an official cue.

The buffet would have taken on a life of its own, with a dynamic mix of chatting, laughing, and flowing back and forth between tables and the food. It would have been wonderfully informal and entirely driven by the moment, as everyone found their way to the food in their own schedule.

In short, people from a flexible-time culture prioritize spontaneity, making decisions based on the moment. In contrast, sharp-time cultures take a structured approach, organizing everything to maximize efficiency and minimize effort.

This wedding was the perfect fusion of cultures. The Germans brought efficiency and order, while the Mexicans added spontaneity and warmth.

Restaurant bill in the USA

I've seen plenty of puzzled looks when taking international clients out for lunch or dinner in the U.S. In some casual American restaurants, it's customary for the server to place the bill on the table without being asked, often with a cheerful, "Whenever you're ready, no rush." This typically happens when the server thinks you're done or nearly done with your meal, and it seems like you won't be ordering anything else.

This move can confuse foreigners— "No rush?" my clients often ask, completely bewildered. "Why would they bring the bill if there's no rush?" They glance around nervously to see if there's a crowd waiting for the table, but usually, there isn't. Or they check their watches, thinking maybe the restaurant is about to close. To them, the bill's early arrival feels like a subtle push to pay up and leave. They feel rushed as if someone's giving them the boot, and they can't help but find it a bit rude.

Welcome to the USA, a sharp-time Culture where time is money. Here, it's common for the bill to arrive unsolicited—not because they're trying to hustle you out the door (well unless there's a line). But more often than not, they're trying to do you a favor. They assume you might need to rush back to work or head to another commitment, and they want to maximize your efficiency by having everything ready. From their perspective, they're just being considerate of your schedule.

This same "time is of the essence" mindset runs through American culture. Fast-food restaurants, for example, are built around the principles of speed and convenience. They accommodate travelers and busy professionals who need a quick, efficient meal. It's no wonder the U.S. has more fast-food chains than any other country. White Castle, one of the oldest American hamburger joints, is even considered the world's first authentic fast-food restaurant. And then, of course, there's Henry Ford's assembly line invention, revolutionizing car manufacturing to maximize efficiency. Coincidence? I think not.

Whether it's food preparation or car production, Americans have mastered the art of doing things quickly, massively, and cost-effectively.

When working or interacting with a sharp-time culture, be ready for their deep respect for punctuality and their expectation that you reciprocate. They prioritize efficiency and meticulous planning. So, the next time the bill arrives with a smile and a "No rush," just remember they're not trying to push you out. They're being thoughtful in their own uniquely American way.

CHARACTERISTICS OF SHARP-TIME-CULTURE

Sharp-time cultures prioritize schedules, punctuality, and completing one task at a time. Time is viewed as a limited resource, making efficient management essential. In these cultures, lateness is often seen as disrespectful, and there is a strong focus on deadlines and punctuality.

For them, time is money, and efficiency is a priority. They are focused on tasks, results, and productivity, preferring meticulous planning with detailed agendas and schedules. Deadlines are crucial, and they place high importance on completing tasks promptly.

People in sharp-time cultures prioritize logic and facts. They work in sequential order, finishing one task before beginning the next and avoiding getting lost in irrelevant details. Their work conversations are short and direct, and strict punctuality is expected. Wasting your own or another person's time is considered unacceptable.

Some countries that embody sharp-time culture include the United States, Germany, the United Kingdom, Switzerland, Austria, the Netherlands, and Scandinavia.

In these cultures, business meetings begin precisely as scheduled, and lateness is often viewed as disrespectful. Projects follow strict schedules with closely monitored milestones, and any delays prompt immediate corrective actions. People rely on calendars and planners to structure their days, ensuring maximum efficiency. Every moment is accounted for, prioritizing productivity. Conversations, especially in professional settings, are direct and goal-oriented, with minimal small talk to maintain focus on achieving objectives.

INTERACTING WITH SHARP-TIME CULTURE

As a Flexible-Time Culture

The best way to deal with a sharp-time culture is to respect their time. This rule applies to messages, conversations, and deadlines. Speak directly and go straight to the point. Summarize your messages by including only the main topics. Meet your deadlines and arrive and leave promptly.

People do things in sequential order. You have their undivided attention when they're with you, and they expect the same from you. Interruptions?

Absolutely unacceptable. Silence your phone, and don't glance at it during meetings or dinners. If possible, leave someone else in charge of urgent matters unrelated to the meeting so you can focus 100%.

Plan your day in advance. Check traffic conditions and prepare essentials like clothes, keys, and your briefcase the night before. Use reminders and alarms to stay on schedule. Monitor how long tasks take, set timers, and stick to them. Since unexpected delays can arise, allow yourself a buffer to stay on track.

Some people thrive on the adrenaline rush of doing things at the last minute, and that adrenaline is addictive. If you're constantly in a rush, plan as if the meeting or activity starts 30–60 minutes earlier than scheduled (plus an extra 10 minutes, just in case).

Try to plan meetings or gatherings when you expect fewer interruptions or delays. Avoid distractions before and during your event.

As a Recurring-Time Culture

In most sharp-time cultures, you can directly contact the person in charge of a task. There is no need to contact their supervisor. Only involve people directly working on a project unless specified otherwise.

Keep conversations brief and to the point. People might be confused if you don't explicitly communicate your needs and expectations.

These cultures prioritize efficiency over socializing at work. If you want to contact them, let them know in advance so they can schedule it. They like to know where they're standing and have a clear plan. So, for example, you can say, "Our work meeting will start at 9 am with an icebreaker, introductions, and chat, and then at 10 am, we'll move to work issues."

RECURRING-TIME CULTURES

Wax on, wax off

Japanese culture is endlessly fascinating. This country has survived wars and tsunamis, rebuilding itself stronger and wiser each time. It's a society that seamlessly blends modernity and tradition, with ancient customs dating back thousands of years coexisting alongside cutting-edge technology and art. Japan stands as one of the world's most potent and industrialized countries.

A key aspect of Japan's multifaceted culture is its blend of religions: Buddhism and Shintoism. Shintoism focuses on this world, life, and every living thing in nature, offering wisdom for a better life. Buddhism, on the other hand, deals with the soul and the afterlife, helping believers see death as a new beginning rather than an end.

Japan also masterfully mixes sharp-time and flexible-time cultures. The Japanese are known for punctuality and loyalty to their groups and families. They work hard, create deep relationships, and learn how to relax and enjoy nature. Expect them to be punctual for both work and social events yet generous with their availability when it comes to friends and colleagues, excelling in hospitality.

While sharp-time cultures emphasize productivity, efficiency, and planning, flexible-time cultures focus on flexibility, socializing, and spontaneity. Japanese culture emphasizes loyalty to the group, thinking of others, and developing discipline and perfectionism while maintaining productivity and punctuality.

A key distinction of Japanese culture is its focus on long-term outcomes. Decisions are made carefully, aiming for precision from the start. Time is viewed as cyclical, mirroring nature's rhythms—seasons, day and night, life and death. This deep connection to nature shapes their daily routines and approach to planning.

Just as the natural cycle cannot be rushed, the Japanese take a deliberate approach to pacing and decision-making. They believe opportunities, risks, and mistakes will resurface, allowing experience to guide wiser choices. There's no need to hurry before thoroughly assessing and minimizing risks.

These cultural differences are beautifully illustrated in the 80s classic film, *The Karate Kid*. If you remember the film, Daniel, a teenager, wants to learn karate to defend himself from bullies. Mr. Miyagi, a Japanese karate master, offers to train him using methods that seem like labor abuse to Daniel.

Mr. Miyagi asks Daniel to paint fences, wax cars, and sand floors in specific ways. These tasks seemed pointless to Daniel, who felt like a servant. However, Mr. Miyagi later reveals that hand and arm movements are essential karate skills[13].

I'm not saying this is the standard Japanese method of teaching karate, but Mr. Miyagi's technique imparts essential lessons, values, and philosophical insights.

What Can We Learn from Mr. Miyagi?

Mr. Miyagi (representing recurring-time culture) didn't explain his plan to Daniel (sharp-time culture). He just put him to work on tasks that didn't seem related to karate without explaining why. The Japanese often value silence and are masters of reading body language. They observe, listen, and think before communicating, which can be puzzling for those accustomed to verbal communication.

Daniel wanted fast results, while Mr. Miyagi focused on building his character, patience, focus, and discipline for long-term results—essential values in Japanese culture. He trained Daniel's physical strength and mind.

In the movie, Mr. Miyagi famously tries to catch a fly with chopsticks, *declaring that a man who can do that can accomplish anything*. This scene perfectly exemplifies Japanese values of patience, precision, focus, and perfectionism. Sure, he could have used any tool to catch the fly more quickly, but he deliberately chose a method that demanded skill and restraint, highlighting traits essential for success in life.

The choice of chopsticks isn't just for dramatic effect—it's a symbol of mastering the art of control and calm. It demonstrates how the slower, more challenging path can sometimes build resilience, cultivate patience, and ultimately lead to a greater sense of achievement. By choosing the challenging route, he showcases the profound belief that true success isn't just about getting things done but about doing them with intention and mastery.

Mr. Miyagi is also a master gardener, and his meticulous care for his bonsai trees reflects the Japanese dedication to detail and craftsmanship. Tending bonsai requires patience, precision, and a deep understanding of nature—qualities ingrained in Japanese culture.

This philosophy extends to teamwork. In Japanese culture, each person's role is vital, and collective success is as crucial as individual accomplishments. Just as Mr. Miyagi nurtures every branch of his bonsai with care, Japanese teams cultivate an environment that values and encourages every member. Their organized and harmonious way of working reflects a shared commitment to excellence in every task. An example of this is the Nemawashi.

Nemawashi: The Art of Preparing for Change

Nemawashi (根回し) is a Japanese gardening term that translates to "turning the roots." Before transplanting a plant, gardeners pay special attention to each portion of the roots, gradually loosening them before relocating them to ensure healthy growth. Rushing this process could kill the tree[14].

This concept is deeply embedded in Japanese life and business. Toyota, for example, describes nemawashi as a key first step in decision-making—sharing information and seeking opinions to involve all employees. Decisions are not made independently but as a deliberate, collective process[15].

In Japan, decision-making emphasizes meticulous preparation to minimize mistakes and risks. Unlike cultures that prioritize quick actions to seize opportunities, the Japanese believe that if something is worth doing, it's worth doing right, even if it takes more time. High-ranking leaders and entire teams collaborate to reach group consensus, ensuring harmony and collective ownership of the decision.

This methodical approach fosters unity and strengthens team bonds by involving everyone, from senior executives to junior employees. Although the process may be slower, it reflects a deep respect for shared responsibility and collective wisdom, ultimately reducing risks and minimizing errors.

While some cultures may worry about missed opportunities due to slow action, the Japanese prioritize thorough preparation to ensure accuracy from the start. This commitment to precision often results in smoother execution and fewer errors.

For those unfamiliar with this culture, the length of the decision-making process can feel frustrating. However, appreciating this thoughtful approach can prevent costly mistakes and build long-term relationships. Perhaps, by embracing this mindset, you may even develop the patience to catch a fly with chopsticks.

CHARACTERISTICS OF RECURRING-TIME-CULTURE

Recurring-time cultures respond and make crucial decisions at a measured pace; however, they value punctuality. They value silence for thinking and analysis. They are people, tradition, and history-oriented. They rarely initiate action or discussion; instead, they prefer listening first to better understand the other person's position.

First, they observe thoroughly, then proceed to action. Decision-making often involves the entire team, reflecting a collective approach.

Honesty, loyalty, hard work, and caring for others are highly valued. Bringing pride to the family is a significant motivator. Some countries in this category include Japan, Hong Kong, Korea, Vietnam, and Taiwan.

INTERACTING WITH RECURRING-TIME CULTURE

As a Flexible-Time Culture

When interacting with recurring-time cultures, it's crucial to be punctual, avoid distractions, and adhere to their principles. This means respecting their schedules, staying focused during meetings, and communicating clearly and concisely.

As a Sharp-Time Culture

Patience is key when engaging with recurring-time cultures. Don't rush things, especially when making significant decisions. These decisions typically undergo an extensive process and require approval from a large group.

Take time to get to know your counterparts and allow for socialization. Behave modestly and avoid talking excessively about yourself or your company. Remember, for them, you're not just a business associate but a potential long-term partner. Cultivating this relationship requires time and effort.

INDUSTRIALIZED VS. AGRICULTURAL AREAS

Perceptions of time can vary widely within the same country, such as between the north and south, small towns and cosmopolitan cities, or coastal and central areas. A notable example is the contrast between industrialized and agricultural regions, where the nature of work and societal priorities shape differences. Agricultural regions often lean toward more relaxed, Flexible-Time approaches in Sharp-Time cultures, while industrialized areas may exhibit the opposite tendency.

Industrialized Areas

In industrialized cultures (sharp-time), time is viewed as a finite and precious asset that must be managed precisely. Factories, offices, and other workplaces run on tightly controlled schedules to ensure maximum productivity and minimal downtime. Punctuality is more than a virtue—it's a fundamental requirement. Even slight delays can disrupt entire production lines, causing costly inefficiencies and throwing off carefully planned operations. This meticulous approach ensures efficiency, keeps operations on track, and supports the smooth functioning of the organization.

The mantra "time is money" is especially relevant in industrialized settings, where every minute holds value. Professionals in these areas must be disciplined and organized, using planning, goal-setting, and structured routines to maximize efficiency and output.

Agricultural Areas

In agricultural societies (recurring-time cultures), scheduling is more fluid, prioritizing flexibility and adaptability. Daily life follows natural cycles, such as seasons and weather patterns, with tasks completed as needed rather than on a strict timetable. Rigid agendas are often seen as unnecessary and stressful.

So, flexible, structured, and cyclical approaches to scheduling can coexist within a single country, blending industrial and agricultural influences.

***

Dealing with people who have a different sense of timing than ours can be frustrating, stressful, and confusing. However, understanding these differences can help us adjust our expectations, work, and interact effectively when our clocks are not synchronized.

KEY TAKEAWAYS

- Golden Rule: Punctuality is valued in all cultures, even if not always expected or reciprocated. Strive to be on time, but be ready to wait.
- Flexible-Time Culture: Values relationships, embraces multitasking, accommodates frequent interruptions, and adapts quickly to changes.
- Best characteristics: Flexibility, patience, and people carrying.
- Time-Sharp Culture: Emphasizes punctuality and thrives on agendas, schedules, deadlines, and structured plans.
- Best characteristics: Discipline, efficiency, and planning.
- Recurring-Time Culture: Prioritizes partnerships and relationships while maintaining punctuality. Decision-making is lengthy, requiring group consensus and careful consideration to minimize future errors.
- Best characteristics: Harmony, gentleness, and discipline.

CHAPTER 5

Who is the boss?

Leadership is about making others better as a result of your presence and making sure that impact lasts in your absence!
--Sheryl Sanberg

Power distribution is a cornerstone of human societies, influencing governance, business, relationships, communities, and personal perspectives. This chapter delves into the contrasting paradigms of egalitarianism, hierarchy, inequality, and equality, examining how these cultural models shape and define human interactions.

RANKS AND BIKES

Does driving a luxury car indicate that the owner has more power than someone who relies on public transportation? Are public transportation options accessible and widely used across all social classes, or is there a clear distinction between who uses public transit versus private vehicles? Have you ever seen a company CEO, prime minister, or royalty riding a bike or using public transport? How would this be perceived in your country? These questions highlight how wealth is perceived across cultures.

In some highly unequal and hierarchical societies, wealth often represents more than financial success—it signals power, prestige, and access. Wealthy people often feel entitled. Material possessions, like luxury cars, high-end watches, or designer clothing, are used to assert one's position in the social hierarchy. In cultures like Mexico, social standing is deeply intertwined with visible markers of wealth, such as extravagant parties or the latest high-end car—

these symbols of affluence project success and open doors to exclusive groups and opportunities.

Figure 6: Egalitarian and Hierarchical Cultures

In Mexico, it is uncommon to see high-ranking individuals using public transport or biking to work, while many lower-level employees cannot afford a car. These disparities underscore and reinforce societal hierarchies both within and beyond the workplace. This phenomenon is particularly prominent in countries or cultures with a pronounced gap between different social or economic classes, where visible symbols of wealth are immediate indicators of one's place in the social order.

By contrast, wealth is less likely to be linked to power, privileges, or entitlement in more egalitarian cultures. In countries like Sweden, Denmark, and the Netherlands, leaders, including CEOs and royalty, often use public transportation or ride bicycles. For example, Crown Princess Victoria of Sweden and Norway's Crown Prince Haakon and Crown Princess Mette-Marit have been seen taking public transportation, blending seamlessly with their fellow citizens. Similarly, former Dutch Prime Minister Mark Rutte famously commuted by bicycle, even arriving by bike at meetings with King Willem-Alexander at the royal offices in The Hague.

Such actions reflect societal values prioritizing equality, practicality, and sustainability over material status. Similarly, Scandinavian principles like "*Jantelagen,*" or the Law of Jante, discourage flaunting wealth or superiority, favoring modesty and contributions to the community instead. This ethos does not prohibit owning luxurious clothing, accessories, or cars; instead, it underscores that wealth should not warrant preferential treatment or elevate one's status above others.

When I lived in Mexico, I remember how important it was for some people to have the best and fanciest party, car, house, watch, accessories, or clothing. It was a way to showcase success and project a certain status within the community. Whether throwing an elaborate celebration or investing in luxury brands, these displays were often seen as symbols of power and prestige. In cultures like Mexico, respect for social and economic status, authority, rank, titles, and social and economic status is big.

In the United States, it's slightly harder to determine someone's job position or power based on their car or clothing. Employees across various levels usually drive cars, and people like to dress casually, so the differences in status are less evident.

In Belgium, company cars are usually practical rather than luxurious, emphasizing utility over status without promoting inequality.

Economic inequality often shapes the extent to which wealth translates into power. Material wealth holds significant social and political influence in countries with high Gini Index scores—such as Mexico (0.459) or the U.S. (0.398). The Gini coefficient, which measures income inequality on a scale from zero (perfect equality) to one (total inequality), highlights these disparities. In such societies, luxury items are seen as symbols of achievement and authority, while reliance on public transport may imply lower status.

Conversely, nations like Belgium (0.259)[16] and Scandinavian countries, with their robust welfare systems, achieve a more equitable distribution of wealth. This promotes social stability and an enhanced quality of life, reducing the cultural emphasis on material displays as markers of success.

While money and economic status are valued in most countries, they hold even greater importance in societies with high Gini scores. Wealth opens doors, grants power, and commands respect in these places.

Interestingly, even in hierarchical societies, not everyone equates wealth with power. Some individuals or organizations embrace egalitarian principles regardless of their cultural context. Companies like Google and Facebook foster environments where informality and egalitarianism are prioritized, with CEOs dressing casually and interacting on a first-name basis. Similarly, wealthy individuals in unequal or hierarchical societies may choose humility and down-to-earth values, underscoring the diversity within every culture.

Ultimately, while no country is entirely egalitarian, equal, unequal, or hierarchical, each society blends elements of both, but some lean more towards one end of the spectrum. Nations like Sweden, Norway, Finland, Austria, Denmark, Israel, and the Netherlands lean toward egalitarianism, valuing humility and shared prosperity, whereas countries like South Africa,

Brazil, and India emphasize wealth as a means of power and status. Japan, meanwhile, strikes a balance, maintaining a hierarchical structure while not placing undue importance on wealth as a social marker.

The perception of wealth and power reflects economic realities and cultural values, influencing how people relate to one another and define success. Whether wealth equals power and entitlement or is merely a resource depends on the cultural perspective.

TITLES AND BUSINESS CARDS

Wealth is just one factor that influences a country's level of inequality or hierarchical structure. Social class, occupation, titles, education, gender, age, religion, and race also play crucial roles. Each society has a unique approach to these factors.

For instance, rank, titles, and age may carry more weight than income or wealth in Japan, reflecting a deep-seated respect for hierarchy and seniority. In India, the caste system may hold more importance than age or wealth in determining one's societal place. Meanwhile, in Saudi Arabia, gender roles are highly influential, often taking precedence over other factors. Each culture emphasizes different aspects, shaping how individuals interact and how status and power are defined within that society.

One example is the use of titles and business cards in Japan. Business cards hold distinct cultural meanings in different parts of the world. In Japan, for instance, exchanging business cards, or *Meishi Koukan*, is a ritualized practice embedded with respect and etiquette. How a business card is presented and received can reflect one's professionalism and understanding of Japanese business culture.

Cards are presented with both hands, accompanied by a slight bow, and should be examined carefully before being placed in a cardholder, never in a pocket. This ceremony underscores the value placed on first impressions and formal introductions in Japanese society.

During and after *Meishi Koukan*, the business card must be respected and treated as an extension of the person who gave it to you. The card is given and received using both hands, and it must be displayed for the duration of the meeting; it must never be put in a pocket or wallet.

The order in which business cards are exchanged in Japan is also crucial. The highest-ranking employees always exchange cards first, following the hierarchy.[17] This protocol shows who has authority and decision-making power and who is at the rank you need to contact. Japanese professionals prefer to work with someone at the same organizational level.

Typically, a Japanese business card will list the company name first, followed by the person's position and occupation, and finally, their name. This order reflects[18] the relative importance of these components. The company's size and prestige influence the employee's social status, which is why it appears first. The position indicates the employee's length of service and company loyalty, while the occupation shows their educational background. These elements highlight hard work and career growth. The employee's name comes last, reflecting Japan's collectivist culture (see chapter #6), where the group is more important than the individual.

Job titles are significant in Japan. How you address a person changes based on their position relative to yours, making business cards essential for showing the proper name and title as a sign of respect and courtesy. This applies to all professions and includes distinctions between junior and senior positions. If you work with Japanese professionals, you may need to get used to many bowing, titles, and formalities and learn to address people courteously.

Similarly, in many East Asian countries, business cards are both convenient and necessary. In China and South Korea, exchanging business cards signifies mutual recognition and a willingness to engage in a business relationship. In these cultures, a business card is more than contact information; it represents the individual's role, rank, and company. Thus, the presentation of a business card demands a level of decorum and respect that reflects the hierarchical nature of these societies.

In contrast, Western cultures, such as those in the United States and Europe, may treat business cards with less formality but no less importance. In these regions, business cards are tools of efficiency and clarity, quickly conveying essential information during introductions. While the ritual may lack the ceremonious nature of its Eastern counterparts, the business card in the West still serves as a crucial first step in networking, providing a tangible reminder of a new connection.

In contrast, Scandinavian countries such as Norway, Sweden, and Denmark exhibit a more egalitarian approach to business practices and social interactions. In these cultures, business cards are exchanged with a simple handshake without elaborate rituals or specific orders. Scandinavian business culture, shaped by the principles of *Janteloven* or the "Law of Jante," promotes equality and humility, often discouraging the display of status or hierarchy.

Business card job titles are straightforward, focusing on one's role rather than academic accolades or honorifics. Academic titles are not used on their cards. Corporate titles like "finance director" or "sales manager" are used to clarify their work area. Interactions are generally first-name based, regardless of rank, reflecting a society where titles are less emphasized and equality is paramount. Calling a Scandinavian by their title or profession or using Mr. or Mrs. is not expected and may be considered rude and arrogant even for CEOs or seniors.

Denmark and Sweden, for example, are among the few countries that legally require equal work rights between men and women and have some of the lowest poverty and Gini rates globally.

When dealing with an egalitarian culture, be ready to roll up your sleeves and leave your titles and diplomas behind.

THE PRIVILEGE OF CHILDBIRTH ORDER AND AGE

In many cultures, birth order and age carry significant benefits and responsibilities, influencing family dynamics and individual roles. As the eldest child, I have experienced firsthand the unique privileges and pressures associated with it. Being the firstborn comes with a set of expectations and opportunities that shape one's character and life path in profound ways.

I am the first child of three and the first grandchild of eighteen on my maternal side. Even before I was born, my family had already labeled me the "leader" of the new generation. This title came with the honor of making several choices. For instance, I often decided what games we played and set the rules for my brothers and cousins, who typically followed my commands. When we wanted candy, snacks, or drinks from the nearby store, my parents, uncles, and aunts would give me the money to pay for and distribute the treats.

At six, I was the only grandchild who could add and subtract, naturally making me the designated money handler for our cousins' treat fund. It became a tradition as we grew older, even after the others caught up with their math skills. My oldest cousin and I took on managing the treat's funds for the group, a task we continued for some years until we became an egalitarian clan.

While the privileges of being the eldest were rewarding, they came with considerable pressures and expectations. My parents wanted me to set a good example for my siblings and cousins, to be the one they could rely on, and to keep an eye on them whenever the adults weren't around. As my brothers and cousins got older, the perks of being the oldest started disappearing, but the expectations and responsibilities kept building up.

Birth order and age in different cultures

In many cultures, gender, birth order, and age significantly influence hierarchy and authority—not just for small matters like treats and candy but also in more formal structures. Monarchies provide a clear example. The right to rule traditionally goes to the eldest child of the reigning monarch. In the United Kingdom, for instance, Queen Elizabeth II was the firstborn child of King George VI and Queen Elizabeth. Historically, the crown was passed to the eldest son, but without a male heir, it went to the eldest daughter, Queen Elizabeth II. Prince Charles, Queen Elizabeth II's first son, is next in line for the throne, followed by Prince William, his eldest son. This tradition continues, though it has evolved slightly. Since 2013, the eldest child inherits the throne regardless of gender, reflecting a move towards gender equality while maintaining the privilege of being the oldest.

[19]In Saudi Arabia, the order of succession follows agnatic seniority, meaning the king's brothers stand higher in succession than his sons. This absolute monarchy, where the king holds complete control and authority (such as in Saudi Arabia, Oman, Afghanistan, Brunei, Jordan, and the United Arab Emirates), is significantly different from absolute monarchies and constitutional monarchies, where the monarch's power is limited and more symbolic (as seen in many European countries).[20]

Family capitalism: inheriting professions in Italy

In Italy, people may not inherit a crown, but they often inherit a profession or a role within the family's longstanding trade or business. Family businesses, particularly in traditional sectors like winemaking, fashion, or craftsmanship, are passed down through generations, with each member assuming a specific position within the family hierarchy. The head of the family, typically the eldest male, wields the most authority and power. He oversees the family's assets, makes significant financial decisions, and guides the family's direction.

Power within the family is distributed hierarchically, often along gender and age lines. The oldest son usually holds the second-most authoritative position, followed by the second son, and so on. This structure extends to their children and the broader family network, encompassing uncles, cousins, and distant relatives, each with a defined place within the family hierarchy. In this system, family loyalty and unity are vital, as younger members are expected to uphold family traditions, contribute to the family's success, and respect the chain of authority. Through this hierarchy, Italian families maintain continuity, preserve their heritage, and ensure their family legacy endures across generations.

When the father dies or retires, the next in the hierarchical family chain takes his place. This practice is encapsulated in the Italian expression *capita-*

lismo familiare, or family capitalism, which refers to the tradition of passing down a privately owned company from one generation to the next.[21]

The luxury fashion industry provides a good illustration of this practice. Companies like Missoni, Fendi, Salvatore Ferragamo, and Ermenegildo Zegna have successfully transferred ownership and management from one generation to the next.

Although this concept has evolved recently, with new generations often seeking different career paths from their family's traditional endeavors, it remains the norm for many Italian family businesses. This hierarchical structure also influences everyday life. Typically, the oldest couple in the family makes most of the critical decisions, reflecting the same respect for seniority and experience seen in the business realm.

Age and respect in East Asian cultures

In many East Asian cultures influenced by Confucianism—such as China, Japan, Korea, Vietnam, Taiwan, and Hong Kong—age significantly shapes social hierarchy, respect, and responsibilities within families and organizations. As Confucius taught, these societies emphasize the importance of maintaining harmonious relationships through respect for superiors and elders.

According to Confucian teachings, five principal relationships outline the structure of social order: ruler to subject, father to son, husband to wife, older brother to younger brother, and friend to friend. In three of these relationships, age provides individuals with greater authority and responsibility, reflecting a paternalistic dynamic where the eldest holds the role of protector and mentor, passing down wisdom to the younger.

Elders are deeply respected for their wisdom, spirituality, and life experience. Their opinions carry significant weight; younger individuals are expected to honor them by respecting and following their guidance. In many East Asian workplaces, for instance, seniority is often a requirement for advancement, with specific years of experience needed before someone can move up the organizational ladder, even if they meet the job's knowledge and skill requirements. This approach underscores the value placed on age and experience over mere qualifications.

Within families, the eldest members are viewed as guardians responsible for making crucial decisions for the family's welfare. They mediate conflicts, offer advice, and provide guidance, while younger members are expected to show respect, use honorific language, obey their directives, and care for them, particularly as they age.

This respect extends to social and religious ceremonies, where elders often take leading roles, symbolizing their status and the reverence they command. Social etiquette reinforces this deference to elders through various acts, such as bowing, offering them the best seats, and serving them first during meals. In these cultures, honoring elders is not merely a custom but a foundational aspect of societal values, ensuring that age equates with respect and responsibility.

Joint family groups in India

Joint family groups, or extended families, are traditional family structures in India where multiple generations live together under one roof. This family system has been an integral part of Indian culture for centuries, embodying values of unity, shared responsibilities, and deep-rooted respect for elders. Typically, the household includes grandparents, parents, children, and sometimes even great-grandparents, along with extended relatives such as uncles, aunts, and cousins. Each family member has specific roles and duties contributing to the family's welfare and harmony.

The joint family is usually headed by the eldest male member, who assumes the role of the family patriarch. This leader is responsible for making significant decisions, guiding the family, and resolving conflicts, often with the support of other senior members. The structure emphasizes respect for age and experience, and the younger members are expected to seek guidance from the elders in important matters.

Caring for elders is a central aspect of the joint family system, with younger members supporting their aging relatives. Sending parents or grandparents to retirement homes is widely considered dishonorable and contrary to cultural values, as it signifies a failure to uphold the family's duty of care. In this system, the well-being of each individual is closely tied to the collective support of the family, fostering a sense of security, belonging, and continuity across generations.

Aging in an egalitarian culture

While many cultures venerate age, in egalitarian societies like the Netherlands, Sweden, Finland, and Australia, respect and influence are not based on age. Here, the young and old's opinions are valued equally, and everyone's voice is heard with the same level of importance. Independent thinking and self-exploration are highly regarded, and parents instill these principles in their children from a young age.

In these cultures, families often embrace democratic relationships; independent thinking and exploration are highly valued. Children are encouraged to engage in discussions, share their opinions, and participate in decision-making processes within the family. This approach fosters a sense of equality and mutual respect for individual perspectives, allowing everyone, regardless of age, to contribute their thoughts and ideas even if they are different from their parents. Children learn to negotiate, communicate effectively with adults, and develop logical solutions, cultivating a sense of agency and self-expression.

As they grow older, young people are free to carve their paths without the pressure to conform to family expectations or adhere to traditional roles. They are free to pursue careers and passions based on personal interests rather than family legacies, allowing them to shape their identities. This autonomy is considered essential to personal development and is respected by parents, who support their children's independent choices.

In the workplace, it's a comparable situation. All contributions are valued, regardless of age, and opportunities for advancement are based on merit and individual achievements rather than seniority. This meritocratic approach fosters a fair and dynamic work environment, where ideas are judged by their substance rather than the age or rank of the person presenting them.

Interpersonal interactions also reflect these egalitarian values. In social and professional settings, younger individuals address older adults by their first names rather than by formal titles or last names, promoting equality.

WHEN INEQUALITY VIOLATES HUMAN RIGHTS

This chapter explores how societies structure hierarchies, the dynamics of power, and their impact on individuals. Both hierarchical and egalitarian systems offer advantages and challenges. Viewed through the lens of human diversity and meritocratic principles, inequality is not inherently harmful; it reflects differences in abilities, efforts, and development stages. Human diversity enriches society, whether in skills, intelligence, or creativity.

A world where everyone had the same abilities would lack innovation and creativity. Differences drive progress, inspire new ideas, and enrich cultures. In this sense, inequality reflects the natural diversity of human potential and interests. It would be unreasonable to expect someone who does not train or lacks athletic skills to be treated the same as an Olympic champion. In this sense, inequality is a fair acknowledgment of individual effort and excellence.

Another essential aspect of inequality is the necessity of age-appropriate privileges and responsibilities. Expecting children and adults to abide by the same rules and standards is neither practical nor fair. In this context, inequality is not a form of discrimination but rather an acknowledgment of the different stages of human development. It ensures that people receive the support, resources, and opportunities appropriate to their age and maturity level, fostering healthy growth and development.

Similarly, considerations of gender, ability, and other facets of diversity often call for different forms of support or tailored expectations.

However, inequality becomes harmful when rooted in systemic injustice, such as racism, gender, or socioeconomic status discrimination, which denies individuals their rights and opportunities. These forms of inequality perpetuate exclusion, hinder progress, and create barriers that prevent people from reaching their full potential. They are unjust and harmful, perpetuating cycles of poverty and exclusion.

For this reason, this chapter was the most challenging to write. My goal in this book is to foster tolerance and acceptance among cultures with distinct ways of thinking, showing their variances without casting judgment or assigning blame. Yet, it is challenging to remain sympathetic when cultural differences cross a line, leading to injustice, discrimination, or even human rights violations. I encourage you to read the following two sub-chapters cautiously as they delve into complex issues that, while necessary to understand, can be profoundly disheartening and depressing.

CLASS ENTITLEMENT

Individuals from privileged social or economic classes believe they inherently deserve special treatment, opportunities, or resources. This entitlement stems from a deep-rooted sense of superiority that can be perpetuated through societal structures, upbringing, and long-standing systemic inequalities. It often leads to behaviors where the entitled expect preferential treatment, disregard the struggles of lower classes, and are resistant to changes that challenge their elevated position in society. Class entitlement reinforces social hierarchies and perpetuates inequality by justifying the uneven distribution of wealth and power.

This class entitlement is still practiced in many places. One of the most notorious is the caste system in India. This traditional social hierarchy has been deeply ingrained in Indian society for centuries. It divides people into different groups based on birth and occupation and has significant social, economic, and political implications.

The caste system, known as "*varna*" in *Sanskrit*, is believed to have originated from ancient Hindu texts such as the *Rigveda*. The *Rigveda* mentions four primary varnas or social classes: *Brahmins, Kshatriyas, Vaishyas, and Shudras.*[22]

The *Brahmins* are at the top of the hierarchy, traditionally responsible for religious rituals, teaching, and maintaining sacred knowledge. The second tier consists of *Kshatriyas*, who traditionally served as warriors, kings, and administrators. The third group, *Vaishyas*, are involved in commerce, agriculture, and trade. At the bottom are the Shudras, who perform manual labor and service jobs.

Outside the *Varna* system are the *Dalits*, historically considered "untouchables" and subjected to severe discrimination and exclusion from mainstream society. Over time, the *Varna* system evolved into the more complex *Jati* system, which includes thousands of sub-castes based on occupation, region, and ethnicity.

The caste system enforces social segregation, dictating marriage, dining, and social interaction based on caste. Castes have traditionally determined one's occupation and economic role, leading to a rigid division of labor. Higher castes have historically had better access to education, resources, and political power, while lower castes have faced systemic exclusion and poverty.[23]

The *dharma* (duty) concept in Hinduism has been used to justify the caste system, with each caste assigned specific duties and responsibilities. The belief in karma (actions in past lives affecting one's present life) reinforces the idea that one's caste results from one's previous actions.

The Indian Constitution, adopted in 1950, abolished *"untouchability"* and prohibited caste-based discrimination[24]. India has implemented affirmative action policies, including reservations in education and government jobs, to uplift historically disadvantaged castes. However, despite legal measures, caste-based discrimination and social prejudices persist, especially in rural areas.

Class entitlement, where individuals or groups believe they inherently deserve privileges and advantages due to their socioeconomic status, is a phenomenon seen around the globe. It manifests in various forms, such as within aristocratic circles and royal families, elite schools, and exclusive social clubs that preserve class distinctions, perpetuating a sense of entitlement among those born into privilege. Russian oligarchs, with vast economic and political power, often expect preferential treatment due to their wealth and connections. Similarly, in China, the *Princelings*—children of high-ranking officials—benefit from inherited political influence, granting them privileged access to wealth and power. Likewise, white supremacy in the United States has historically upheld systemic advantages for certain groups, reinforcing disparities in opportunity and influence.

These examples highlight how class entitlement reinforces social stratification across cultures and political systems, often creating barriers that prevent equal opportunity access. Addressing these entrenched advantages remains a critical step toward fostering fairness and dismantling systemic inequalities worldwide.

GENDER ROLES AND EQUALITY

Gender inequality, though deeply rooted in societies worldwide, is increasingly being challenged as the world moves toward greater equity. Significant progress has been made, with many countries making meaningful strides to close the gap in opportunities and rights for men and women. However, ingrained norms and biases still subtly influence behaviors, perceptions, and access to opportunities, reminding us that the journey toward full equality is ongoing.

While biological differences between men and women are undeniable, they do not justify inequalities in rights, privileges, power, opportunities, or safety.

The following sub-chapters on gender equality draw insights from key resources, including the Global Gender Gap Index, the Women, Peace, and Security Index, and UN reports. The Global Gender Gap Index ranks 156 countries based on economic opportunity, education, health, and political empowerment, while the Women, Peace, and Security Index evaluates 170 nations on security, justice, and inclusion. Together, these tools highlight persistent gender disparities and the multifaceted factors driving inequality, emphasizing the ongoing need for progress toward true equality.

My experience with gender roles in the US

As the owner of a real estate company in the US, I manage everything from hiring labor and approving projects to overseeing contract execution. This involves working closely with electricians, plumbers, realtors, and contractors. However, despite my role, I encounter situations where these professionals seek confirmation from my partner before proceeding.

For example, they might ask questions like, "Should we wait for your husband's approval before starting?" or "Would you like to call him for confirmation?" These interactions imply that my decisions alone aren't sufficient and that my partner's approval is needed to validate them. This is frustrating and disheartening, as it diminishes my authority and undermines my role as a business owner.

What's striking is that these questions are never directed at my husband.

His decisions are taken at face value, while mine are second-guessed. Even though it doesn't happen often, this disparity underscores the persistent gender bias in the industry, where women's authority is frequently questioned, and men's decisions are rarely challenged.

Although societal views are evolving, there remains a lingering, unspoken belief that men are the primary decision-makers and providers or hold more authority than women. This raises important questions: Are there instances where traditional gender roles serve a purpose? Do biological factors justify these conventional roles? Are gender roles still necessary to protect women?

I value traditional acts of chivalry, such as feeling protected by men or enjoying the courtesy of doors being opened for me. These gestures make me feel appreciated and cared for. At the same time, I strongly advocate gender equality, especially in areas like job opportunities, equal pay, and the freedom to make my own decisions without requiring validation or approval. I believe it's possible to balance appreciating traditional roles with maintaining a woman's independence and authority, particularly in professional settings.

I support sharing responsibilities with my husband at home, but not necessarily in a strict 50-50 split. Instead, we divide tasks based on our schedules and commitments outside the house. This flexible approach allows us to contribute to household chores and childcare in a way that respects our strengths and availability. It fosters a harmonious partnership where both of us feel supported and balanced.

Globally, gender roles and power dynamics between men and women vary widely, shaped by a complex interplay of cultural, religious, economic, and social factors. These influences create diverse expectations for how men and women should behave across different societies. Two contrasting examples of approaches to gender equality are Iceland and Afghanistan.

Iceland

In Iceland, young girls can confidently aspire to become anything they dream of—whether president, astronaut, or doctor—thanks to a society where laws, government policies, and social systems work together to achieve these ambitions.

Iceland and other Nordic countries like Denmark, Finland, Norway, and Sweden consistently lead the world in closing the gender gap. In 2022, Iceland ranked first in the World Economic Forum's Global Gender Gap Report, achieving a 90.8% score, and placed third on the Women, Peace, and Security Index (WPS) in 2021 with a near-perfect score of 0.907. [25]Icelandic men and women enjoy nearly equal power and opportunities, a reality shaped by progressive laws and regulations that have ranked the country at the top in gender equality for thirteen consecutive years.

One inspiring figure for Icelandic girls is Vigdís Finnbogadóttir, who made history in 1980 as the world's first democratically elected female head of state. Her 16-year presidency (1980-1996) [26]is a powerful example of female leadership. Politically, Iceland also ranks highly, with 52% of its parliament consisting of women, and it holds the highest share of female heads of state in the past 50 years.[27]

Iceland was the first country in the world to require companies with more than 25 employees to prove they pay men and women equally for the same work.[28] This progressive approach is enforced by an external certification system that imposes daily fines on companies failing to comply. Although women still earn between 14% and 18% less than men, their labor force participation rate is above 80%,[29] supported by policies that ensure job flexibility, equal pay for equal work, and legal job protection after childbirth.

Iceland's parental leave policies are equally groundbreaking. They offer 12 months of leave per family, split equally between both parents. This legal mandate entitles each parent to six months off at 80% of their income and promotes shared responsibility in family care[30]. As a result, it's common to see fathers actively involved in childcare, helping to dismantle traditional gender roles.

Public company boards, government councils, and committees must maintain gender balance, ensuring at least 40% representation of either gender. By 2021, women held approximately 42% of managerial roles and 52% of parliamentary positions.[31]

Both girls and boys have full access to education, and public colleges are tuition-free. Iceland's educational attainment score stands at an impressive 0.993[32], 1.0 representing total equality. Gender-based discrimination is prohibited in all areas of life, including schools, extracurricular activities, sports, advertising, language use, workplaces, insurance costs, and the trade of goods and services.

Iceland is widely regarded as the safest country in the world, boasting the lowest crime and murder rates.[33] Women can confidently walk alone at night without significant concern for their safety. While the risk of assault is low, it's still advisable to remain cautious, especially in environments where alcohol is prevalent, such as bars and nightclubs.[34]

Iceland enforces strict punishments for domestic violence and sexual harassment, the latter encompassing any behavior perceived as disrespectful. Citizens are encouraged to report any abuse or discrimination. While violence against women has not been wholly eradicated, Iceland's rates are notably lower than in many other countries.

In conclusion, Iceland is a nation where women can feel safe, access education and employment, receive equal pay, share family responsibilities with their partners, and live free from gender-based discrimination. Icelandic women are supported by strong female role models and a society that promotes gender equality.

Afghanistan

Many girls dream of feeling loved and cherished. They hope to find their soulmate, fall in love, get married, and start a family. They aspire to live healthy, beautiful lives, express themselves through fashion, and enjoy simple pleasures—dancing, laughing with friends, traveling, and pursuing careers that bring them fulfillment and purpose.

However, in Afghanistan, these dreams are far from reality for most girls. Chasing such aspirations can come at the cost of their lives or freedom. In a society where women are often regarded as inferior to men, they have little to no voice and minimal control over their own lives. From birth until death, the decisions that shape their futures are made mainly by men. This has been the cultural norm for generations.

Afghanistan consistently ranks at the bottom of the Global Gender Gap Index, reflecting the severe limitations placed on women. The restrictions are profound—Afghan men forbid women from interacting with, speaking to, or even being seen by male strangers, including doctors, nurses, teachers, or police officers. This creates a web of isolation that begins early and affects every aspect of a woman's life.

The consequences of these societal taboos start even before birth. Afghanistan has one of the highest maternal mortality rates in the world[35], as most births occur at home without the aid of professional healthcare workers, primarily due to a shortage of female doctors and nurses.

If a girl survives childbirth, her life continues to be governed by male relatives, starting with her father, who will likely control significant decisions about her future, including her marriage. Less than 20% of Afghan girls have any say in choosing their spouse. Forced and arranged marriages are the norm, with over 30% of girls married before the age of eighteen and about 15% before the age of fifteen.[36]

UNICEF partners recorded 183 child marriages and ten cases of child trafficking within just one year in only two of Afghanistan's thirty-four provinces. These cases involved girls ranging from six months to seventeen years old, often married to men twenty to fifty years their senior.[37]

Married life for Afghan women is fraught with hardship. Husbands often view their wives as possessions and frequently justify physical abuse as a form of "correction." Many men consider it acceptable to beat their wives for reasons such as burning food, arguing, leaving the house without permission, neglecting children, refusing sex, or failing to care for in-laws. Shockingly, nearly 90% of Afghan women have endured domestic abuse, and their husbands have physically assaulted 40%.[38]

Both the Afghan Constitution and Islamic Sharia law permit polygamy, allowing men to have up to four wives, while women are restricted to only one husband. Men can divorce their wives unilaterally, without the woman's consent, whereas women do not have the same rights and require their husband's approval for most decisions, including divorce. Divorced women often face intense societal shame for the rest of their lives, and in extreme cases, they may even be subjected to honor killings.

The aspirations of pursuing a college degree or a professional career are often shattered. Before the Taliban's return to power in 2021, 87% of Afghan women were illiterate, two-thirds of girls were unable to attend school, and only 20% of the teaching workforce was female[39]. Now, under Taliban rule, girls have been instructed not to attend secondary school and are barred from most forms of employment, except in the health sector, making access to education even more difficult than before.

Traditionally, Afghan women's clothing was vibrant in color, with intricate designs unique to each province. Though modest, these garments reflected the culture's diversity and allowed women to express their identity while covering most of their bodies, not entire faces. However, in recent years, women have been stripped of the freedom to choose their attire—an integral part of their heritage and self-expression.

Afghanistan's climate can be harsh, with summer temperatures averaging between 28 and 32 degrees Celsius (84-90°F) and sometimes soaring to 43 degrees Celsius (109°F).[40] Despite the oppressive heat, women are prohibited from wearing weather-appropriate clothing like summer dresses, shorts, or short-sleeved shirts. Under Taliban rule, they are compelled to cover their faces or wear a burqa in public. The burqa is a loose, solid-colored garment that conceals the entire body and face, with a mesh screen covering the eyes. Worn over regular clothing, it offers little relief in the sweltering heat and is ill-suited for such extreme weather conditions.

Afghan women face severe restrictions, with limited rights and numerous obligations. The legal system imposes harsh rules and brutal punishments for defying societal norms. Many lack access to education, healthcare, or employment and are denied the freedom to choose their clothing, husbands, or travel without a male guardian. Divorce is often inaccessible, leaving women vulnerable to abuse and entrenched inequality.

Similar hardships exist in countries like Yemen, Syria, Pakistan, and Iraq, where women often need permission from male relatives to leave their homes. Venturing out without a guardian or adhering to strict dress codes can result in physical punishment, perpetuating a cycle of oppression.

EGALITARIAN, EQUAL, HIERARCHICAL, AND UNEQUAL

Cultural attitudes toward hierarchy, equality, and power distribution vary worldwide, shaping how societies function and individuals interact. These differences can be broadly categorized into four types: egalitarian, equal, hierarchical, and unequal cultures.

Egalitarian cultures

Egalitarian cultures prioritize fairness and equality and minimize displays of status, fostering shared responsibility and mutual respect. Hierarchical structures are deemphasized, with power and opportunities distributed equitably to ensure everyone can succeed. Decision-making is often democratic, emphasizing collaboration, consensus, and open communication, which leads to innovation, adaptability, and higher job satisfaction.

Rooted in Indigenous traditions of communal living and influenced by Enlightenment thinkers like Jean-Jacques Rousseau.[41] Modern egalitarianism champions equal rights, social justice, and individual freedoms. These principles are central to participatory democracies, where power is decentralized, and citizens play an active role in governance. Social interactions in egalitarian cultures are typically informal. People from diverse educational and socioeconomic backgrounds work and socialize together and address each other by first name, with less emphasis on titles or honorifics, encouraging relationships built on mutual respect and equality while promoting social mobility and inclusivity.

Examples: Scandinavian countries and the Netherlands.

Key Characteristics

- A core belief in the equal value and dignity of all individuals.
- Collective decision-making processes where everyone's voice is heard.
- Roles and responsibilities can be fluid, with less emphasis on rigid structures.
- Strong focus on social justice, inclusivity, and equal opportunities for all.

Equal cultures

Egalitarian and equal cultures emphasize fairness and minimize power, status, and resource access differences. However, subtle differences exist in how these principles are applied and perceived. Egalitarian cultures downplay status and power differences but do not necessarily strive for identical outcomes. Equal cultures seek to level the playing field in tangible ways, like through economic and social policy. While these cultures may sometimes overlap—many egalitarian cultures also strive for equality in resources, and equal cultures often incorporate egalitarian principles—the distinction lies mainly in focusing on equal opportunity or outcomes.

Equal cultures focus on providing everyone with the same resources, opportunities, and rights. The emphasis is on achieving parity in outcomes, not just in opportunity. Equality here means that differences in status, wealth, or power are minimized, with systems in place to ensure that no one is significantly advantaged over others.

Equal cultures aim to achieve equal outcomes through systemic measures. Decision-making may be focused on policies that ensure fair distribution of resources, even if that requires some centralized control. Equal cultures advocate for inclusivity and strive to break down barriers that could exclude people based on arbitrary or historical divisions.

Examples: Sweden, Denmark, Norway, Australia, and New Zealand.[42]

Key Characteristics

- Fair distribution of resources, including healthcare, education, and social services.
- Legally protected from discrimination based on race, gender, religion, or sexual orientation.
- Income inequality is addressed through minimum wage laws, social benefits, and support programs.
- Healthcare, education, and transportation are universally accessible.

Hierarchical cultures

Hierarchical cultures prioritize order, structure, and clear roles, where authority and leadership are respected and stability is maintained. While roles differ within the system, each is considered valuable, emphasizing harmony and tradition. Governance in these cultures is typically centralized, with power concentrated at the top and decisions flowing downward. Historical examples include feudal Europe, imperial China, and the caste system in India, often justified by religious or philosophical doctrines like the divine right of kings or Confucian ideals of harmony.

Social interactions in hierarchical cultures are formal and structured, with titles, honorifics, and class distinctions playing significant roles. Respect for elders and those in higher positions is expected, while social mobility is often limited. Communication tends to be formal, and subordinates rarely question authority, relying on superiors for guidance. Though hierarchical, these systems highlight stability and the value of defined roles in maintaining social order.

Hierarchical structures are deeply entrenched, and employees may rely heavily on their superiors for direction and decisions. Subordinates are less likely to question or challenge authority. Often exhibit formal communication, with clear distinctions between different levels of hierarchy.

Examples: Japan, South Korea, Malaysia, the Philippines, and Mexico.

Key Characteristics

- Clear lines of authority and respect for hierarchical positions.
- Emphasis on maintaining social order and stability through established roles.
- Deference to elders, superiors, and those in positions of power.
- Rigid roles and responsibilities with well-defined social stratifications.

Unequal cultures

Unequal cultures refer to societies where significant power, wealth, or status disparities are often acceptable or inevitable. These cultures can involve a hierarchical structure, but the focus is on the gaps between levels rather than the structure itself. In unequal cultures, resources and opportunities are unevenly distributed, and upward mobility can be restricted, with structural barriers and limited opportunities, making it hard for people to change their status.

Income distribution and access to resources like healthcare and education are unequal. In unequal cultures, authority can be viewed as reinforcing privilege and restricting others' access to power or resources. Those in power may exploit their position for personal gain or to oppress others. Violation of rights could lead to practices that violate fundamental human rights and dignity.

Examples: South Africa, Namibia, Honduras, Guatemala, and Brazil

Key Characteristics

- Significant gaps exist between the wealthy and the poor.

- Structural barriers make it difficult for individuals to climb the socio-economic ladder. Factors such as family background, education access, and social connections play a significant role in determining one's ability to improve one's socio-economic status.
- Unequal access to education and healthcare is often influenced by wealth or social status.
- Concentration of power and influence in the hands of a minor, elite group.
- Abuse of power and lack of basic rights result in practices that undermine fundamental human rights and dignity.

Cultural clashes

When individuals from hierarchical and egalitarian cultures interact, misunderstandings often emerge due to different expectations and norms surrounding respect, authority, and social conduct.

Imagine a Dutch student studying in Korea who addresses professors by their first names and shares opinions freely in class, as is customary in their home country. This behavior is encouraged in the Netherlands as a sign of confidence and active engagement. However, in Korea, where respect for hierarchy is deeply rooted, this approach could be perceived as disrespectful and inappropriate. Such behavior might affect the student's grades and relationships with professors and peers, who expect a more formal and respectful manner in the classroom. The student's intent to be approachable and participative could unintentionally signal a lack of respect for authority in the eyes of their Korean counterparts.

Conversely, misunderstandings can arise when someone from a hierarchical culture interacts in an egalitarian setting. For example, a friend from India, a doctor in his sixties, recounted an experience that left him feeling disrespected. He ordered the bill after dinner while on vacation with his wife, daughters, and their husbands. However, when the waiter brought the bill, she handed it to one of his sons-in-law instead of him. This action deeply offended him, implying disregard for his seniority and authority within the family. In his view, the waiter had, perhaps unknowingly, undermined his role as the elder by prioritizing his younger relative.

In many hierarchical cultures, the eldest or most senior person is typically accorded the highest respect, with specific gestures, such as handling the bill and reinforcing their status. By overlooking these cultural nuances, interactions that might seem trivial in egalitarian cultures can lead to discomfort or offense for those from hierarchical backgrounds.

Interacting with hierarchical cultures

- A hierarchical culture has a clear authority structure with well-defined levels of power and responsibility.
- Use titles and last names.
- Be cautious when talking to or inviting people of a different rank or social status than yours, as this may be inappropriate.
- Accept higher-ranking or elders' opinions, especially in public, and seek their approval before making decisions.
- Follow the hierarchical chain for all communications, speak with the person at your level or social status, or ask for permission to hop from one level to another.
- Make sure you know who to include in the decision-making process.
- Invite individuals below your rank to share their ideas. Don't expect spontaneous input.
- Understand that if a hierarchical team member gives you a plan without asking for your opinion or ideas, it's not a sign of disrespect.

Interacting with egalitarian and equal cultures

- An egalitarian culture is characterized by minimal hierarchy, where power and responsibility are equally distributed, and all individuals are treated as equals.
- Seek input from other team members.
- Understand that disagreeing with a higher-ranking individual or bypassing hierarchy is not necessarily a sign of disrespect.
- Speak directly to the person you must communicate with—no need to copy or include their boss.
- Manage by objectives, ensuring they are concrete and specific. Consider linking them to rewards or recognition.
- Act as a facilitator rather than a supervisor.
- Don't take it personally if someone disagrees with you; it's not a sign of disrespect.
- Interacting with unequal cultures
- Use your privileges to contribute to a more inclusive, equitable, and fair world.

KEY TAKEAWAYS

- Egalitarian cultures prioritize fairness and minimize status displays, fostering a sense of shared responsibility and mutual respect.
- Equal cultures emphasize balanced opportunities and equitable treatment, ensuring individuals have similar chances to succeed.
- Hierarchical cultures rely on structured authority and clear power distinctions to maintain order and respect for roles.
- Unequal cultures, often marked by significant wealth, privilege, and access disparities, reflect deeply entrenched social divides.
- Use your privileges to contribute to a more inclusive, equitable, and fair world.

CHAPTER 6

Me or we

"The strength of the team is each member.
The strength of each member is the team."
- Phil Jackson

A h, the age-old question: Am I a lone wolf or part of a pack? This concept goes beyond simple preferences and dives deep into how we're raised and the societal norms we adopt. Do parents in your culture teach their children to be independent, stand tall, and chase their dreams? Or are they taught from the beginning that they are first and foremost members of a group, a family, or a community, with their identity interwoven with others? What role do elders and authority figures play in personal decisions?

This chapter delves into these distinctions between individualist and collectivist cultures, focusing on how they shape individual vs. group interests and goals[43].

LUNCH TIME AT WORK

I worked for the same company in Mexico and later in the US. One of the most noticeable cultural differences was around lunchtime.

In Mexico, lunchtime was a significant and communal affair. The company had a massive cafeteria that comfortably seats more than 400 employees. It also offered a banquet service that prepared buffet-style meals for over 1,000 employees, fostering a sense of community and providing ample time for employees to socialize and enjoy a meal together.

In contrast, the lunchtime experience in the US was much more individualized and often shorter. Employees typically brought their meals or grabbed a quick bite, and the dining areas were smaller and less communal.

My friends and I had a ritual of eating lunch together around 2 p.m., which is the most popular lunchtime in Mexico. A few minutes before 2, we would walk toward the cafeteria, gathering some friends from their offices on our way. We'd sit in a group of ten to fifteen, chat, and wait for everyone to finish their meal before leaving the table. After lunch, we often took a short walk together, continuing our conversations, before returning to our offices around 3 p.m. On other days, we'd head out as a large group to a restaurant, spending about an hour to an hour and a half enjoying our meal before returning to work.

When I moved to Memphis, a Human Resources representative gave me a plant tour. Everything felt familiar—the offices, plant layout, desks, and meeting rooms, everything except the cafeteria. Instead of the large, bustling dining area I was used to, there were just 6 or 8 small tables, a fridge, a sink, and a microwave. I assumed there must be another cafeteria somewhere in the building, but this was it.

When I asked about the buffet, she kindly explained that they didn't provide that service and that I would need to bring my food. She pointed out that I could use the fridge, microwave, and kitchen facilities and suggested marking my lunch with a Post-it if I planned to leave it in the shared fridge.

On my first day, I brought my lunch box and Post-it notes with my name on them. I worried there wouldn't be enough room in the fridge for my food—how could one fridge fit food for at least 400 employees? Surprisingly, I never had a fridge space issue in my two years there.

But what surprised me the most was that many employees ate alone. They came, warmed their food in the microwave, devoured it, and returned to work within 10-15 minutes. Initially, I thought the timing was off because I ate at 2 PM, which is late for Americans who usually eat around noon. So, I switched my lunch to noon. While a few more employees were eating then, it was still a small group, considering the company's size.

Where did everyone eat? I noticed that some ate at the cafeteria, some at their desks, some outside, a few in their cars, and others just grabbed a snack and continued working to leave on time. However, compared to Mexico, a significant percentage of people ate alone.

Eating lunch at their desks or alone isn't unusual in the United States. Several factors contribute to this behavior, perhaps the main reason being productivity and time efficiency. Many employees feel that eating at their desks allows them to continue working through lunch, which can be especially important in high-pressure jobs or environments with tight deadlines.

This practice can also provide more flexibility for managing their daily workload and leaving the office on time for dinner with their families.

In some workplaces, there might be an implicit expectation to be always available or to demonstrate dedication to the job. Employees may feel that taking a more extended lunch break away from their desks could be perceived negatively by employers or colleagues.

Some people might also prefer to use their lunch break for personal activities, such as running errands, making personal calls, or simply enjoying quiet time alone. Also, not all workplaces provide adequate communal spaces for employees to gather and eat lunch together. In many offices, the break room or cafeteria might be small, poorly equipped, or uninviting, leading employees to choose the convenience of eating at their desks or outside.

Eating alone in Mexico and other collectivist cultures may be seen as antisocial, isolating, and, frankly, a bit sad. Some people even drive 30-60 minutes to have lunch with their families. Does this mean they slack off at work? Absolutely not! They stay late to finish their tasks, but family meals remain a top priority.

Collectivist cultures place a high value on social interactions and community. Mealtime is not just about filling your stomach but also about building and maintaining relationships. This practice helps build teamwork and a sense of belonging within the company. Eating alone can be seen as missing out on crucial social bonding opportunities.

In many East Asian and Latin-American cultures, for example, sharing meals is vital to maintaining harmony and strengthening group cohesion. Eating together is about food, fostering relationships, networking, and respecting and caring for colleagues and family members.

Eating alone or at one's desk can be viewed negatively, suggesting that the person is not interested in participating in the collective social life. The person may also be perceived as unsociable or disengaged.

Another dining-out experience is when individuals from an individualist culture visit a restaurant. Often, each person orders their meal, eats their food, and pays their bill. The focus is on individual preferences and choices. In collectivist cultures, especially in Asia, multiple dishes are ordered for the whole table, placed in the center, and everyone shares the food. The focus is on communal eating and sharing, highlighting the collectivist principle of group harmony.

In summary, while eating alone is a practical option in some cultures, it is a missed opportunity for essential social interactions in collectivist societies. So, the next time you're in Mexico, Colombia, South Korea, or Japan, grab a friend or a coworker and share a meal—it's more than just good manners; it's a cultural necessity.

NURSING HOMES

One of the most emotionally difficult choices a family caregiver faces is whether to place a loved one in a nursing home. When my grandmother became old and required specialized medical care and assistance with daily activities that family members were unable to provide at home, I suggested to my mom that we consider a nursing home. My mom replied that if we put her in a nursing home, she would die of sadness.

A nursing home was never an option for my mom or grandmother. My grandmother would have felt like a burden, believing her children didn't love her anymore and had abandoned her. Even though this wouldn't have been the case—since the family would have visited her often and ensured she was doing fine—her perception of being in a nursing home would have been profoundly negative.

In many collectivist cultures, like mine, there is a strong belief that parents who have devoted their lives to raising their children deserve to be looked after in their old age within the family home. The intense emotional bond between parents and children reinforces the expectation that children will look after their parents personally. Providing emotional and physical support within the family is deeply ingrained, making placing parents in a retirement home highly dishonorable, selfish, and disgraceful.

In China, filial piety (孝, Xiào) is a Confucian moral tenet that requires children to respect and serve their parents and elders.[44] It emphasizes respect, obedience, and care for one's parents and elders, placing a strong moral obligation on children to care for their aging parents personally within the family home. Sending them to a nursing home can be perceived as neglectful and disrespectful.

Indian culture places considerable social pressure on caring for elderly parents at home, facilitated by the joint family system where multiple generations live together. This setup naturally supports the care of elderly family members within the household. The community often views those who send their parents to nursing homes as neglectful or ungrateful.

In the Dominican Republic, children are not only obligated by a sense of responsibility to care for their parents, but it's also the law. Section 5 of the Commonwealth of Dominican Maintenance Act states: "Every person who is not a minor has an obligation, to the extent that the person is capable of doing so, to maintain the person's parents and grandparents who need such maintenance because of age, physical or mental infirmity or disability."[45]

In the U.S., caring for elderly parents is considered a moral responsibility and a significant family value. However, unlike in some collectivist cultures where filial piety is a deeply ingrained expectation, there is less social and emotional pressure for children to provide direct, hands-on care. While many Americans prioritize their parents' well-being, professional caregivers and nursing homes are often seen as practical and acceptable solutions. This approach is not due to a lack of familial devotion but rather a cultural emphasis on individualism and the realities of demanding work schedules, which make full-time personal caregiving less feasible for many families.

Nursing homes are often considered crucial when elderly parents require specialized medical care and assistance with daily activities that family members cannot provide. Modern life demands, such as full-time jobs, make it difficult for adult children to provide full-time care. Some individuals believe nursing homes offer better medical care, social interaction, and safety than what might be available at home. Professional caregivers and medical staff can provide expertise and attention that can be difficult to match in a home setting.

There are cultural variations in how nursing homes are perceived. While sending an adult parent to a nursing home is often viewed as a practical solution to meet complex care needs, it is also a decision laden with emotional and cultural considerations. The perception of this choice varies widely among individuals and is influenced by practical realities, cultural backgrounds, and evolving societal norms. Regardless of practicality, many collectivist cultures strongly emphasize family and filial piety, making the idea of placing parents in a nursing home far less acceptable and often viewed negatively.

LEAVING THE NEST

I grew up in a close-knit family that valued tradition, community, and family bonds. My parents expected my brothers and me to live with them until we married, so I did. As the nursing home example shows, some parents wish their children to live with them and support each other until they get married. This lifestyle choice is influenced by the cultural importance of family and economic and social factors, reflecting deeply rooted traditions and contemporary economic challenges.

I started working at a multinational corporation when I was 20 and still in college. Even though I covered some of my expenses, like gas, dining out, and clothing, I didn't have to worry about rent, utilities, or groceries. This allowed me to save up and buy my apartment, which was utterly mortgage-free, before getting married. I didn't have to worry about cooking or cleaning, allowing me time to focus on studying and working. I was at college from 7 am to 1 pm, went home for a quick lunch with my family, and worked from 3 to 7 pm every weekday for two years. After work, I had to do my homework or study for tests. I couldn't have made it without my family's support. After graduating, I started working full-time but still lived with my parents until I married at 25.

Another advantage (which I perceived as a disadvantage then) was that part of the courtship occurred at my parents' house. My now-husband would visit me at my house, where my family warmly welcomed him. They got to know each other through family gatherings and dinners at home. Of course, sometimes we wished for more privacy.

After the wedding, we moved to our apartment near our parents' houses. The proximity allowed us to stay in close contact, often visiting for Sunday dinners and family gatherings filled with laughter, music, and delicious food. My parents were supportive but emotional about their only daughter leaving home. They had always known this day would come, but it was still a bitter-sweet moment.

***

In Italy, "mammoni" (mama's boy) describes a significant cultural phenomenon where many Italian men live with their parents well into adulthood, often until they get married. Living at home until marriage is not merely a convenience but a reflection of strong familial bonds and mutual dependence. In this context, the family home serves as a haven where children, particularly sons, remain under the protective wing of their parents.

The high cost of living, particularly in urban areas, and the scarcity of affordable housing exacerbate this situation. For many young Italians, living at home is not just a cultural tradition but a practical and economic necessity. It protects against financial instability and allows them to save money for future investments, such as purchasing a home or preparing for marriage.

In Hispanic, Asian, and Mediterranean cultures, living with your parents until you get married is commonly viewed positively.

On the other hand, individualistic cultures might view living with parents as a sign of failure to launch. Some might perceive it as a lack of independence or ambition. Another concern is that adults living with their parents might delay their personal development and independence. Some argue that living independently teaches valuable life skills and fosters individual growth.

For example, according to a 2018 Statista survey, around 6% of undergraduate students in the United States reported living with their parents during the school year. [46]This percentage increased after the onset of COVID-19, when schools were closed, and living costs rose.

In the United States, most college students move out of their parents' house during their first year, typically around age 18. Some colleges even require students to live in campus dormitories during their first year to help them acclimate to college life, foster independence, and build community. This requirement varies by institution but is a common practice aimed at enhancing the overall student experience.

More than 70% of young adults (ages 18 -34) in Croatia, Greece, Portugal, Serbia, and Italy live with their parents. In contrast, in Scandinavian countries such as Finland, Sweden, and Denmark, the percentage is much lower, with fewer than 20% of young adults living with their parents. In the US, that percentage is 32%, varying significantly between those with and without a college degree.[47]

These differences reflect both cultural values and economic conditions. Southern and Eastern European countries, which tend to have more collectivist cultures, emphasize strong family ties and often face higher economic pressures that encourage multigenerational living. Living with parents into adulthood is a practical response to financial challenges and cultural expectations of family support and cohesion in these regions.

In contrast, Northern European countries, characterized by individualistic cultures, often have more robust social safety nets and cultural norms that favor early independence. These nations typically offer extensive state support for housing, education, and social services, allowing young adults to move out and live independently earlier. This reflects a cultural emphasis on self-reliance and personal responsibility.

WEDDINGS AND PARTIES

When planning our wedding, my husband mentioned he wanted a small party. I said, "Yes, just family and close friends." We invited 400 guests to our "small" party, and more than 380 showed up.

We started with a guest list that included our direct and extended family, grandparents, some cousins, uncles, aunts, and our closest friends. Simple enough? Then, my parents added more second cousins, uncles, aunts, and their friends. My in-laws did the same. My brothers went solo, and my in-laws' siblings invited some of their friends. So, our initial guest list of 200 doubled before we could say, "I do."

Our families extended the guest list to include people we barely knew, Rotary Club friends, Domino game buddies, and uncles we hadn't seen since we were in diapers. And we didn't mind. Why? It was also a momentous day for them, and they wanted to celebrate it by sharing the joy with their circles. We understood that this event wasn't just about us; it was also a meaningful occasion for them to connect with those who had been part of their lives.

Our parents also wanted to be deeply involved in the wedding planning process. They had opinions on everything: which church was better, which priest was the best if the venue was too small or too far. They offered to make desserts, help with invitations, and hire a violinist for the reception. We planned it for 14 months; during those 14 months, they were involved in every step.

For instance, I initially decided against a wedding cake since my mother-in-law insisted on making her brownies with ice cream instead. However, my mom opposed: "How can you have a wedding without a cake? It's tradition for the bride and groom to cut the cake at the reception." So, she went out and bought the largest, most beautifully decorated cake she could find—but she also ensured it was the most affordable one, knowing its sole purpose was a photo op. We took the traditional picture of us cutting the cake, and that was it. No one ate the cake, but it made my mom happy, and we had our photo.

Weddings are significant cultural rituals that reflect the values and social structures of the societies in which they are celebrated. How weddings are conducted in collectivist cultures differ significantly from individualist cultures, illustrating contrasting attitudes toward family, community, and individual identity.

Collectivist cultures prioritize the group over the individual, emphasizing family, community, and social harmony. This cultural orientation is evident in the way weddings are planned and celebrated.

In collectivist societies such as those in many Asian, African, and Latin American countries, weddings are not just a union of two individuals but a coming together of two families or communities. The extended family plays a crucial role in planning and executing the wedding ceremony.

In some more collectivist cultures, parents and family are often deeply involved in decision-making, from selecting the wedding date to arranging rituals and ceremonies. Their blessings and approval are considered essential for the marriage to be auspicious. Some weddings involve the entire community. For example, in Indian weddings, hundreds or thousands of guests are often invited, reflecting the importance of social networks and community bonds.

Collectivist cultures strongly emphasize rituals and traditions, which are meticulously followed and passed down through generations. In Chinese weddings, traditional practices such as the tea ceremony, where the bride and groom serve tea to their elders as a sign of respect, are integral to the celebration. Similarly, Indian weddings are known for their elaborate rituals, including the Saptapadi (seven steps) and the exchange of garlands, symbolizing the couple's union.[48] The symbolism in these weddings often reflects cultural values such as respect for ancestors, the importance of fertility and prosperity, and the sanctity of marriage.

In several cases, the bride's family pays for the wedding expenses. In collectivist cultures, family members often share financial and logistical wedding responsibilities. For instance, in many Middle Eastern cultures, it is customary for both families to share the wedding expenses, reducing the burden on the bride and groom. Wedding planning is a collective effort, with relatives and friends taking on various roles to ensure the event's success.

In contrast, couples in individualist cultures frequently opt for customizable ceremonies that align with their beliefs and preferences. This might include non-traditional venues, personalized vows, and unique themes. In most cases, weddings are seen as a celebration of their relationship rather than a formal union of families. While family involvement is still significant, it is generally less pervasive than in collectivist cultures.

In some individualist cultures, while parents and close family members often offer support and guidance, the couple generally has more control over wedding decisions than those in a collectivist culture. The focus is primarily on fulfilling the couple's preferences and desires rather than meeting broader family expectations. This autonomy allows the couple to shape the wedding to reflect their tastes, from the venue and decor to the ceremony style and guest list. While family opinions are valued, the couple usually prioritizes their vision for the big day.

The guest list tends to be more selective, often limited to the closest friends and family, reflecting a more intimate celebration. Individualist cultures usually emphasize financial independence, even when it comes to weddings. It is common for couples to fund their weddings, reflecting the value placed on self-sufficiency. While parents may contribute, it is not always expected. Weddings are planned carefully considering the couple's budget and financial situation, often leading to more modest and practical celebrations than the lavish affairs in some collectivist cultures.

***

The same goes for parties and social groups. In collectivist cultures, social gatherings are often larger and more inclusive, with extended family members, friends, and neighbors attending. The aim is to bring the community together by keeping the guest list broad enough to include as many people as possible. Frequent gatherings and celebrations are a common occurrence.

In individualist cultures, parties and gatherings tend to be smaller and more intimate, reflecting the individual's or host's close circle of friends and acquaintances. The focus is on quality interactions rather than quantity, and invitations are often more selective. Social gatherings or parties are less frequent and often with a smaller, more intimate group of friends.

INDIVIDUALIST AND COLLECTIVIST CULTURES

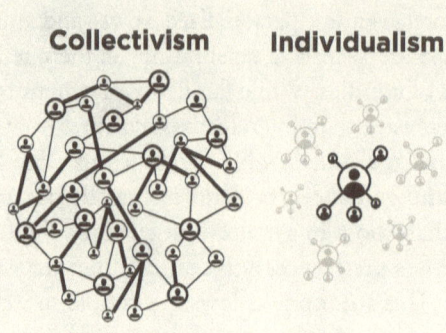

Figure7: Collectivism and Individualism

INDIVIDUALIST CULTURES

Individualistic cultures prioritize personal autonomy and self-expression, encouraging people to pursue their goals and make independent choices with less influence from family or societal expectations. While relationships may take longer to build, people are friendly and care for others, though social pressure is less dominant than in collectivist cultures.

Success is often defined by individual achievements and career milestones, with performance-based rewards in workplaces. Direct communication is valued, with openness in expressing opinions and addressing disagreements.

In education and careers, personal interests guide decisions rather than group expectations. Countries like the U.S., Australia, the U.K., Germany, and the Netherlands embody individualism, promoting self-reliance, innovation, and entrepreneurship. The American Dream exemplifies this mindset, celebrating personal effort and success stories like Steve Jobs and Oprah Winfrey.

Respect for personal space and privacy is also fundamental, reinforcing the belief in individual rights and freedom of choice.

COLLECTIVIST SOCIETIES

Collectivist cultures prioritize the group's well-being over individual interests, emphasizing community, harmony, and loyalty in both personal and professional interactions. Decisions are often made through consensus, aligning personal ambitions with group objectives, while family and societal expectations influence education and career choices.

In workplaces, conflicts are resolved through mediation to maintain harmony, and group achievements are celebrated over individual recognition. Teamwork and collaboration are highly valued, as seen in countries like Japan, China, Korea, and many Asian, African, and Latin American societies.

For example, Japan embraces consensus-building through the ringi system, where proposals circulate through multiple levels to gather input before a final decision. Japanese expressions like itadakimasu (gratitude for a meal's preparation) and otsukaresama desu (recognition of hard work) reflect a deep respect for collective effort. Filial piety, or honoring parents and elders, is also a core value.

In Korea, the concept of Jeong (정) embodies deep emotional bonds and mutual care, fostering strong bonds within families, friendships, and communities. This lasting sense of attachment and support strengthens social harmony and a shared sense of belonging.

Ultimately, collectivist cultures emphasize relationships and cooperation and prioritize the group's needs, ensuring social cohesion and long-term stability.

CHARACTERISTICS OF INDIVIDUALIST AND COLLECTIVIST CULTURES

Individualism and collectivism are cultural dimensions that reflect how people view their relationships with others and their society. These characteristics influence different societies' behaviors, communication styles, decision-making processes, and values. Here is an overview of the key characteristics of each:

Individualist	Collectivist
People tend to maintain distinct boundaries between their personal and professional lives.	Family and groups invade private life and influence professional life choices.
An enjoyment of challenges and an expectation of individual rewards for hard work.	Responsibilities and duties are often distributed among family and community members.
Task prevails over relationships.	Relationship prevails over tasks.
Individuals are encouraged to be self-reliant and independent.	There is an expectation to support and rely on one another.
Personal goals and desires often take precedence over group goals.	The needs and goals of the group are prioritized over individual desires.
People are expected to look after themselves and their immediate family only.	Family ties and social networks are fundamental. Individuals see themselves as part of a larger collective, such as a family, community, or workplace.
Individual accomplishments and personal achievements measure success.	Achievements often are seen as the result of collective efforts.
Competition is often seen as a positive. Pushing innovation and progress.	Success is shared among the group, and so is failure.
Individuals place a high value on self-expression and personal freedom.	Elders and leaders often play significant roles in decision-making.
Opinions, ideas, and personal preferences are freely expressed and respected.	Maintaining harmony and avoiding conflict is crucial.
Communication is typically direct and explicit. People say what they mean, and there is less emphasis on reading between the lines.	Indirect communication is expected to preserve relationships and prevent disagreements.
Everyone is expected to have an opinion, even if it differs from that of others.	There is a strong focus on saving face and respecting social norms.
Occupational mobility is higher.	Occupational mobility is lower.
Value standards are supposed to apply to everyone.	Value standards differ for in-groups and out-groups.

Individualist	Collectivist
Friendships are voluntary and should be fostered.	Some friendships are predetermined.
Adult children leave their parent's house.	Adult children live with their parents.
Countries: United States, Canada, Australia, the United Kingdom, and many Northern European	Countries: China, Japan, South Korea, India, Mexico, and many Middle Eastern and African.

[49]Both perspectives offer unique strengths and weaknesses. However, individualists in a collectivist society may struggle with the group's extensive expectations for conformity and cooperation. In contrast, a collectivist in an individualist society might find the lack of communal support and emphasis on personal achievements challenging.

Note that the counties named here don't necessarily fit all the characteristics of one group or the other. Instead, they often lean more toward one side while incorporating elements from both without being rigidly defined by either.

Interacting with an Individualist Culture

- Celebrate achievements and support self-reliance in decision-making.
- Foster open expression by encouraging idea-sharing, initiative, and constructive debate.
- Respect personal boundaries, including time, space, opinions, and choices.
- Communicate clearly and assertively to advocate for your needs.
- Emphasize autonomy by promoting independent work with minimal supervision.

Interacting with a Collectivist Culture

- Prioritize group needs by fostering collaboration and teamwork.
- Strengthen bonds through relationship-building and active participation in group activities.
- Value community by engaging in discussions and striving for consensus in decision-making.
- Communicate harmoniously and humbly, avoiding open conflict and appreciating others' contributions.

- Demonstrate reliability by fulfilling responsibilities and sharing time, skills, and resources to support others.

KEY TAKEAWAYS

- Individualistic Cultures: Emphasizes the autonomy and interests of the individual over those of the group. They value personal independence, self-expression, and the pursuit of individual goals.
- Collectivist Cultures: Prioritize the group's interests over individual priorities. Relationships and group loyalty form the foundation of social structure, profoundly shaping personal and professional interactions.

CHAPTER 7

Joyful alignment

*"We all need both moments of quiet reflection
and times of joyful expression to experience life fully."*
— Anonymous

Cultural expression is as diverse as the people who inhabit the world, with enthusiasm and reservation forming two distinct poles on the spectrum of social behavior. This chapter explores how people express emotions through body language, voice tone, signs, and other gestures.

DECIBELS

My family is big—truly enormous! Between my parents' sides, they each have six siblings, so just among my immediate aunts and uncles, there are 25. And don't even get me started on cousins, nieces, nephews, siblings, and other close relatives—I'm too lazy to count, but we are easily in triple digits. A "small family gathering"? We don't know what that means. It's not just because of our family size but also because we do everything we can to never miss a significant event. Whether it's New Year's, Christmas, milestone birthdays, weddings, or graduations, you can bet the entire (or the majority) extended family will be there, celebrating together.

My family is energetic, empathetic, attentive, helpful, compassionate, and caring—and they're loud! Conversations often evolve into lively and engaging debates. Someone starts talking, then another jumps in to add a point, and before long, more people chime in. Soon, everyone's talking at once, creating sub-conversations across the table, where someone might be chatting with another one across the room while also engaging with the person beside them.

Then, suddenly, everyone reconnects to the main discussion.

When someone in my family has a good point, joke, or important message, they raise their voice to get everyone's attention. The more exciting and engaging the conversation becomes, the faster and louder we speak. This is the environment I grew up in—it was normal for me to follow and participate in multiple conversations without losing track of any. For someone unfamiliar with this dynamic, it can seem chaotic, hard to follow, and even disrespectful due to the volume and pace. But for us, it's our way of expressing enthusiasm and engagement.

For us, mealtimes are the perfect opportunity to connect, share our day, and discuss plans, making them a cherished time for gathering. While we respect the food and family traditions, meals are typically lively social events, especially during larger gatherings or special occasions. It's not unusual for dinner to stretch out over hours, filled with conversation, laughter, and bonding over the food. Although our mealtime discussions aren't overly loud, sitting in silence or speaking very little while eating with family or friends would make us feel like something was wrong—like we were upset, sad, or unhappy with each other.

When my Korean friend, Jiwoo, told me that her parents preferred her to stay quiet, ideally in silence, during meals to appreciate the food thoroughly, I was utterly puzzled. I asked her, "Do you mean speaking softly?" She responded, "No, in complete silence." Confused, I asked, "So, if not at mealtime, when do you talk?" She explained that they chat throughout the day but keep conversations minimal during meals. It was such a different concept from what I had known.

In Buddhist traditions, particularly in Japan, Thailand, and China, some families may observe silence during meals to foster mindfulness and gratitude. This practice emphasizes the importance of being present and fully appreciating the food without distractions, with silence allowing for reflection and contemplation.

In some Finnish families, the preference for quiet meals stems from cultural norms that value peace and introspection. Conversations during meals are often minimal or absent, not out of awkwardness but as a sign of comfort and understanding. Silence is deeply embedded in Finnish communication styles, reflecting a cultural appreciation for meaningful conversation and calm interactions. In this context, silence conveys respect and creates a serene dining environment.

Worldwide, the volume and tone naturally shift depending on the environment and situation. For instance, in formal, intimate, professional, or religious settings, silence or quiet conversations are valued in most, if not all, cultures. In some cultures, speaking too loudly or fast can be perceived as intrusive or disrespectful.

For example, in Japan or Finland, conversations are often soft-spoken and carefully measured. Silence is highly prized, serving as a vital part of communication and offering moments for reflection and understanding. Silence is a comfortable part of interaction, reflecting a deep connection rather than a lack of engagement.

In traditional settings in China and Korea, especially in the presence of elders, conversations are typically soft and respectful. In certain Buddhist and Taoist communities, quiet speech signifies reverence, with silence during meals or spiritual practices being a form of mindfulness. Across several cultures, maintaining quiet conversations is a way to promote harmony and avoid disturbing others, reflecting a deep cultural respect for the environment and the people around them.

Conversations in countries like Brazil, Italy, Greece, Spain, Colombia, and Mexico tend to be lively and animated. Participants engage passionately and often speak over one another as a sign of enthusiasm rather than rudeness. Silence here isn't typically seen as a positive or comfortable space; it can be perceived as awkward, disengaging, or dull in social gatherings. For many, the energy of a conversation reflects connection and excitement, and a soft-spoken, restrained dialogue might feel lacking in warmth or depth.

These cultures often view lively interaction, including expressive gestures, animated tones, and frequent interruptions, as essential to meaningful communication. Being vocal and expressive shows involvement and interest, while silence may suggest disinterest or discomfort.

There are so many variations in conversational style that you can always find someone who speaks louder or softer than you're used to. I used to think my family was the loudest around—until an experience in downtown Memphis changed my perspective. My husband and I noticed a large group of African American men talking so loudly that I initially thought they might be arguing or even fighting. But as we got closer, it became apparent they were having a great time, filled with laughter and energy. This experience highlighted how cultural norms around speech volume can vary. What might seem chaotic or confrontational in one culture can be an expression of joy, enthusiasm, and connection in another.

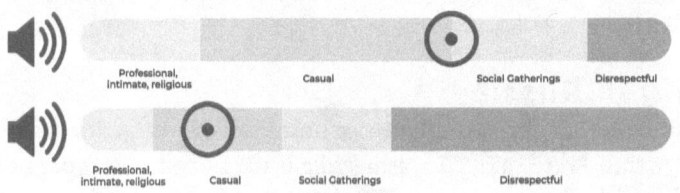

Figure 8: Decibels

This graph compares two perspectives on acceptable speech volume across different settings, highlighting cultural differences. One culture prefers generally quieter conversations, while the other tolerates or encourages louder volumes, especially in social gatherings. For example, the acceptable volume for a professional setting in one culture could be noisy in another. Both perspectives, however, agree that very loud or shouting levels can be deemed disrespectful, particularly in formal or intimate situations.

BODY LANGUAGE

Oh my! I've lost count of how many times I've sent or misinterpreted a message purely because of body language! It's incredible how a simple gesture, facial expression, or even posture can completely change the meaning of what's being said. Sometimes, what feels like a harmless gesture can be considered hostile or dismissive, leading to awkward confusion or unintended signals. It's a reminder that non-verbal communication is just as powerful—if not more than words. Whether it's crossing arms, a raised eyebrow, or even how close you stand to someone, these small cues can alter the entire tone of interaction, often without us even realizing it!

Like voice volume, cultures with an enthusiastic communication style tend to use more expressive and exaggerated body language than those with a reserved approach. In enthusiastic cultures, people often rely on hand gestures, facial expressions, and body movements to emphasize their points, convey emotions, and enhance storytelling. This adds dynamism and meaning to conversations, allowing individuals to express themselves fully and passionately and making conversations visually animated. People in countries like Brazil, Kenya, Colombia, Morocco, Italy, Spain, and Mexico tend to express themselves more freely.

In contrast, individuals from reserved cultures typically employ subtler, more restrained gestures and may prioritize eye contact or a calm posture over large movements. They often value composure and minimal physical expression. Countries like Japan, Korea, Sweden, and Thailand may fall into this category.

Smiling in Russia

I grew up believing that a smile was a universal sign of gentleness; as poet William Arthur Ward said, "A warm smile is the universal language of kindness."[50] Similarly, Stanley Gordon West's words, "Smile, and the world smiles with you," reinforced my belief. To me, a genuine smile at a stranger always conveyed something positive—a sign of happiness, gratitude, or a friendly greeting.

When I visited Russia, I instinctively smiled at the store clerk who helped me find the perfect Matryoshka in the right color. It was my way of showing gratitude for her effort. Later, I smiled at the waitress to express thanks for her attentive service and even at a little girl whose peaceful, beautiful face made me happy. Yet, to my surprise, no one smiled back. The store clerk didn't return my smile, even though I was pleased with my purchase. Despite my good tip and the fact that we thoroughly enjoyed the meal, the waitress remained neutral. Even after I picked up and returned the doll that had fallen unnoticed, the little girl and her parents said " Спасибо " (spasibo), or thank you, but not a hint of a smile. Not one!

Curious and a little perplexed, I asked our Russian tour guide why people in Russia didn't seem to smile back at strangers. She explained that, in Russia, smiling at strangers is considered inappropriate and even impolite. Showing teeth can be regarded as insincere, unprofessional, or mocking. There's a Russian saying: "Only fools smile without reason." While I thought I had plenty of reasons to smile, in Russian culture, smiling at someone is reserved for moments of authentic joy, after a good joke, or when you're with close friends.

I learned that if Russians don't smile at you, it doesn't mean they dislike you or are unfriendly; it simply means they are not accustomed to smiling at people they don't know well. After this revelation, I tried to refrain from smiling at strangers in Russia, understanding that it might send the wrong message. However, I continued to smile freely at our French tour group, and being more accustomed to such gestures, they happily smiled back.

Winking in Belgium

In contrast, Belgian men have a charming habit of winking at women. So there I was, surrounded by all these handsome men casually winking at me, and I had no idea how to respond. It completely caught me off guard! Should I avoid eye contact? Flash my wedding ring to show I was unavailable? Run? Hide? Ha! Thank goodness I didn't do any of those—imagine how embarrassing!

After a few months, I realized that winking comes naturally to them. Just as Americans smile at strangers as a friendly gesture, Belgian men wink at women as a casual, playful greeting. Unlike in some cultures where a wink might be seen as flirtatious or suggestive, in Belgium, it's often a lighthearted way to acknowledge someone with no romantic intent. It can convey a sense of camaraderie, playfulness, or simply a non-verbal "hello." Once I understood this cultural nuance, my initial surprise and self-consciousness disappeared. The feeling that I was attracting extra attention quickly faded, and I saw it for what it really meant to them—just a friendly social gesture.

Indian Head Wobble

I have several Indian friends and have worked with many more. However, I had never noticed them doing the characteristic head wobble. This might be because they've lived in the U.S. for several years or perhaps because they come from regions in India where this gesture isn't as common.

Recently, though, I had a new experience. A gentleman who had just moved from India rented one of my properties. While explaining the details about the house, how to make the deposits, and providing general information about the neighborhood and city, I noticed he frequently wobbled his head quickly from side to side as I spoke.

At first, I was confused and thought he might disagree with the terms, mainly because he didn't verbally express his opinion. So, I asked, "Does this work for you?" He responded, "Yes," while wobbling his head again. I asked another question: "Are you still set on moving in on that day?" Once more, he replied, "Yes," with the same head wobble. As I continued talking about the city, his head kept wobbling similarly.

Eventually, he signed the lease and handed over the check for the deposit and first month's rent. I left the meeting uncertain, unsure if he fully understood or agreed to everything. When I got home, I looked up what "head wobble" means in Indian culture.

A fast, continuous head wobble means the person understands what is being said. The more vigorous the wobble, the more they know.

A quick side-to-side wobble generally means "yes," "good," or "all right."

A slow, gentle wobble, often with a smile, is a sign of friendliness and respect.[51]

Ultimately, I realized he was probably five steps ahead of me the entire time—perfectly understanding everything, while I was the one wobbling in confusion!

Hand gestures

Head gestures vary significantly across different cultures, and what may seem like a familiar gesture in one country could carry a completely different meaning in another.

For example, forming a circle with your thumb and index finger to signal "OK" is widely understood (or so I thought!) as a positive sign, indicating that everything is fine. However, this seemingly harmless gesture takes on a very different meaning in other parts of the world. In Brazil and Turkey, for instance, it's equivalent to flashing a middle finger, carrying strong insulting and scatological undertones. In parts of Southern and Central Europe, this same gesture implies that someone is worthless or insignificant—basically calling them a "zero." And in Mediterranean countries like Turkey, it takes an even more offensive turn, translating to a vulgar, sexual insult. It's fascinating (and a little nerve-wracking) how the same gesture can shift from reassuring to rude, depending on where you are!

The thumbs-up, another seemingly innocent gesture in many Western countries that is common to show approval or agreement, can land you in trouble in places like Greece, the Middle East, and some African countries, where it carries an offensive and vulgar insult, where it may be equated to the middle finger in the US.

Crossed arms in Western cultures can indicate defensiveness, resistance, or discomfort. In Finland, however, they are often interpreted as a relaxed or thoughtful position, not necessarily defensive. Another example is the "peace" sign (index and middle fingers raised), widely seen as a symbol of peace or victory. Still, it can be disrespectful if it is done with the palm facing inward, especially in the UK or Australia.

Certain cultures are particularly expressive, where emotions, communication, and social interactions are infused with enthusiasm and gestures. Italians, for example, are famous for their dynamic communication style, using hand gestures, facial expressions, and passionate vocal tones to convey their thoughts and feelings. For them, gestures are more than habits—they are essential tools for adding emotion, emphasis, and clarity to their words. Whether it's a wrist flick to indicate impatience, fingers pinched together to express disbelief, or an open hand showing frustration, these gestures breathe life into conversations, making them more vivid and engaging.

Nearly every finger gesture is likely to offend someone, somewhere, at some point. As a general guideline (pun not intended!), avoid using any single finger in a gesture unless you're sure it's appropriate for that specific culture or country.

How can someone avoid making these kinds of cultural faux pas when traveling? The best way to prevent cultural faux pas when traveling is to research before visiting a new country. Learning about the local customs, gestures, and etiquette helps prevent misunderstandings. Additionally, observing locals in real-time is an effective way to pick up on what's acceptable in the area. When in doubt, a subtle smile without showing teeth, a simple nod, or open-handed gestures with fingers kept together tend to be the safest option across most cultures.

Head gestures

If hand gestures aren't complex enough, let's bring head movements into the mix. In Western cultures, a nod typically signals agreement or "yes," while a horizontal shake of the head from side-to-side means "no" or disagreement. However, the opposite is true in places like Bulgaria and Greece: nodding can mean "no," and shaking the head might mean "yes." It's one of those cultural quirks that can easily lead to confusion if you're unaware.

In Filipino culture, raising the eyebrows (often accompanied by a slight upward tilt of the head) can indicate "yes" or acknowledge someone. It is frequently used as a friendly or informal greeting. A quick side-to-side movement of the head can mean "no," often without verbally expressing it.

In Italy and some Mediterranean cultures, a quick upward tilt of the chin can be used to dismiss someone or something or say "no," especially when paired with a "tsk" sound. It's often a gesture to convey disinterest or dismissal rather than agreement.

In Japan, a slight head tilt while someone is speaking can show active listening or agreement. This gesture, often paired with sounds like "hai" (yes), demonstrates attentiveness and understanding. It tends to be subtle and conveys politeness.

Japan and South Korea commonly use bowing as a gesture of respect, greeting, or apology. Different degrees of bowing can indicate various levels of formality, from a slight nod of the head to a deep bow at the waist. In Thailand, a slight lowering of the head or bow is a gesture of respect, particularly when greeting or showing deference to someone of higher status. The depth of the bow can indicate the level of respect being shown.

In parts of Greece and Southern Europe, a head tilt to the side, often with a slight chin raise, can indicate confusion or that the person is seeking clarification, almost as if saying, "What do you mean?"

In Western cultures, touching or patting someone on the head might be seen as an affectionate gesture. In Thailand, the head is considered sacred, and touching someone's head can be deeply disrespectful.

Eye contact

Eye contact is a powerful form of non-verbal communication. In Western, Russian, and Eastern European cultures, direct eye contact shows confidence, honesty, and attentiveness. Maintaining eye contact during conversations shows that you're engaged and respectful. However, prolonged or intense eye contact can be considered aggressive or overly assertive, depending on the context.

In East Asian cultures, direct eye contact, especially with superiors or elders, can be seen as disrespectful or aggressive. People in Japan, South Korea, and China often avoid prolonged eye contact to show respect and humility. Instead, they may look downward or use brief glances to maintain a polite distance. Looking down or away can be a sign of respect or deference.

In many Middle Eastern cultures, direct eye contact between men and women, particularly in public or formal settings, may be considered inappropriate or suggestive, especially if they are not closely related or married. Avoiding eye contact in such interactions is often a sign of respect and modesty. Eye contact between men is more acceptable and can show respect and engagement. However, overly prolonged or intense eye contact might be interpreted as confrontational or aggressive. Direct eye contact with elders or those of higher status may be limited out of respect.

In Latin American and Mediterranean cultures, eye contact during conversations is generally positive and conveys engagement and warmth. People may use eye contact more expressively and combine it with gestures and facial expressions to emphasize emotion and build rapport. Avoiding eye contact can be interpreted as disinterest or insecurity.

Eye contact norms vary depending on age and social hierarchy in many African cultures, especially in West African countries. Direct eye contact with elders or authority figures can be seen as disrespectful while making eye contact with peers is generally acceptable and a sign of engagement.

Feet and legs

Leg and foot gestures, often unnoticed, can carry significant cultural meaning. In Western cultures, crossing your legs or showing the soles of your feet is generally acceptable. Middle Eastern Cultures, crossing your legs so that the sole of your shoe faces someone is considered disrespectful and offensive. Showing the bottom of your foot, especially in Arab cultures, is seen as an insult, as the foot is regarded as the dirtiest part of the body.

In Japan, crossing legs while sitting, particularly in formal settings, is considered disrespectful. Instead, sitting with legs together and feet flat on the ground (for men) or knees together and feet tucked under (for women) is more appropriate.

In India and Southeast Asia (Thailand, Laos, and Cambodia), the feet are considered the lowest and dirtiest part of the body, both literally and figuratively. Pointing your feet at someone, touching someone with your foot, or even pointing your feet toward sacred objects like Buddha statues is seen as deeply disrespectful.

In China and India, it's important to keep feet flat on the ground in formal settings, when seated with elders, or in a religious context. Sitting with legs elevated on chairs or resting feet on desks can be seen as lazy or disrespectful.

Wearing shoes indoors is a major faux pas in several countries, including Sweden, Finland, Norway, Japan, India, Korea, Iran, Lebanon, Turkey, and Thailand. In Japanese and Korean households (and in some public spaces like temples or traditional restaurants), removing shoes at the entrance is a sign of respect. Wearing shoes inside is seen as disrespectful and unhygienic.

In Indian culture, touching someone's feet (usually an elder) signifies respect and reverence. It's common during certain religious or familial ceremonies. In contrast, touching or kissing someone's feet is rarely practiced and might be viewed as overly submissive or strange in most Western cultural settings.

How to read body language

- Observe the distance and eye contact the locals keep from strangers.
- Notice if the person looks uncomfortable, annoyed, or mad.
- Observe if they avoid eye contact or look around while you talk.
- Pay attention if the person moves away from or toward you. Let them mark their comfort distance by remaining in the same place.
- Consider your surroundings, especially in closed spaces or places without easy escape. Standing too close may feel like harassment.
- Speak up if you feel uncomfortable or unsafe.
- Practice.

SOCIAL DISTANCE

"The distance you keep from others is an elaborate, instinctive dance.
- Michael Graziano

When you read those two words, I'm sure you immediately thought of COVID-19. We hear these two words quite often. Stay with me; this is a significant cultural difference not associated with viruses. I promise.

Bridging the gap

Just a few days after COVID-19 was declared a global pandemic, governments around the world put out a flurry of new regulations for everyone to follow: only leave the house if necessary, wash your hands frequently, wear a mask, and keep six feet (or two meters) away from anyone not in your quarantine bubble. Suddenly, "social distance" became a household phrase, and we quickly learned to measure a six-foot space.

Fast forward a few weeks into April 2020. There I was, in line at the grocery store, doing my best to follow all the safety rules, when the guy behind me—apparently unaware of the whole "global pandemic" thing—started chatting on his phone, pulled his mask down, and drifted right up to about a foot behind me. We knew very little about the virus at the time other than that it spread fast, it was deadly, and distance was our best defense. Feeling a mix of horror and indignation, I desperately wanted him to back up, change lines, or that the person on the line was his wife, reminding him to bring something he had forgotten so he would have to leave the line.

No such luck. My discomfort only intensified. Instead of just turning around and saying, "Hey, buddy, could you give me a little space?" I went for the indirect approach (see Chapter 3 for more). I gave him a sideways glance over my shoulder, hoping he'd pick up on my unease. No response. So then, I pointedly looked at the stickers on the floor, clearly marking where everyone was supposed to stand—still, he didn't budge. It's a classic case of a direct communicator missing all the subtle signs and, of course, me hesitating to ask outright!

Finally, the woman in front of me moved forward, and I seized my chance. I slid around my cart, leaving it as a makeshift barrier between us. That cart was an excellent shield, and I felt relief for the first time in that line.

We don't need a virus to feel uneasy when our personal space is invaded. When someone crosses our invisible, comfortable bubble space, it can lead to feelings of discomfort, irritation, or anxiety. Personal space is the physical boundary we place around ourselves to feel relaxed and safe, and its size can vary depending on culture, context, and individual preferences. When someone crosses this invisible boundary, our instinctive reaction may be to step back, create a barrier (like holding something in front of us), or use body language to communicate our unease.

Breaking in or offering help

Two weeks after moving to Belgium, I was home alone, surrounded by unpacked boxes, trying to make sense of our new space. Suddenly, there was a knock at the door—but no one rang the bell. Our house, which had no fence, was encircled by tall, dense Emerald Green Arborvitae Trees for privacy. With large, curtainless windows, we had motorized shades for nighttime privacy. During the daytime, everyone walking behind those trees had an unobstructed view inside.

The doorbell and mailbox were on a brick column at the edge of the property by the street. A pathway from this spot wound through the trees to our front door, which didn't have a bell; the only bell was out by the street.

Not expecting anyone, I was surprised to hear a knock at the door instead of the bell ringing. After a few moments, I opened the door to find a young, tall, athletic Kenyan man who appeared to be on his way out. When I called out, he returned and offered to mow our lawn. As we talked, he moved closer, narrowing the distance between us to about 30 cm (12 inches). Each time I stepped back, he unconsciously moved forward, keeping the same proximity.

Anxiety began to build; he was invading my personal space, making it hard to focus on what he was saying. My thoughts raced: Why is he standing so close? Is he here to mow the lawn, or is this a setup to get inside? I felt vulnerable—alone, in a new country, with no neighbors close enough to hear me if I screamed. He was tall and strong, while I was petite; he could easily overpower me. Just one more step back, and we'd be inside the house, leaving me nowhere to escape. Am I safe?

I panicked and blurted out, "No," quickly closing and locking the door in his face. (Not my most polite moment, I admit.) He didn't move immediately; he might have been trying to assimilate what happened, which only heightened my anxiety. My heart pounded, and my hands shook as I bolted upstairs to my room, locking the door and grabbing my phone, ready to call the police. Of course, nothing happened, but my fear lingered.

A few days later, my husband met him and decided to hire him for lawn care. I got to know him better over time, realizing he was the sweetest, friendliest, and most respectful gardener I'd ever met. The issue wasn't him—it was our differing sense of personal space. His comfort zone was much closer than mine. Eventually, I apologized for my rudeness. Despite my remorse, I realized that, given the same situation, I'd likely react similarly. When a stranger encroaches on our personal space, especially in unfamiliar surroundings, it can trigger feelings of unease, unsafe, or danger. In such moments, trusting our instincts is crucial; apologizing afterward is easier than ignoring that possible threat.

Although we don't physically measure personal space, we mentally gauge the expected distance during interactions. When someone stands closer than anticipated, it raises the question: Why are they so close? Hall's theory of proxemics, or personal space, offers insight into this. Sometimes, a close distance might be culturally customary, while it may feel intrusive or aggressive in others.[52]

Cross-cultural miscommunication often arises when we misinterpret the intentions behind someone's proximity. For example, suppose someone stands closer than we're accustomed to. In that case, we might view it as a personal intrusion (personal attribution) rather than understanding it as a difference in cultural norms regarding social distance (situational attribution). Recognizing that comfort zones vary widely across cultures, what feels too close in one may be friendly in another.[53]

My personal, social, and public distance

Since kindergarten, my teachers have taught me to keep a respectable distance from others. No floor stickers or signs showed us exactly how far to stand. Instead, we used a more straightforward method: extending our arms until our fingertips touched the other person. This was the "proper distance."

Of course, this rule didn't apply in specific spaces, like the school line, church, concession store, or playground, where physical space was limited, and we stayed closer to each other. As I grew, my understanding of personal space evolved. The distance around a person forms an invisible "bubble" that changes in size depending on context and relationship. My distance is about 70 cm (27.5 inches) for family and close friends. For acquaintances, referred to as a social distance, it is around 81 cm (32 inches). And for strangers, my comfort zone, or public distance, is typically no less than 1.2 meters (48 inches).

But once again, these distances depend on the context and adjust accordingly. In crowded places like a nightclub, Disneyland, an elevator, or on public transportation, my "bubble" naturally shrinks to fit the environment. Yet in situations where I feel vulnerable, like being alone in the dark, that bubble widens if a stranger approaches.

Other factors influence the size of our personal space: age, gender, personal status, religion, beliefs, and even the weather. My "bubble" also expands or contracts based on the level of trust or familiarity with the person I'm speaking to and the nature of my relationship with them. Additionally, living in a densely populated area can influence how much space we're accustomed to having around us.

Class experiment

During my MBA in Belgium, I took a course on cross-cultural communication. In my class, there were students from at least 20 different nationalities. The professor, a lady with remarkable international experience, divided the group into two. One group stayed in the classroom while the other went outside, and then she strategically paired us off.

I stayed in the room. She explained how social space varies worldwide and asked us to observe the movements of the student pairs while they talked. One by one, she invited the pairs to come back to the room. She invited them to start in the right corner of the room. The short-distance personal space culture stood on the right in front of their partner (long-distance social space) on the left. Then, they started a conversation on a topic she had previously selected.

All the pairs started on the right side and ended on the left side of the room. During their conversation, the person on the right got closer to the person on the left, so the person on the left stepped backward. The person on the right stepped forward, and so on, until they reached the opposite corner. This frequent phenomenon occurs when people with different social space preferences interact. It was interesting to watch.

Proximity

Social distancing may seem like a recent concept, but it has existed for centuries. In medical terms, it helps prevent the spread of disease, while in sociology, it refers to the comfortable distance between individuals—often called personal space, peripersonal space, or a space bubble. This unspoken boundary isn't fixed; it varies across cultures, contexts, genders, and personal preferences.

Figure 9: Proximity

Our brains unconsciously calculate a flexible shield around our bodies, influencing how close we stand to others. This spatial awareness is so instinctive that we rarely think about it, yet it plays a crucial role in shaping interactions and social dynamics. The distance we maintain depends on factors like familiarity—closer with loved ones, moderate with colleagues, and greater with strangers.

Anthropologist Edward T. Hall introduced the concept of proxemics, which explores these subconscious spatial zones and their variations across different cultures. He explained varying comfort levels during social interactions and how different cultures perceive and navigate these invisible boundaries. For example, Latin American, Middle Eastern, African, and Mediterranean cultures often favor closer proximity, viewing it as a sign of warmth and engagement. In contrast, Northern European and Scandinavian cultures tend to prefer more personal space as a sign of respect, particularly in professional or unfamiliar interactions, to create a professional atmosphere.

Our unique distances profoundly impact how we interact, indicating the nature of our relationships and perceptions. They serve as a nonverbal cue, revealing our comfort levels and boundaries with others.

According to the World Population Review, Romania has the largest preferred social space at 1.39 meters, while Argentina has the smallest at 76.5 cm.[54] Here are some examples from various countries:[55]

Country	Preferred Social Space	Country	Preferred Social Space
Romania	139	United States	95.3
Hungary	130	Greece	91.2
Saudi Arabia	126	Spain	90.5
Turkey	123	Russia	89.1
Uganda	121	Slovakia	88.8
Pakistan	119	Austria	88.1
Estonia	118	Ukraine	85.5
Colombia	117	Bulgaria	81.3
Hong Kong	116	Peru	79.6
China	115	Argentina	76.5
United Kingdom	99.4		

Imagine two people talking: an Argentinian who prefers 76.5 cm (30 inches) of social space and a Romanian who needs 1.39 meters (55 inches). The Argentinian would move closer, making the Romanian uncomfortable and potentially prompting them to step back.*

The Argentinian might think the Romanian is:

---

* You can find a complete list at: "Personal Space by Country 2024". World Population Review, 2024. https://worldpopulationreview.com/country-rankings/personal-space-by-country. Personal Distance: "Personal Space by Country 2024." World Population Review, 2024. https://worldpopulationreview.com/country-rankings/personal-space-by-country
Miller, Christina. "Ranked: Countries with the most (and least) personal space, 2024". CEO World Magazine. 2024. https://ceoworld.biz/2024/02/02/ranked-countries-with-the-most-and-least-personal-space-2024/#google_vignette

- Cold
- Distant
- Not interested in the conversation
- Not wanting to be there
- Repelled by their presence

The Romanian might perceive the Argentinian to be:

- Close-Talker
- Space-Invader
- Disrespectful
- Aggressive
- Intrusive
- Pushy
- Harassing

If you catch yourself adjusting your distance—whether closing in or pulling back—take a moment to check your spacing and adapt accordingly. Personal and social space preferences can vary widely, so being mindful of these subtle shifts can help create a more comfortable interaction for you and the other person. Adjusting your distance to match theirs can show attentiveness and respect. Here is an overview of the different types of distances:

Intimate Distance
This physical space is reserved for interactions with people who are emotionally very close to us. It is used for intimate interactions with loved ones, including family members, close friends, and romantic partners. It's used for physical contact and whispering and is usually only shared with those we trust deeply. It varies from 0 to 18 inches (0 to 45 cm).

Personal Distance
This space is typical for casual conversations with family, friends, or close acquaintances. It maintains comfort and a sense of connection without being too intrusive. Invading this space can cause discomfort and anxiety. It is where informal conversations and personal interactions occur. It typically ranges from 18 inches to 4 feet (45 cm to 1.2 meters).

Social Distance
This is common for interactions with people we aren't particularly close to,

such as colleagues or new acquaintances, and people in social settings where they do not know each other well. This space suits formal interactions, business meetings, and social gatherings. It allows for comfortable conversation while maintaining a professional boundary. It ranges from 4 to 12 feet (1.2 to 3.6 meters).

Public Distance

This zone is used for public speaking, presentations, large gatherings, and events where the interaction is impersonal and there is no need to interact closely. It also applies to public events where there is little or no personal interaction between the speaker and the audience. Usually, it starts from about 12 feet (3.6 meters) or more.[56]

GREETINGS AND PHYSICAL TOUCH AROUND THE WORLD

One day in Columbus, my brother visited us and invited me to eat. While at the restaurant, one of my American friends came to our table to say hi. As customary in Mexico, my brother stood up, reached his hand to shake her hand, and instinctively leaned in to greet her with a customary Mexican cheek kiss.

She froze and pulled back; her face turned all tones of red, and her eyes widened in surprise. She didn't know what to say or what to do. She clearly didn't expect that kind of greeting at all. I quickly apologized, explaining, "In Mexico, we greet with a cheek kiss to show warmth and friendliness." She smiled, appreciating the cultural insight. "No worries," she said, laughing lightly. "It's just different here. A handshake or a wave is more common.". Then, my brother realized his cultural misstep and apologized, and now his face turned red.

Awkward!

Physical touch is a fundamental aspect of human interaction, and its interpretation varies widely across cultures. Misinterpreting these norms can lead to discomfort or misunderstanding. For instance, a person from a low-contact culture might feel uneasy with the frequent touch in high-contact cultures, while someone from a high-contact culture might perceive the reserved behavior in low-contact cultures as cold or unfriendly.

Social interaction styles also differ significantly across regions. Physical contact and expressiveness are central to communication in countries like Spain and Greece, and many Latin American nations—such as Mexico,

Argentina, and Brazil—are known for their warm and friendly interactions, often involving hugs, cheek kisses, and pats on the back. Physical closeness is a sign of friendship, affection, and social bonding.

On the contrary, Asian and Northern European cultures may prefer less contact and more personal space to show respect.

In countries like Brazil, Argentina, Mexico, Italy, Spain, Portugal, and Greece, people frequently greet each other with cheek kisses, 1 to 3 kisses, and often maintain close physical proximity during conversations. In the Netherlands, Belgium, Switzerland, and some parts of France, people kiss three times on the cheeks (right-left-right) for close relationships, while a handshake suffices for less intimate greetings. In Russia and Ukraine, three air kisses are customary.

In countries such as Saudi Arabia and the UAE, same-gender friends often hold hands, hug, and kiss on the cheeks as a display of camaraderie. However, physical contact between men and women in public is generally limited due to cultural and religious norms.

In the UAE, Saudi Arabia, Oman, and many Gulf countries, nose bumping is a traditional greeting. In New Zealand, the Maori greeting "hongi" involves pressing foreheads and noses together, symbolizing sharing the "breath of life."

A firm handshake is the most common greeting in the United States and Canada. Hugs are typically reserved for close friends and family, and personal space is highly valued. People maintain about an arm's length distance during conversations. Similarly, countries like the United Kingdom and Germany prefer handshakes and maintain a moderate distance in social interactions. Physical contact is more reserved than in Southern Europe but still present in close relationships.

In Japan, handshakes are less common than in Western cultures, as bowing is the traditional greeting. However, handshakes occur in business or international settings, but their grip is softer than that of Western countries. A firm grip may appear aggressive, so a light, respectful grip is preferred.

In Japan, Nepal, Cambodia, India, Thailand, and China, bowing is a standard greeting in many Asian cultures, reflecting respect and humility. Physical contact, such as hugging or kissing, is rare and usually reserved for close family members. Maintaining a greater personal distance is seen as polite.

Bowing is different and has different meanings in these countries, i.e., In Thailand, the "Wai" involves pressing hands together and bowing slightly. In Japan, "ojigi" is a traditional greeting that expresses respect, gratitude, or apology. The depth and duration of the bow vary depending on the situation and the status of the individuals involved.[57]

In Scandinavian countries like Sweden and Norway, physical touch is minimal, and people value personal space. Handshakes are common in formal settings, but other forms of physical contact are less frequent.

In Tibet, greeting someone involves sticking out your tongue and touching your chest. This gesture, especially among Tibetan monks, signifies peace and demonstrates that the greeter is not the reincarnation of the cruel 9th-century king Lang Darma, known for his black tongue.

In Zimbabwe and Mozambique, clapping hands rhythmically is part of the greeting tradition. In Malaysia, people greet each other by touching their fingertips, then bringing their hands to their chests and nodding slightly. Men should wait for women to extend their hands first.

In many Asian and African cultures, elders are greeted first. In the Philippines, young people touch their foreheads to an elder's hand. In India, people touch elders' feet. In some African countries, young people kneel to show respect.[58]

Another exciting aspect of physical touch is how often people touch each other in different settings. Canadian psychologist Sidney Jourard conducted research called the Coffee Study in the U.S., France, the UK, and Puerto Rico. He watched people sitting in cafes and recorded the rate at which they touched each other in one hour. Puerto Ricans touched 180 times, the French 110, the British 0, and the Americans touched twice.[59]

In many cultures, touching, handshakes, kisses, or gestures like putting a hand on the shoulder can be uncomfortable, even between friends. Recognizing and respecting these differences helps foster better interactions and avoid turning faces red.

ENTHUSIASTIC AND RESERVED CULTURES

Enthusiastic and reserved cultures represent two distinct approaches to communication, expression, and social interaction. These cultural styles reflect how people engage with each other, manage emotions, and navigate social dynamics, often influenced by historical, social, and geographic factors.

Enthusiastic cultures

Enthusiastic cultures are expressive, emotionally open, and thrive on vibrant communication. In these societies, interactions are lively, with passionate conversations, animated gestures, and visible emotions such as joy, excitement, or frustration.

People in these cultures use hand gestures, facial expressions, and physical touch—like hugs or cheek kisses—to emphasize points and convey warmth. Conversations are often fast-paced, loud, and engaging, where interruptions signal enthusiasm rather than rudeness. Personal space is smaller, and close physical proximity is common.

Emotional authenticity and openness are valued. Social gatherings are vibrant and communal, centered around family, friends, and collective enjoyment. People in enthusiastic cultures thrive in social settings, seeking environments that encourage active participation, spontaneous plans, and energetic discussions.

Argentina, Mexico, Brazil, Venezuela, Italy, Spain, Greece, Lebanon, Turkey, Morocco, Nigeria, South Africa, and Kenya are examples.

Reserved cultures

Reserved cultures emphasize calm, introspection, and composure, favoring thoughtful communication over overt emotional displays. Conversations are measured and reflective, with personal space deeply respected. Silence holds meaning, and social interactions prioritize modesty, order, and discretion rather than expressiveness.

People in these cultures use minimal body language, controlled gestures, and limited physical touch. Conversations tend to be quieter, slower-paced, and interruption-free, valuing deep listening and reflection. Emotions are typically kept private, with polite smiles replacing loud laughter, and direct eye contact may be avoided to maintain comfort.

Social interactions are often formal or purpose-driven, with relationships developing gradually through trust and shared experiences rather than immediate emotional openness. They prioritize patience, restraint, and quiet contemplation.

Examples of reserved cultures are Japan, South Korea, China, Finland, Sweden, and Norway.

***

People in enthusiastic cultures may perceive reserved settings as overly restrained, cold, or distant, while those in reserved cultures may view enthusiastic interactions as overwhelming or intrusive. Each style offers unique strengths: enthusiastic cultures excel in forming quick relationships and building community, while reserved cultures offer stability, respect for personal boundaries, and a reflective approach to communication.

While everyone possesses elements of both, the degree to which someone leans toward one or the other shapes their energy, social preferences, and overall approach to life.

KEY TAKEAWAYS

- Enthusiastic Culture: Distinguish by their high energy and expressiveness. Often louder and faster-paced, they talk more and listen less. Have a deep need for connection.
- Reserved Culture: Communication is calm, measured, and polite, focusing on brevity and clarity. Pauses in conversation are standard, allowing time for careful reflection. People tend to listen more than speak. Body language is subtle, with minimal gestures or movements. Personal space and privacy are highly valued, with limited physical touch and a preference for respectful distance in conversations.

CHAPTER 8

Joyful alignment

"We may have different religions, different languages, different colored skin, but we all belong to one human race."
— *Kofi Annan*

B ecoming a responsible global citizen means embracing an identity transcending national and cultural boundaries. It involves recognizing our shared humanity and taking responsibility for the well-being of people and the planet. A global citizen is committed to understanding diverse perspectives, promoting social justice, and contributing to the worldwide community. This mindset encourages active participation in addressing global challenges, fostering cross-cultural understanding, and advocating for positive change, both locally and globally.

AN AMBASSADOR

At some point, I dreamed of becoming an Ambassador of Mexico. My love and passion for Mexican culture, its people, rich history, stunning architecture, diverse geography, and vibrant ecosystem fueled this aspiration. I've always loved traveling and envisioned a life where I could explore the world and promote the country I love. As an Ambassador, I would have the opportunity to do just that—represent Mexico on a global stage and contribute to its positive image worldwide.

Years later, when I told my family that I was moving to Memphis, USA, my aunt said something that resonated with me: "You're finally going to be an Ambassador for Mexico." Initially, I didn't fully grasp what she meant, but she explained, "You're moving to another country, and this is your chance to represent and promote Mexico there. You can challenge negative stereotypes, create a positive image of our country, and lay the groundwork for future generations. Isn't that what you always wanted to do?"

She was right. Although my job title was different and I didn't have the same platform or reach as an official ambassador, I realized I could still fulfill the core of my dream. Wherever I go, I carry her words with me: "I'm not just representing myself; I'm representing my country. I must leave a good impression and make thoughtful decisions."

Over time, my perspective has expanded. While Mexico always holds a special place in my heart, I feel connected to something bigger. I believe I'm not just a representative of one nation but of the world. This isn't because of my citizenship or the countries I've lived in or traveled to, but because our actions—no matter how small—impact the world.

We all share this beautiful planet called Earth. In that sense, we are all GLOBAL CITIZENS.

THE BUTTERFLY EFFECT

The butterfly effect, a concept from chaos theory, suggests that small actions can lead to significant, sometimes unpredictable, outcomes. This idea, famously illustrated by a butterfly's wings potentially triggering a tornado, highlights how tiny changes can ripple through complex systems over time.

This principle applies beyond science, influencing fields like economics, psychology, and global citizenship, emphasizing how interconnected our world is. Everyday choices—such as using eco-friendly products, supporting ethical businesses, or promoting cultural understanding—create ripples that shape broader social, environmental, and economic systems.

The butterfly effect also fosters humility, reminding us that we can't always predict the full impact of our actions. This perspective encourages respect for diverse cultures and values, promoting empathy, inclusion, and deeper social connections. Even small gestures, like engaging with others with curiosity and kindness, contribute to a more understanding and peaceful world.

Being a good global citizen means recognizing that each decision shapes the future, no matter how small. The journey isn't about grand gestures alone. It's about consistent, meaningful actions that collectively make a difference over time.

Figure 10: Global Citizen

BECOMING A GLOBAL CITIZEN

In a broad sense, we are all global citizens, sharing the planet and interconnected through social, economic, environmental, and technological systems. Whether we realize it or not, our actions have far-reaching effects beyond our immediate surroundings.

However, true global citizenship goes beyond mere existence. It requires a conscious awareness of this interconnectedness and an active commitment to global issues, social justice, and sustainability. While not everyone identifies as a global citizen or engages in global advocacy, the responsibility and opportunity to do so are universal.

Being a global citizen isn't about how many countries you've visited; it's about adopting a mindset that embraces our shared humanity beyond borders. It doesn't replace local, national, or cultural ties but expands them to include a broader, global perspective.

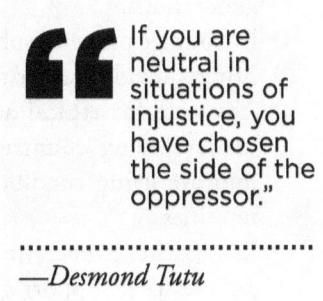

If you are neutral in situations of injustice, you have chosen the side of the oppressor."

—*Desmond Tutu*

Recognizing that our actions have worldwide implications, global citizenship fosters empathy, respects diverse cultures, and advocates for social justice.

Ultimately, it's about making informed, responsible choices that contribute positively to beyond borders.

Global citizen responsibilities

As global citizens, our influence comes with certain rights and responsibilities to improve the world, even when not required by law. By fostering understanding, showing respect, and actively engaging with others, we can help create a more interconnected and harmonious global community.

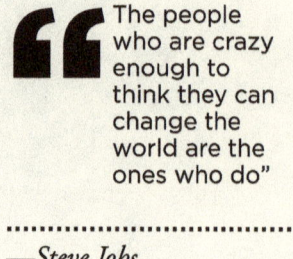

The people who are crazy enough to think they can change the world are the ones who do"

—*Steve Jobs*

The responsibilities of a global citizen encompass a wide range of actions and attitudes that contribute to the well-being of the worldwide community. Global citizens are called to uphold the principles of justice, equity, and sustainability while encouraging understanding and cooperation across cultural and national boundaries.

Here are some key examples of the responsibilities of a global citizen:

- Promote human rights and social justice, standing against discrimination and injustice, supporting equal rights for all people regardless of race, gender, religion, or nationality
- Strive to understand and respect diverse cultures, traditions, and perspectives. Stay informed of global issues, such as climate change, poverty, and conflicts, and make informed decisions and actions.
- Adopt and promote sustainable living practices to reduce one's ecological footprint and help protect the environment for future generations.
- Encourage peaceful solutions to conflicts and engage in dialogue that bridges divides rather than exacerbates tensions.
- Advocate for ethical and fair-trade practices that benefit producers in developing countries and reduce global inequalities, aiming to improve living conditions and opportunities for disadvantaged communities.
- Engage in democratic processes, such as voting, and advocate for policies that support global justice, international communities, and the planet's well-being.

- Work with others across borders to address global challenges, sharing knowledge, resources, and strategies.
- Help build inclusive communities that welcome and support people from diverse backgrounds.
- Make purchasing decisions that reflect ethical considerations, such as labor practices, environmental impact, and corporate responsibility. Support local businesses and economies whenever possible, particularly in disadvantaged or developing regions.
- Advocate for and contribute to efforts that provide quality education and literacy for all, especially in underprivileged areas.
- Cultivate empathy and compassion and strive to understand and share the feelings of others, especially those who are suffering or marginalized. Use your privileges to help others.
- Help to accomplish global goals.

The global goals, known as the Sustainable Development Goals (SDGs), are a set of 17 interconnected objectives established by the United Nations in 2015 to end poverty, protect the planet, and ensure prosperity for all by 2030.

These goals address many global challenges, including eradicating hunger, achieving gender equality, ensuring quality education, promoting decent work, combating climate change, and preserving biodiversity. Each goal is accompanied by specific targets and indicators to measure progress, aiming to foster sustainable economic growth, social inclusion, and environmental protection, ensuring no one is left behind.[60]

Global Citizen Rights

Universal human rights are the essential rights and freedoms to which every person is inherently entitled, regardless of nationality, ethnicity, gender, religion, or other statuses. These rights are founded on equality, dignity, and respect for all individuals. They are codified in international law, most notably in the Universal Declaration of Human Rights (UDHR), adopted by the United Nations General Assembly in 1948.

The UDHR contains 30 articles that collectively establish these fundamental rights and freedoms. The initial articles highlight all individuals' inherent dignity, equality, and rights, including the right to life, liberty, and security. They also explicitly forbid practices like slavery, torture, and any form of discrimination. Further articles focus on the rule of law, ensuring equal treatment under the law, and protecting individuals from arbitrary arrest and exile.

The UDHR also elaborates on civil and political rights, such as freedom of thought, conscience, religion, expression, and peaceful assembly. It also emphasizes economic, social, and cultural rights, including the right to work, education, and a decent standard of living. The final articles stress the importance of a social and international order where these rights can be fully realized while also making clear that no one can exploit these rights to infringe upon the rights of others. Collectively, these 30 articles form a comprehensive human rights framework that has shaped international law and global human rights standards.[61]

Global citizen values

Global citizen values are the guiding principles that shape the attitudes and actions of individuals who see themselves as part of a broader, interconnected world community. These values include respect, responsibility, diversity, justice, empathy, belonging, abundance, peace, advocacy, equity, fairness, collectivism, openness, global perspective, interdependence, cooperation, participation, and curiosity.

An exceptional global citizen might value human rights, religious pluralism, participatory governance, environmental protection, poverty reduction, sustainable economic growth, peacebuilding, humanitarian aid, and cultural diversity.

Global mindset

While global citizenship emphasizes responsibility and action, a global mind is about the intellectual and cognitive approach to understanding and engaging with the world. It is about how we think and engage with the world, marked by openness, curiosity, and a willingness to learn from diverse perspectives. It allows us to see through multiple lenses, appreciate cultural complexity, and understand the nuances that shape different ways of life.

More than awareness, a global mind fosters adaptability, navigating cultural contexts, communicating across differences, and bridging divides. In business and leadership, it enables strategic thinking, recognizing global patterns and shared challenges that drive innovation and success. It's about acknowledging differences and actively learning from them to make informed decisions, solve problems, and build meaningful relationships.

Rather than tolerating differences, a global mind embraces them—dismantling barriers, seeking common ground, and celebrating the diversity that enriches the human experience. It prioritizes collaboration and mutual respect over division, fostering stronger, more connected communities.

By understanding different perspectives, individuals with a global mindset encourage cooperation, personal and professional growth, and cultural exchange. Thriving communities are built on respect, shared responsibility, and a commitment to collective well-being—ensuring everyone feels valued and empowered. Together, we create a more inclusive and unified world.

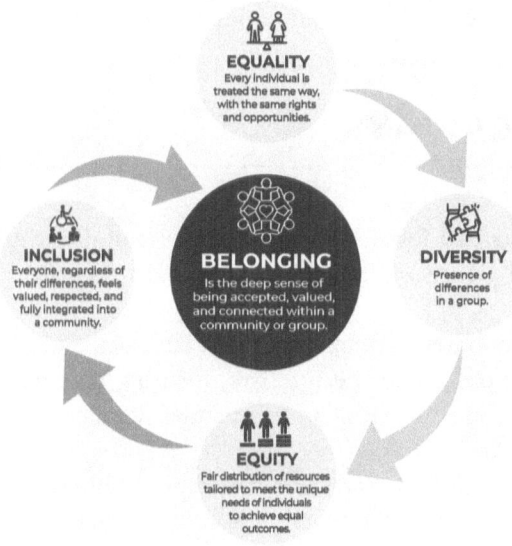

Figure 11: Belonging

Celebrating differences

Differences can encompass race, ethnicity, gender, age, sexual orientation, socioeconomic status, ability, and more. True inclusion goes beyond acknowledging these differences—it values diverse perspectives and experiences, creates an environment where every voice is heard, and ensures that all individuals, regardless of background, feel welcomed, respected, and empowered to participate fully. It also means fostering a culture where people can express their identities freely, without fear

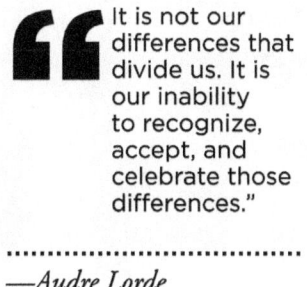

It is not our differences that divide us. It is our inability to recognize, accept, and celebrate those differences."

—*Audre Lorde*

of discrimination or exclusion. When individuals feel genuinely accepted and valued as integral members of a group or community and can be their authentic selves, knowing they are appreciated for who they are.

When global citizenship and a global mindset come together, they create a powerful combined effect that enables individuals to make a meaningful impact on the world. A global citizen with a broad perspective understands their responsibility to the larger community and possesses the awareness and skills to engage across cultural boundaries with empathy and effectiveness.

KEY TAKEAWAYS

- A global citizen fosters empathy, respect, and diversity and advocates for social justice while making choices that benefit the global community.
- A global mindset embraces openness, curiosity, and a commitment to learning from diverse perspectives, focusing on common ground to build a sustainable, resilient, and compassionate world. It seeks unity over division
- Global citizens have rights but also responsibilities.

PART II

Living abroad

Life-Changing Lessons and
Skills From Living Abroad

iving abroad offers a rich adventure filled with both challenges and rewards. Part II of this book guides you through the complex journey of relocation and adapting to life in a new country. This section provides essential knowledge and tools to enhance your experience abroad. With practical advice and strategies for navigating unfamiliar surroundings, you'll learn how to overcome common obstacles and make the most of your time in a new place. The insights shared here are invaluable for fostering successful adaptation, personal growth, and a more profound, expansive worldview.

Whether you are contemplating a move, already navigating the complexities of life in a foreign land, or supporting loved ones through this transition, this section offers invaluable insights and practical advice to make the experience enriching and transformative.

I hope these chapters become your trusted companion, a source of comfort where you feel heard and supported during the most challenging moments, and inspiration and upliftment, empowering you to step forward with confidence and courage on this remarkable journey ahead.

CHAPTER 9

To move or not to move?

*"With changes, you may lose something good,
but something even greater might come with it."*
—*Unknown*

This chapter offers insights to help clarify and guide your decision on whether to move abroad or stay. By 2022, an estimated 281 million international migrants lived worldwide, making up 3.6 percent of the global population. [62]Among these, over 75 million are expatriates, each with their reasons, conditions, and expectations for moving. Your motivations and circumstances are unique, and your outcome will inevitably differ from others—and that's perfectly okay. Choose wisely.

While many move for economic reasons, there are countless other motivations. They may include career advancement, education, retirement, finding a partner, a fresh start, improved quality of life, new adventures, political stability, personal safety, or a desire to volunteer and make a difference.

Before you decide to move, there are crucial factors to consider, whether your stay will be short-term or long-term. Your decision will depend on your goals, risk tolerance, and the trade-offs you're willing to make for this experience. Moving abroad can be an enriching, transformative journey but often complex. This is why it's essential to approach this choice thoughtfully: research your destination, weigh the pros and cons, and seek advice from those who have lived abroad.

If you're relocating with a spouse, children, or family members, involve them in decision-making. Ensuring they also have something to look forward to in the new environment can be key to a smooth transition and a successful adjustment for everyone.

Living in a different country was one of the best decisions I've ever made, and I can't stress enough how valuable the experience has been. For anyone considering it, I highly recommend embracing the opportunity. Of course, not every country is the right fit for everyone. Your decision to move will depend greatly on your personality, values, interests, and goals.

With 195 countries worldwide, there is likely a place that matches your needs and satisfies your adventurous spirit. And if, after careful thought, you decide staying is the best choice, that's perfectly okay, too. The journey toward making the right choice for yourself is a fulfilling one in itself.

MY PROS AND CONS

My husband and I have lived in three different countries: Mexico, the United States, and Belgium. So far, I have no regrets, not even a little. Naturally, there are moments of melancholy and anxiety—that's unavoidable. But those moments are balanced by the excitement and joy of new experiences.

We moved from Mexico to the U.S. in 2001. What started as a plan for just a few years extended into the present. Our main reasons for moving were to gain the experience of living and working in another country, which we knew would enrich our personal and professional lives. We also wanted to improve our language skills, access better-paying jobs, and take advantage of the opportunity to travel to places that would have been harder to visit otherwise.

We considered staying in Mexico primarily because of our close-knit family and friends, the vibrant social life, the weather, domestic help, and the food. But when the opportunity to explore a new land presented itself, it didn't take long for us to decide to go. Why? Because it was a fantastic chance to learn, grow, and expand our horizons. The downsides, aside from being away from family, seemed minor, and after all, it was only supposed to be for two years, right?

Living in the U.S. allowed us to visit family and friends once or twice a year. Naturally, we missed the familiar comforts of Mexico—like the warm weather and the ease of having domestic help. Although it wasn't quite the same, we did have conveniences in the U.S., such as air conditioning, heating, dishwashers, and dryers, making everyday life more manageable and compensating for our Mexican comforts. After thoughtfully weighing the pros and cons, we thought it was the right choice.

Then, in 2003, we relocated from the U.S. to Belgium. The advantages of moving to Belgium were somewhat different. While the experience of living in another country and learning a new language remained, the chance to explore Europe and the legal entitlement to at least 21 days of vacation plus ten national holidays was impossible to resist.

The main drawback was that we would be even farther from our families. But again, it was only for a few years, and our family and friends were excited to visit us in Europe. Looking back on both relocations, I can confidently say that living abroad exceeded our expectations in countless ways. It changed our lives for the better, and though we had to sacrifice some things, it was worth it.

BENEFITS OF LIVING ABROAD

Moving abroad is a gateway to a life-changing adventure beyond mere relocation. It offers unparalleled personal and professional growth opportunities, cultural enrichment, and self-discovery. Immersing in a new environment fosters adaptability, resilience, and a global perspective, making the experience enriching and transformative.

It exposes you to diverse traditions, beliefs, and perspectives, fostering cultural sensitivity and appreciation while broadening perspectives. Daily interactions smooth language acquisition, offering a dynamic and practical alternative to traditional learning.

Professionally, international experience is highly valued. It opens doors to unique career opportunities and enables the development of a global network. It enhances problem-solving, independence, and adaptability. Furthermore, moving abroad often leads to improved living standards, access to world-renowned educational opportunities, and the chance to align life with personal values and goals through self-discovery.

It often leads to greater self-awareness and clarity about your values and goals. In one's home country, people are typically surrounded by others who behave similarly, making it less necessary to question whether their actions align with their values or the cultural norms they have grown accustomed to. However, when living abroad, exposure to new cultural values and norms encourages us to regularly evaluate our own beliefs and behaviors, leading to either reinforcing or reassessing those values.[63]

Some benefits

Cultural Enrichment	Personal Growth	Networking and Connections
Language Acquisition	Independence	Improved Quality of Life
Career Advancement	Enhance Global Perspective	Educational Opportunities
Self-Discovery	Adaptability	Cross-Cultural Communication
Problem-Solving	Empathy	Open-Mindedness
Resilience		

The endless benefits of living abroad make it a transformative experience that fosters personal and professional growth, enhances quality of life, broadens perspectives, and deepens one's understanding of the world.

KEY CONSIDERATIONS

Before moving abroad, it's essential to consider several key factors that will significantly impact your experience. From understanding visa and legal requirements to assessing the cost of living, healthcare, and job opportunities, every aspect is crucial in ensuring a smooth transition. Additionally, cultural differences, language barriers, and the emotional challenges of living in a new environment can shape your journey. Carefully evaluating these considerations will help you make informed decisions and better prepare for life in a foreign country.

Safety

Safety is one of the most important aspects to consider. Living in a safe place can make your life easier, more enjoyable, and less stressful.

Of course, not even the safest places can guarantee your safety. There is risk everywhere. However, there are countries or cities where the risk is lower than others. To get a better idea, you can check some websites listed below, which offer global crime rate information.

- United Nations: unodc.org
- World population Review: worldpopulationreview.com
- U.S. Department of State: travel.state.gov
- Global Initiative: globalinitiative.net
- Global Peace Index: visionofhumanity.org

Every country has areas that vary in safety, so it's essential to thoroughly research crime rates for the city or town you're interested in. For example, the U.S. crime rate is 47.70 per 100,000 people, but in Louisiana, it jumps to 3,711 per 100,000, and in Hammond, a city in Louisiana, it skyrockets to 11,790. By contrast, Vermont has an impressively low rate of 0.0017 per 100,000. Safety can differ dramatically within a single country, so for accurate insight, check local news and specialized websites or, better yet, ask a local.

Keep in mind that the news often highlights the worst incidents, rarely showing the daily life of most people. Crime rates can also appear higher in countries where people feel more comfortable reporting crimes, unlike others where fear suppresses reports. Additionally, laws may differ in what is classified as a crime versus an offense, skewing comparisons. For example, in Sweden, if a spouse abuses their partner twenty times in a period, each abuse is reported individually, while other countries may count them as a single offense.

So, don't be discouraged by high crime rates—conduct more in-depth research, speak with locals, or even better, with ex-pats living there. They can provide invaluable insights into safety precautions and whether they feel secure. For example, they might say the city is generally safe as long as you avoid the downtown area, which is known to be more dangerous. Or perhaps they suggest precautions like staying indoors after a particular time, avoiding specific neighborhoods when walking alone or even when driving, and refraining from wearing flashy jewelry in public. They might also recommend installing a home alarm system, opting for a house with high fences and no street-facing windows, living in a gated community with security, and, for women, avoiding walking alone.

When I first moved to the U.S., I was shocked to see people leaving their car engines running, doors unlocked, keys in the ignition, and valuables like purses on the passenger seat while they shopped. I assume it's to keep the car cool with the AC running. And as for leaving the purse? It's probably just for convenience. Whatever their reasoning, attempting this in other countries might leave your car cool—but with a new driver by the time you return.

I have several Brazilian and international friends who live or have lived in São Paulo, Brazil. They all rave about the city's vibrant atmosphere, diverse cuisine, and warm people, describing it as a beautiful place to live. However, when asked about safety, their responses are consistent: crime is a concern, as it is in most populated cities worldwide.

They live safely but within a bubble—residing in apartments with 24-hour surveillance, driving with windows up and doors locked, and often detouring to avoid high-risk areas like certain favelas. They stay vigilant, safeguarding their belongings in crowded places and avoiding walking alone at night. Locals know which streets and stations to steer clear of, and this knowledge is crucial for navigating the city. Despite the precautions, most expats enjoy living there and find the experience rewarding.

Here are some essential tips if you're considering moving to a high-crime area:

- Speak with locals for insider advice and safety tips.
- Keep your home country's embassy or consulate contact information handy.
- Before committing to any agreements, visit your potential neighborhood and workplace at different times, day and night, ideally with someone familiar with the area.
- If something feels off, trust your instincts—safety should always be your priority.
- Listen to your intuition; it's often your best guide in unfamiliar environments.

Cost of living

A common oversight when relocating is failing to account for the cost of living in your destination. A seemingly generous salary might not stretch as far in cities like New York, Tokyo, or London, where expenses can dramatically surpass your current situation.

I've met people thrilled by a promotion with a significant salary bump, only to find that their anticipated savings quickly evaporated due to the high cost of living. What once afforded them a spacious house in their home country barely covered a small apartment at their new destination.

When we moved to the U.S., I was shocked by how much grocery costs differed from Mexico. Items I once considered everyday staples—like lemons and avocados—became premium purchases. Two lemons for a dollar? An avocado for $2.50? I could buy three pounds of lemons or eight avocados in Mexico for the same price! To make matters worse, sometimes the avocados that looked fine on the outside were spoiled inside. Bummer!

Research recurring expenses—housing, utilities, groceries, transportation, taxes, and healthcare- to avoid financial surprises. Use cost-of-living calculators like Living Cost, The Economist Intelligence Unit, or Expatistan to compare. Local real estate agents, relocation companies, and colleagues can provide valuable estimates.

Additionally, consider factors like exchange rate fluctuations, which can affect your purchasing power if paid in a foreign currency, and tax implications on foreign investments.

Job opportunities

If you or your significant other wants to secure a job abroad, exploring opportunities before making big moves is wise. A good starting point is to research the unemployment rate in your desired country. In some countries, job opportunities may be limited even for locals, and foreigners may find it challenging to secure work unless they possess in-demand skills that are hard to find locally.

Investigate the country's work visa requirements, documentation, and regulations if the unemployment rate looks favorable. Embassies are a valuable resource for this information and can also provide details on entrepreneurial programs or work visa prerequisites. Make sure all your formal documents are current and in order.

Other critical factors to consider include salary expectations and benefits in your field, tax obligations, working hours, maternity, paternity, or sick leave policies, vacation, corporate culture, and any economic, political, or cultural restrictions that could impact your work and lifestyle.

Gather essential information about obtaining a work visa, required documents, and other legalities. Then, you're ready to start the job search. Your current employer is an excellent place to start, especially if it's a multinational company—ask about international opportunities and the specific requirements.

The Internet and networking are powerful tools for finding job opportunities abroad. Explore company websites for international roles, apply online, and search for job sites specific to your destination country. Networking is equally valuable—reach out to your social network, join ex-pat or professional groups on LinkedIn or Facebook, and connect with like-minded professionals through platforms like Meetup or Business Networking International.

Attend international job fairs and monitor local media in your chosen country for job openings. If your skills aren't immediately in demand, consider short-term positions or enroll in a study program to build connections and improve language fluency, easing your entry into the local job market.

Review the specific requirements for positions you're interested in, as certain qualifications may be implied but not listed in the job posting, such as certified translations of official documents, local language fluency, or specific local certifications. For example, a friend from Spain who moved to the U.S. due to her husband's job found this out firsthand. She was a certified dental hygienist, cosmetologist, and esthetician in her home country with years of experience and fluency in French and Spanish but no knowledge of English. Although highly qualified, she couldn't work as a dental hygienist or in any of her specialties without U.S. certification, highlighting the importance of verifying required credentials before moving abroad.

Volunteering is another excellent option for meeting people, improving language skills, and improving one's chances of finding paid work later.

Healthcare

While vacationing on a Caribbean island, I asked my husband, "Wouldn't it be nice to retire somewhere like this?" I imagined us waking up to sunrises, walking on white sandy beaches, soaking up the sun, sipping mojitos, and enjoying fresh tropical fruits and Caribbean dishes—all with the turquoise sea and nothing to worry about.

He replied, "No, not here."

The next day, we were at sea on a cruise when the ship slowed down. We heard an announcement over the speakers: "Code Blue, Code Blue," summoning a medical team to respond immediately. The captain reduced the ship's speed and soon informed us that we'd return to Miami due to a medical emergency. Though we were closer to several Caribbean islands, he chose to head back to the U.S. with over 4,000 passengers and 1,500 crew members on board.

The captain didn't explain his decision, nor did he have to. He had a life in his hands and did what was necessary. I guessed that the island hospitals weren't equipped to handle the emergency. My husband's "no, not here" answer about retiring in paradise made sense then. This paradise was missing one critical thing: a well-equipped hospital.

The last thing you want to think about when planning to move abroad is a hospital visit, but if you're considering it, preparing for medical emergencies is essential, especially if you have a medical condition. Understanding the basics of the healthcare system in your new country is critical.

Some questions to consider: Are there enough hospitals, doctors, or even essential medications? Do doctors speak your language, or are interpreters available? How far is the nearest hospital? Does your insurance cover you abroad? Are there any restrictions or limitations for foreigners? Some countries lack high-quality hospitals, have limited facilities or medical personnel, or have complex, expensive healthcare systems. Necessary medications might also be unavailable.

We were healthy when my husband and I moved to the US, so I hadn't thought much about healthcare. My first medical experience in the U.S. was soon after moving to Memphis, just before our wedding anniversary. We were in our honeymoon phase and wanted to wait a few years before having children. I'd been taking birth control in Mexico, so I packed the remainder of a 28-day pack plus an extra to last about six weeks in the U.S.

In Mexico, contraceptives are available at any pharmacy without a prescription unless you're a minor. I assumed it would be the same in the U.S., so

I waited until I had less than a week's supply. At the pharmacy, to my surprise, the pharmacist told me they couldn't sell birth control without a prescription.

I figured it wouldn't be a big problem; I'd make a quick appointment with an OB/GYN and get the prescription. But when I called the first doctor, the receptionist said, "We're not accepting new patients." I called another doctor, who informed me I'd need to complete a new patient application and that the next available appointment was two months away.

Two months? I was a newlywed, needing a prescription within days, and all I heard were waitlists. Doctor after doctor, the answer was the same. So, I had no choice but to wait two months for an appointment.

Thankfully, this was only for birth control. Had I known in advance, I would have brought a longer supply from Mexico or scheduled an appointment sooner, saving myself unnecessary stress and hassle. But imagine this scenario for something more serious.

Another challenging experience came when my daughter, about nine months old, developed a high fever on a Sunday night when everything was closed. We tried alternating ibuprofen and acetaminophen and cooling her down with gradual baths, but her fever didn't budge. Anxious, I called the on-call doctor, who told me I couldn't give her more medication yet.

The fever persisted, and my worry grew. I've always been concerned about fevers, probably because a second cousin suffered permanent neurological damage as an infant due to meningitis-induced fever. After trying everything, we took her to the emergency room since neither her pediatrician nor any other doctors in the group could see her in person.

We waited more than an hour in the ER waiting room as more urgent cases were ahead of us. Eventually, a nurse called us in, took her temperature, checked her pulse, measured and weighed her, and left the room. After another hour, she returned and repeated the same procedure, leaving us again. The fever finally dropped after several hours, and we decided to leave.

A few weeks later, the bills started arriving. There wasn't just one but several: one for the nurse, one for the ER admission, one from the hospital, and more, totaling over $1,000. After disputing it, they reduced it to $850. We had insurance, but even with coverage, we were left with this hefty bill for a visit where we saw only a nurse, no doctor, and received no treatment or tests.

This was an expensive lesson in how different the U.S. healthcare system is from what we were used to in Mexico. There, patients often have direct contact with their doctor, even in emergencies, and may receive support over the phone or via a house visit, all at minimal cost compared to the U.S. In the Mexican healthcare system, costs are usually disclosed upfront, so there are few surprises. We discovered clinics and other affordable options for people without primary doctors several dollars later.

Navigating an unfamiliar healthcare system in the middle of an emergency is no one's idea of fun. That's why it's essential to understand how the healthcare system works in a new country before moving. You never know when you'll need it, but having a plan and knowing what to expect can make all the difference.

Health systems around the world

No country has a perfect healthcare system, but it's essential to ensure that the system in your new country meets your priorities. Confirm that you'll have access to medical care if needed, and it will be affordable. For example, if hospitals are far away, you may need to arrange for emergency transport options, such as a helicopter service, to reach a treatment facility.

When evaluating healthcare options in a new country, consider factors like affordability, accessibility, hospital infrastructure, medical equipment, technology, innovation, the skill level of doctors and medical staff, quality of services, wait times, availability of hospital beds per 1,000 inhabitants, and healthcare outcomes (such as mortality rates, maternal and child health, and life expectancy).

One way to assess hospital standards is to check for certifications from international accreditation organizations. Hospitals accredited by bodies like the Joint Commission International (JCI, based in the U.S.), Trent Accreditation Scheme (UK-Europe), Accreditation Canada International (ACI), Australian Council for Healthcare Standards International (ACHSI), or QHA Trent Accreditation are held to specific international standards. These accreditations evaluate the quality of patient care and the facility's commitment to continuous improvement using objective global criteria.

It's also essential to understand the type of healthcare system in the country. There are five main types of healthcare systems. Universal health coverage ensures everyone can access necessary health services, medications, and technology without financial hardship. A universal system may be public, privately managed, or socially funded by the government. In contrast, a non-universal system requires individuals to pay out-of-pocket, making it less affordable for all citizens.

Here's a look at different healthcare systems around the world.

Universal Public System (Bismarck Model / Social Health Model)
Funded through mandatory payroll deductions, with contributions from employees and employers. It's accessible to everyone, with tax revenues supplementing it. Both public and private institutions provide services under government regulation. In some countries, those without formal

employment may not qualify for free care, but private insurance is available for those who can afford it.

Examples: Belgium, France, Japan, Singapore, China, India, South Korea.

Universal Government-Funded Healthcare (Beveridge Model)

Centrally funded through taxes, healthcare is available to all citizens, regardless of income or employment. The government is the sole payer for medical services delivered through public institutions.

Examples: Australia, Canada, Spain, Norway, Italy, Sweden, New Zealand, UK. (Similar to the U.S. Veterans Health Administration.)

Universal Private Health Insurance System

Managed by the government and offered by private insurers. The government subsidizes low-income citizens who cannot afford insurance.

Examples: The Netherlands, Israel, and Switzerland. (Similar to the US Medicare)

Universal Private-Public Health System

A hybrid where some people use private insurance while public healthcare is available to all, funded through taxes.

Examples: Mexico, Germany, Argentina, Turkey.

Non-Universal Insurance System

In this model, consumers pay directly for healthcare from private or public providers. Some citizens have private insurance, and a limited public healthcare system may be available, often with minimal access for those without insurance.

Examples: Democratic Republic of Congo, Nigeria, and the USA[64]

Some Considerations

If the country ha**s a universal healthcare system, ensure you meet eligibility requirements for these benefits. In a non-universal system, familiarize yourself with medical costs, especially if you have a preexisting condition. If you aren't eligible for local health coverage immediately, consider getting an International Medical Plan, as most domestic health insurance plans don't cover treatment abroad. Compare policies carefully for cost, coverage, and ratings.

....

** You can find a more detailed list at toyirodriguez.com

Additionally, bring copies of your insurance card, contact information for your insurance provider, and vaccination records for all family members. Confirm whether your current medications are permitted in the new country and if you can restock them.

Before You Move

- Familiarize with the new country's health system.
- Schedule doctor, dentist, and optometrist appointments in your current country to address any health needs.
- Refill any necessary medications, keeping them in their original containers with labels and prescriptions for easier customs clearance.
- Ensure your medications are permitted in the new country and if you can re-stock up on those there.
- Verify your insurance covers any preexisting conditions.

Once in the New Country

- Identify local doctors and clinics and check appointment timelines for new patients, as waits can be extended.
- If waiting times for new patients are lengthy, consider scheduling a general checkup early to establish a relationship with a provider. This will make it easier to access timely care in the future.

Taking these steps will help you to reduce stress in emergencies.

Healthcare Summary

Universal
Everyone is automatically covered at birth (in most countries) or after a certain age or condition (US Medicare and Veterans Administration).

Non-Universal
People have to acquire insurance. Some people will remain uninsured.

Country Data Source
World Health Organization 2021. OECD Health Data 2016 or Work Bank 2014.[65]

The U.S. is the only industrialized country without universal healthcare coverage, despite spending 17.4% of its GDP on healthcare.

Coverage	Universal			Non-Universal	
	Single-payer, Single-provider (Beveridge model or socialized medicine)	Single-payer, Multiple-providers	Multiple-payers, Multiple-providers (Bismarck model, Sickness Funds, or Social Health Insurance)	Multiple-payers, (private insurance) **Multiple-Providers**	Out-of-pocket
Model					
How it works	Healthcare is funded and supplied by the government through tax revenue.	Healthcare is delivered by private doctors in private facilities, with the government covering the majority of medical expenses.	Employers and employees were covered by national health insurance funded through mandatory payroll taxes. Health insurance companies are private, non-profit organizations that the government regulates.	Healthcare providers are reimbursed fee-for-service by various payers, including state and federal entities and private health insurance companies. Employers provide insurance coverage.	Patience pays out-of-pocket for healthcare.
Countries and % GGP spend in healthcare. 2021	Cuba 13.79% U.K. 12.36%	Canada 12.33% Taiwan 6.7%	Japan 10.82% Switzerland 11.8% Germany 12.93%	U.S 17.36%	China 5.38% India 3.28%

Environmental, geographical, and natural phenomena to consider

Too hot? Too cold? Tornadoes, tsunamis, earthquakes? Almost every place has some weather or climate-related drawbacks. Research these environmental factors to know what to expect and to ensure the new setting is a good fit for you and your family. Not everyone can comfortably handle extreme cold or heat; some may be more sensitive to altitude or pollution, exacerbating existing health conditions.

When moving to a city with a significantly different climate or geography, several factors should be considered, especially if you have a chronic health condition. Air quality, pollution levels, average temperatures, precipitation rates, climate, altitude, sunshine, and snow days per year are just a few examples.

Adapting to a new climate can be challenging, with factors like age, lifestyle, weight, and health playing an important role. People adjust to different temperatures, climates, and environments uniquely. For example, my children adapt quickly to cold weather and wear short-sleeve t-shirts most winter days, even at -10°C, while I bundle up in multiple layers. However, for someone with arthritis, cold weather often worsens joint stiffness and pain, limiting mobility and increasing discomfort.

Through experience, I've learned how weather affects my health and mood. Living in Indiana, where winters are long, cold, and gray, I must take vitamin D supplements from September through May to compensate for the lack of sunshine; otherwise, I'd feel fatigued, down, and sometimes even sad. I also discovered, after several years, that I have seasonal allergies to tree and ragweed pollen and mold spores—something I didn't encounter in Mexico due to the climate in San Luis Potosí, where these seasonal allergies are far less common.

Most people eventually adapt to new environments, but the more you know about your new ecosystem, the easier it will be to make informed choices to protect your physical and mental well-being, identify potential triggers for any symptoms, minimize risks, and respond effectively to natural events.

Understanding the climate of the new city also helps inform decisions about purchasing a home, selecting insurance coverage, and budgeting for expenses you may not have in your current location, like air conditioning, heating, window treatments, a 4x4 vehicle, or appropriate weather gear.

For example, if you plan to live in a hurricane-prone area, you may need to research if the property is in a high-risk area. Consider a higher-elevation house with impact-resistant windows, reinforced doors, and hurricane shutters. A backup generator can be helpful to keep essential systems running during power outages. Adequate drainage systems, like sump pumps or storm drains, to manage potential water accumulation, and elevated electrical panels and HVAC systems to protect them from flood damage.

All climates have pros and cons. One of the best ways to acclimate is to get outside for at least 10-15 minutes daily, even when you don't feel like it—choosing the best time of day for comfort and safety. With the proper preparation, you can comfortably ease the transition and embrace the new environment.

Black Ice

Moving to a place with a vastly different climate or weather conditions than you're accustomed to can be exciting and challenging. Whether transitioning from a tropical paradise to a snowy city or swapping desert heat for a humid coastal environment, adapting to new environmental conditions requires preparation. Adapting successfully to a different climate is more than just adjusting your wardrobe; it's about equipping yourself with the knowledge and resources to embrace your new environment safely and comfortably.

Winter took on a new meaning when I moved to Collierville, Tennessee, from Mexico's warm, mild-weathered climate. In over 25 years of living in Mexico, I'd only witnessed a few brief snow flurries on two rare occasions. I had never experienced winter storms, icy road conditions, or cold that could transform everyday streets into slippery hazards. Tennessee winters aren't extreme, but they're significantly colder than most places in Mexico. I'd read about black ice while studying for my driving test, but experiencing it firsthand was another story.

For those unfamiliar, black ice is a thin, nearly invisible layer on roads when temperatures drop below freezing. It gets its name because it blends in with black asphalt, making it hard to see, especially at night or in low light. Unlike thicker layers of ice or frost, black ice appears as a harmless wet spot on the road. Yet, driving on it is incredibly dangerous; cars can lose traction in an instant, leading to skidding and loss of control.

In the U.S., local authorities do a good job of clearing snow and salting streets to melt the ice. But it takes time, and less-traveled roads are sometimes left untreated. My first encounter with black ice happened in Collierville during a winter morning commute to Memphis. The drive usually took about 45 minutes and started on a chilly, humid day. My husband cautioned me about the possibility of black ice. He had driven to work carefully and advised me to stay home as our neighborhood streets had not yet been cleared.

Later that morning, I called my workplace, and most of my coworkers had made it safely to the office; I also noticed a truck spreading salt on our street. Thinking it was safe, I decided to drive cautiously. The roads looked clear, and I'd gently brake or turn the wheel occasionally to check for any signs of slipperiness, and everything looked fine. Ten minutes into the drive, I was heading down a hill when I saw a car approaching from a side street. The distance seemed safe, so I began braking slowly—but the car didn't respond. My four-wheel-drive vehicle seemed helpless on the invisible black ice. I quickly began honking to alert the other driver, who sped up just in time, allowing me to stop inches from his car.

Shaken but relieved, I pulled over to gather myself before returning home.

Living where temperatures regularly drop below freezing (32F, 0C) means learning what to do—and, just as importantly, what not to do—when you encounter black ice. Even the most experienced drivers can suddenly find themselves in a dangerous situation.

We moved in April, giving us plenty of time to learn about black ice and prepare for the winter ahead. Now, imagine it's mid-winter, and someone who has just relocated or is visiting from a tropical paradise—unfamiliar with or unaware of these icy conditions—suddenly encounters these hazards for the first time.

I'm not trying to sound alarmist. Anyone can learn to navigate and adapt to different weather conditions. All I want is to highlight the importance of researching your new environment as soon as you move—or even before-hand—so you can reduce risks and be prepared for situations like this.

***

When moving to a new location, the local climate, weather patterns, air quality, and geographical features significantly impact your lifestyle, health, and comfort. Understanding these factors can help you effectively prepare for, plan, and adapt to your new environment.

Also, understanding your limits regarding climate and the environment is essential. You need to know what works for you and what doesn't, what you enjoy, and what you prefer to avoid. It's critical to consider the level of risk and adaptability you're comfortable with and, more importantly, to ensure that your new environment won't negatively affect your health or exacerbate any existing conditions.

What may seem like minor discomfort to some could pose serious health risks to others. While I might endure cold weather with mild discomfort, someone with respiratory issues could find it dangerous. Likewise, someone who brushes off earthquake fears might live in constant anxiety in a seismic zone. Recognizing these personal thresholds can make the difference between living comfortably and putting your well-being at risk.

Climate
Extreme heat, cold, humidity levels, and seasonal allergies can require lifes-tyle adjustments.

Weather
Weather patterns, such as monsoons, heavy snowfall, fire risk, or storm sea-sons, may disrupt transportation, travel, or outdoor pursuits.

Air Quality

Monitor local air quality indices and understand any pollution regulations that may affect your budget or daily life activities.

Daylight Variation

Extreme daylight variations in polar regions may influence sleep and mood, emphasizing the need for strategies to maintain balance during prolonged light or darkness.

Altitude

If moving to a high-altitude location, consider how it may affect you, especially if you have any heart or lung conditions. High altitudes can cause altitude sickness or exacerbate respiratory issues.

Natural Hazards

Natural hazards encompass a wide range of events, including hurricanes, typhoons, droughts, floods, famines, wildfires, heat waves, cold waves, tropical cyclones, tornadoes, derechos, hailstorms, blizzards, snowfalls, avalanches, volcanic eruptions, earthquakes, landslides, mudslides, sinkholes, tsunamis, and even rare occurrences like meteor or comet impacts.

Certain natural disasters are more prevalent in specific geographic regions. Awareness is your strongest ally when it comes to mitigating disaster risks. Familiarize yourself with the necessary steps to take before, during, and after such events. Proactive measures—such as assembling an emergency kit, identifying evacuation routes, and staying updated via weather alerts—can significantly minimize potential harm.

***

Being informed, prepared, and ready to respond is not about living in fear but taking sensible precautions. Doing so ensures that you and your family can navigate the situation confidently and calmly in the face of the unexpected.

Adjusting to a new climate often requires a period of adaptation. To ease your transition, ensure you're prepared with suitable clothing, skin protection, and indoor climate control. If you're passionate about outdoor activities, consider how the local climate might affect your routines and explore indoor alternatives if needed.

Planning and considering these factors can help you adapt comfortably and mitigate potential challenges.

Housing

One of the most immediate priorities when moving abroad is finding suitable housing. It's crucial to understand local rental or buying practices, including whether housing is typically furnished or unfurnished, the costs of utilities, and the standard of living across neighborhoods. Additionally, be prepared for differences in housing quality, size, and amenities compared to what you may be used to in your home country. Factors such as proximity to work, schools, essential services, and public transportation, as well as the volatility of the local housing market, can significantly impact your housing search and living experience. It's also wise to consider your long-term ability to rent or buy, particularly in competitive markets.

When we moved to Carmel, we were taken aback by the intense competitiveness of the housing market. Homes were selling within hours—I'm not exaggerating—and before we could even offer, many were already off the market, often for prices well above the listing. Fortunately, we had the flexibility of time. We didn't need to rush our move, but for those with a tight relocation timeline, the house-hunting process was incredibly stressful and likely more costly than anticipated.

Understanding the fast-paced nature of specific markets and preparing for potential price surges can make all the difference, helping to ease the transition and avoid unexpected financial strain.

Transportation, traffic, distance, and accessibility

Moving to a new country often means adjusting to a different transportation infrastructure. Consider whether public transportation is reliable, safe, and cost-effective or whether owning a car is necessary. Traffic conditions, distance between home, work, and schools, and accessibility to grocery stores or healthcare facilities can significantly impact your quality of life. Additionally, assess the area's walkable or bike-friendly, local driving laws, road conditions, and parking availability.

Laws and regulations

Navigating the legal landscape of a new country is vital to a smooth transition. Employment, taxes, investments, and real estate laws can vary significantly from country to country. Understand the country's visa, residency, and citizenship processes, especially if you plan to stay long-term or invest in property. Take note of specific regulations that might impact your personal or professional life, such as local business laws, labor rights, and rules about transferring money or assets. Additionally, consider how democratic or stable the government is and how that might affect your rights and security.

Discrimination

Be aware of potential discrimination based on race, gender, religion, or nationality in your destination country. While potential discrimination can pose challenges, there are proactive steps you can take to foster a positive experience and successfully integrate into your new community—research local laws and protections for minority groups to understand your rights and identify available resources. Seek out organizations, cultural groups, or online forums where expats and locals alike promote diversity and inclusion, offering support and guidance.

Engage with your community and demonstrate an openness to learning about their culture while sharing aspects of your own. This mutual exchange can help break down barriers and foster understanding. Approach challenges with an informed and open mindset.

Education / school tests

Evaluating the educational system is essential if you have school-age children or plan to study abroad. Research international schools or local schools that offer programs in the language your child speaks. Consider the quality of education, curriculum, and how local testing systems compare to what your child is used to. Some countries have rigorous national exams that may differ significantly from your home country's. Look into how well the schools accommodate children from international backgrounds and whether they support students who need help adjusting academically or culturally.

Pace of life

The pace of life can vary widely. Some countries, especially in southern Europe or Latin America, have a slower, more relaxed pace. In contrast, others, like North America or parts of Asia, maybe more fast-paced and productivity-driven. This can affect everything from business hours to social interactions and how quickly things get done in your day-to-day life, including banking, government services, or setting up utilities.

The pace of life can significantly influence a person's well-being and ability to adapt to a new environment. While fast-paced countries may provide opportunities for productivity and achievement, they can also lead to stress for those unaccustomed to the pressure. On the other hand, slower-paced countries may offer a more relaxed lifestyle, but for some, this could feel unmotivating or inefficient.

Access to products and services you like

The availability of familiar products and services can significantly affect your comfort level abroad. Whether it's certain foods, brands, or personal care products, research whether these items are available or if there are local alternatives. Additionally, consider access to services such as gyms, salons, or hobbies you enjoy. Check how easily these are accommodated if you have specific dietary needs or preferences, such as gluten-free or vegan options. Consider whether there are international shipping options or specialized stores to help you maintain your lifestyle.

Understand your job offer

If you're relocating through a company transfer, it's essential to understand your job offer thoroughly. Moving abroad for work is a significant commitment, and carefully reviewing the details will help ensure a smooth transition. Beyond your role and responsibilities, several unique factors need attention to avoid potential surprises. Besides the other considerations listed above, here are a few more things you should consider before accepting a job abroad:

Salary and Currency

Research the average salary for your role in the destination country, as salaries can vary widely based on the local economy, cost of living, and industry standards. If paid in a foreign currency, be aware that exchange rate fluctuations could impact your earnings. Confirm how frequently you'll be paid and whether any adjustments will be made for currency changes. Also, clarify if the salary is gross (before taxes) or net (after taxes and deductions), as tax rates vary dramatically by country and will affect your take-home pay.

You should set up bank accounts, understand currency exchange rates, and familiarize yourself with the financial systems of your new country.

Taxation

Understand the local tax system and how much of your income will be taxed. Some countries have progressive tax systems, while others may offer tax benefits for expatriates. Check if your home country will tax your foreign income, as you might face double taxation. To avoid this, see if there is a tax treaty between your home and host countries. Additionally, inquire about social security or national insurance contributions in the new country, as these may impact your net salary.

Benefits and Compensation Package

This includes moving expenses, temporary housing, or assistance with settling in. Clarify pension and retirement plan contributions and how working abroad will affect your benefits. Paid vacation time and public holidays differ widely by country, so check your entitlement to vacation, sick days, parental leave, and local holidays. Ensure you have adequate health coverage and understand the extent of medical insurance offered.

Work Visa and Permits

Confirm that your employer is committed to sponsoring your work visa and fully understand the conditions of your work authorization. Moving abroad without the proper visa can be risky, and visa renewals may require company support. If you're relocating with family, check whether they are included in your visa or if they'll need separate visas. Understand the process and timelines involved.

Cultural and Workplace Adjustments

Every country has its own work culture, from office hierarchy to meeting etiquette. Research these norms to see if they align with your working style. Understand standard working hours, overtime policies, and workplace flexibility. Some countries prioritize work-life balance, while others may expect extended hours or weekend work.

Language Requirements

If you're not fluent in the local language, verify if the company operates in English or your native language. If learning the local language is essential, consider how it may impact your work and social integration.

Legal Rights and Protections

Familiarize yourself with local labor laws. Are employees protected from unfair dismissal? What are your overtime pay, parental leave, and sick leave rights? Ensure you receive a written contract outlining all employment terms, including salary, benefits, and termination conditions. Have a legal professional with local laws review the contract if needed.

Certifications and Accreditation

Check if your qualifications and certifications are recognized in the new country. Some professions require local accreditation or additional exams. This may also apply to family members' certifications if they intend to work.

Cost of Returning Home

Some companies provide repatriation assistance if your assignment ends earlier than planned or when it's complete. Clarify if the company will cover moving expenses and any lease termination penalties. It's wise to have an exit strategy if the position doesn't work out or you must return home for personal reasons. Consider whether you'll have financial stability if you must leave the position earlier than expected.

Spousal and Family Support

If relocating with a spouse, confirm if they will have the right to work in the new country. Some countries don't offer automatic work visas for spouses, which could affect your household income. For those with children, research international or local schools that meet your standards. Some companies may include an education allowance for expat children, so inquire about this benefit.

Visa and legal requirements

Research the types of visas available (work, student, residency, etc.) and ensure you meet the eligibility criteria. Understand the immigration laws and visa application processes, extensions, or permanent residency. Ensure you have all the necessary documentation (passport, health records, financial proof, etc.).

PREPARE BEFORE YOU MOVE

It's never too soon to start preparing for your big move. Proper planning and organization are essential for a smooth transition to your new life abroad.

Research Local Customs and Culture: Understanding your new country's customs, traditions, and social norms can help minimize culture shock. Learn about the pace of life, work culture, and everyday social etiquette to avoid unintentional mistakes, especially in professional settings.

Pack Wisely: Plan your packing based on weather patterns, climate, and the size of your new home. Check which electronic appliances will work, as voltage and plug types may differ. Consider adapters or voltage converters if needed and verify local restrictions on what you can bring into the country.

Language Preparation: If the local language differs from yours, consider language lessons before moving. Basic proficiency can help with essential communication, making integrating and settling in easier.

Visa and Documentation: Ensure you have the correct visa, whether a work visa, student visa, or residency permit. Check the application process, timelines, and specific requirements, such as health or background checks. If applicable, ensure your employer provides the necessary documentation for a work permit. Ensure your passport is valid for at least six months beyond your intended stay, and make copies of all essential documents, including your visa, for easy access.

Driving and Transportation: If you plan to drive, check whether your current license is accepted or if you'll need an international driver's permit or local driver's license. If you plan to bring your vehicle, ensure it meets local regulations and emissions standards. Look into the costs of shipping and registering it in the new country. Research public transportation options, including trains, buses, and taxis, and learn about transit cards or payment apps used locally.

Healthcare and Insurance: Research the healthcare system in your new country (public or private) and whether your current insurance covers you abroad. If not, consider international health insurance. Ensure you're up to date on any required or recommended vaccinations. Bring copies of your medical history, prescriptions, and vaccination records. Verify the availability of any prescription medications you rely on and check for restrictions on specific medicines.

Banking and Finances: Determine if you need a local bank account and what documents are required—research efficient ways to transfer funds internationally. Ensure you have enough savings or an emergency fund for unexpected expenses, especially in the early months.

Education and Childcare: If you have children, research local and international schools, the availability of spots, and the differences in curriculum. If the language of instruction differs, consider language support or tutoring. Some employers offer education allowances, so be sure to inquire about this.

Declutter Before Packing: Evaluate what to take, sell, or leave behind. Downsizing simplifies the move and may reduce shipping costs.

Shipping and Customs: If you're shipping belongings, research international shipping companies, costs, and timelines. Confirm customs regulations to avoid issues with restricted or prohibited items upon arrival.

Essential Document Copies: Keep digital and hard copies of essential documents (passports, visas, birth and marriage certificates) in your carry-on. Mark them as "Do Not Pack" to ensure that movers don't accidentally pack them with the rest of your belongings. Put all the essential documents on a carpet or case, and make sure you have all the required documents to open a bank account, obtain a driver's license, enroll children at school, find work, or find housing—some landlords require identification papers, references from previous landlords, bank statements, letters of recommendation from old neighbors, and copies of old bills showing they had been paid in full. These are easier to do, obtain, and organize before moving. And it's one of the most critical steps.

Communication Setup: Decide whether to get a local SIM card or an international phone plan. Make sure your phone is unlocked and compatible with regional networks. Research local internet providers and arrange for installation in your new home as soon as possible.

Emergency Contacts: Have emergency contact numbers for your new country's police, medical, and fire services accessible. Register with your country's embassy or consulate for assistance in emergencies.

Community and Support Networks: Seek out expat networks and local communities to connect with others who have gone through similar experiences. These groups can offer valuable advice, social opportunities, and emotional support during adjustment.

Family Needs: If you are moving with your family, involve them in planning. Ensure that their needs, from childcare and education to social activities, are met to help them adjust smoothly.

Prepare for Culture Shock: Moving abroad can be emotionally challenging, bringing excitement and homesickness. Adjusting to a new culture may come with frustration, loneliness, or homesickness. Allow yourself and your family time to adapt, and be prepared for emotional ups and downs.

While thorough planning is essential, be realistic and open to surprises. You may experience emotional highs and lows, from enthusiasm for your new surroundings to homesickness. Transition phases can be challenging, but they also offer growth and the opportunity to learn resilience as you adapt to new experiences.***

EMBRACE THE ADVENTURE OF MOVING ABROAD

Embracing the chance to relocate, don't let fear hold you back from the possibilities that await. No matter how overwhelming it can feel, each step forward brings you closer to a life enriched by new experiences, perspectives, and achievements. One day, you'll thank yourself for the courage to try.

A vivid childhood memory taught me the importance of seizing opportu-

---

*** You can find a more detailed list at toyirodriguez.com

nities. When I was about five, my Uncle Paco and Aunt Paulina took me to the circus. As the oldest and only girl on my mom's side of the family, I was lovingly spoiled. They treated me to flashing lights, a plush stuffed animal, prime seats, and plenty of delicious treats making the experience even more magical.

The circus was a whirlwind of color, with dazzling costumes and enchanting music. Act after act captivated the audience until it was time for the clowns. Their antics ranged from playful to slightly mischievous, drawing plenty of laughter. The moment that stuck with me most was when they invited an audience member into the ring—though, looking back, I suspect he was an actor.

They asked the man to climb a folding ladder hanging from the ceiling, and as he did, the clown clumsily attempted to follow behind him. The clown's oversized shoes kept getting stuck, making him stumble repeatedly and lose his balance. He grabbed the volunteer's clothing for support each time he slipped. Eventually, he tugged at the man's pants so many times that they slowly inched down until, to everyone's amusement, they fell completely, leaving him standing in his underwear. I laughed, but I remember thinking how embarrassed he must have felt!

After the clowns left, it was time for the elephants. I was thrilled to see these magnificent, intelligent creatures up close. I have always admired elephants, and while I'm grateful that most circuses no longer use animals in their acts—not because I dislike them, but due to the cruelty often involved—seeing them in person at that moment was unforgettable.

The elephants performed graceful routines—holding each other's trunks and tails in circles, forming towers, and dancing in sync. Suddenly, the ringmaster looked in my direction and invited me to join them in the ring.

What? Me, on stage?

I had no idea what to expect. This was my first circus experience—or at least the first one I remembered. After watching the clowns pull down that man's pants, I couldn't shake the fear that something equally embarrassing might happen to me. Would they make fun of me, too? Or, even worse, would they involve the elephants in a way that puts me in danger?

My mind raced with worst-case scenarios. Fear held me back as much as I longed to get close to the elephants, and I was too scared to accept the invitation.

All around me, other children cheered and raised their hands, eager to be chosen. Eventually, the ringmaster picked up a boy just a few seats away. I watched as he petted an elephant, took a ride, fed them, and even received a piece of cotton candy from one of them!

My heart sank with regret. Why hadn't I said yes? I would have loved every moment—it would have been a story I could excitedly share with friends and family for years. But my fear of the unknown had held me back, keeping me from experiencing something truly special.

I regretted that missed opportunity for years, often dreaming of returning to the circus and finally getting close to the elephants. It would have been a fantastic story—one I could have shared with excitement for years. That experience taught me at a young age that some opportunities come only once—you either seize them or spend a lifetime wondering what might have been.

I want to say this: If the chance to move to a new country or city presents itself, don't let fear hold you back. I'm not suggesting you jump at every opportunity without thought but consider it carefully. I wouldn't have felt the same excitement if I had been invited to get close to a boa instead of an elephant. Likewise, I wouldn't move to a country with high insecurity or instability. It simply wouldn't appeal to me. But if something about the opportunity excites you, don't let fear be the reason you say no. You never know what incredible experiences might await if you say yes.

Welcome the opportunity for new adventures, the cultures you'll explore, and the friendships you'll build. In the end, moving abroad is a bold and transformative choice, filled with extraordinary rewards. While weighing the pros and cons is important, those who take the leap often find it to be one of the most enriching journeys of their lives. It might just lead to experiences beyond anything you ever imagined.

KEY TAKEAWAYS

- Analyze the advantages and drawbacks of relocating internationally.
- Consider safety, cost of living, job opportunities, healthcare, climate, housing, transportation, laws and regulations, potential discrimination, educational factors, pace of life, access to products and services, and a clear understanding of your job offer.
- Living abroad provides many benefits and can be one of life's most enriching and transformative experiences.

CHAPTER 10

Cultural adjustment stages

"A ship is always safe at shore,
but that is not what it's built for."
-Albert Einstein

Moving abroad is like any major life decision; it can bring a whirlwind of emotions—excitement, sadness, joy, anxiety, motivation, challenges, amusement, frustration, and discomfort, to name a few.

Relocating to a new country is a thrilling adventure and a daunting change. It's normal to feel exhilaration and nervousness, happiness and sadness, all at once. This mix of emotions is a natural response to immersing yourself in a different culture and adapting to new ways of life, essential elements of the journey that make it as rewarding as it is challenging.

Moving to an unfamiliar place can be stressful on many levels, from managing logistics to learning a new job and adjusting to different norms and expectations. The ups and downs of life abroad can generally be broken down into several emotional phases. While the length and intensity of these phases vary for each person, the experience is universal.

Some people are almost fearless, ready to explore the world and embark on a new adventure without hesitation. They may move quickly from the Honeymoon phase to Acceptance, Adjustment, and Integration. Others—especially those who moved out of necessity or reluctantly—may experience more prolonged anxiety or culture shock. They might take longer to progress through these phases, spending more time feeling homesick or unsettled. Each journey is unique and depends on the individual's willingness and openness to embrace change.

The concept of cultural adjustment was first introduced in 1954 by

Canadian anthropologist Kalervo Oberg and has since become a widely recognized framework. Although there are various versions of the adjustment phases, they all share a similar progression of emotional highs and lows that most people experience during relocation. The classic four-phase model provides an insightful perspective on what many, including myself, go through in adapting to a new environment.[66]

So, buckle up for this emotional roller coaster!

Wait—don't be alarmed! I'm not trying to scare or discourage you. Instead, I'm here to help you understand these phases so you can move through them smoothly and find fulfillment in your new cultural surroundings. The more prepared you are, the easier your transition will be. Moving abroad doesn't have to be daunting; it can be one of the most empowering experiences of your life.

The Process of **Adjustment**

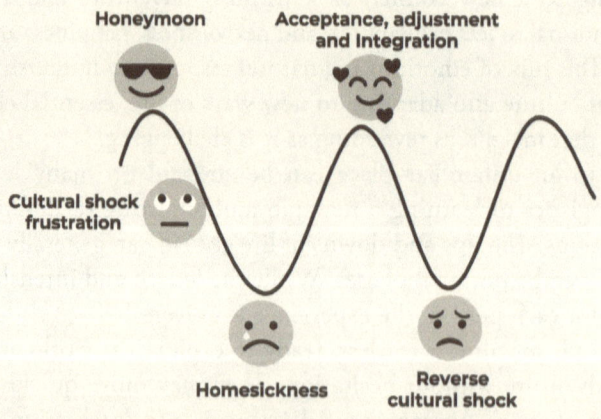

Figure12: The Process of Adjustment

STAGE ONE: HONEYMOON

"If you are brave enough to say goodbye,
life will reward you with a new hello."
-Paulo Coehlo

The first phase is about excitement and wonder; everything feels new and extraordinary. You can't wait to dive into this adventure! It's like a vacation —you have a whole city to explore, snapping pictures of every new sight, sampling local food at unique restaurants, and settling into your new home with awe and curiosity.

During this stage, you're buzzing with things to share. You constantly post on social media, text, and call family and friends back home to tell them about your discoveries. You're brimming with motivation, ready to tackle any challenge that comes your way.

***

For me, living abroad was a lifelong dream. I'd always been intrigued by different cultures, drawn to the sounds of foreign languages, and excited to meet new people and see new places. This made my decision to move a bit easier, and when the opportunity finally came, I was beyond excited. Initially, it did feel like a long, thrilling vacation—exploring every corner, dining out often, and treating my new house or apartment like a temporary retreat.

In this phase, excitement for new experiences is immense, and positive energy is at its peak. I made the most of this time by setting goals and writing down everything I wanted to achieve, from places to visit to new skills to master. I created bucket lists, wish lists, and plans for hobbies I wanted to explore. The more detailed, the better—these lists were filled with dreams and ambitions that gave me direction and purpose.

These lists and goals became more than just ideas; they grounded me, gave meaning to my sacrifices, and offered a sense of purpose when the initial excitement vanished. The following phases can be challenging, and having these goals established early on helps prepare you for what's to come, reminding you why you took this leap in the first place.

How to get the best of this phase
- Savor every moment of excitement and novelty in your new surroundings.

- Channel your positive momentum and energy by setting goals and planning for the months ahead—think about new routines, hobbies, and professional aspirations to explore. Make a wish list with places to visit, foods to try, and activities or skills you'd like to learn.
- Reflect on your journey by writing down your thoughts and expectations about moving abroad. This reflection can be both therapeutic and a valuable reference point as time goes on.
- Write down your reasons for moving abroad; revisiting them during challenging times can keep you focused, motivated, and connected to the excitement that brought you here.

STAGE TWO: CULTURAL SHOCK / FRUSTRATION

"No one ever said it would be easy.
They just said it would be worth it."
—*Anonymous*

The first few months abroad are often the most challenging and overwhelming. After the initial excitement and "vacation feeling" of the Honeymoon phase have faded, reality begins to settle in.

You start to feel the weight of day-to-day life: this isn't a vacation, and now you have responsibilities—work, studies, routines—all without the support system you had back home. Close friends are scarce, family is far away, your routine is a mess, and the language barrier makes essential communication challenging and exhausting. Everyday tasks, like grocery shopping, become frustrating when you struggle to find familiar items for simple meals.

Your mind is in overdrive, constantly absorbing new information, learning a new language, trying to keep up at work or school, and navigating the quirks of a foreign city. Even small tasks feel unfamiliar and unsettling. The new cultural environment feels unfamiliar, and simple things you once did without a second thought now require planning and patience.

Gradually, you realize this place isn't as "perfect" as you may have imagined; it has its challenges and flaws, just like anywhere else. And being away from home magnifies these difficulties.

Some of the cultural shocks I encountered during my first few months included:
- During my first few weeks at work, one of my coworkers celebrated a

birthday. Her cubicle was in front of mine, and I expected the usual festivities: a cake, a lively chorus of "Happy Birthday" from the team, hugs, and good wishes. Instead, colleagues casually stopped by at different times to offer quick birthday wishes and a slice of cake before returning to their cubicles. No singing? No hugs? No group gathering? It felt nothing like the warm, communal birthday celebrations back in Mexico and hardly seemed like a celebration to me.

- One evening at my new apartment, I was steaming vegetables when, suddenly, a loud alarm blared. I had never heard a fire alarm and was completely confused. Once I figured out what it was, I quickly opened the windows to release the steam. To my surprise, a fire truck and a police car arrived at my door minutes later. Where I'm from, seeing a fire truck or police car at your home means something serious; it's not for a bit of steam in the kitchen!

- In Belgium, I discovered that most stores, including grocery stores, are closed on Sundays. Adjusting to this routine wasn't easy; remembering to stock up in advance took several weeks (and several incomplete meals).

- One of the most amusing surprises was our first New Year's Eve in Indiana. We'd invited friends over, and having just returned from vacation two days before, we went shopping the day before New Year's Eve, which happened to be on a Sunday. We loaded our cart with cheeses, meats, appetizers, and a fine selection of red and white wine and champagne.

- We noticed people gave us odd looks, but we shrugged it off—until we reached the cashier. With a straight face, she informed us, "We can't sell alcohol on Sundays." In Indiana, it turns out, alcohol sales were restricted on Sundays. So, there we were, facing the possibility of ringing in the New Year with mocktails!

- Miscommunication was a frequent challenge due to the language barrier. I'd try to say something, but it would often be understood entirely differently.

- In Mexico, we hang clothes in the sun to disinfect, keep whites bright, and remove odors. At my new apartment, however, drying clothes outside was prohibited. Likewise, we typically disposed of mop water outside on the driveway, but I had no idea where it was acceptable to throw it here.

- In some Belgian supermarkets, you need a coin to unlock a shopping cart. When you return the cart, you get your coin back. I lost count of how many times I drove to the store only to realize I didn't have any coins, forcing me to go back home or rely on the kindness of a charitable person willing to lend me one.

All these little experiences build up, making you feel like an outsider. Even small tasks can feel daunting and frustrating at this phase, leaving you feeling out of place or out of control as if you can't quite understand the local system or culture. Moving abroad is, without a doubt, a hassle; it can be uncomfortable and uneasy. In this phase, the thought of returning home, where everything feels simpler, can be very tempting.

But remember, nothing worthwhile comes easily. These challenges are all part of the journey, and each small hurdle makes the experience richer and more rewarding.

How to get the best of it

- Observe how people act and respond in various situations to gain insight into the local culture.
- Resist the urge to compare your hometown with your new location; each place has a unique charm.
- Learn about cultural differences between your home and your new country to build understanding and ease the transition.
- Ask neighbors, friends, or coworkers for guidance on how things are done locally when uncertain.
- Embrace the experience with a sense of humor, and don't be afraid to laugh at yourself as you navigate new situations.
- Shift your perspective to find appreciation for your new environment and discover what makes it unique.
- Explore new hobbies or activities to keep yourself engaged. This can help you integrate, meet people, and feel more connected to your new community.
- Stay open-minded—understand that differences don't equate to right or wrong; they're simply different.
- Accept that you must adapt to your new surroundings, not vice versa.
- Prepare for the unexpected and allow yourself to adapt as things arise.
- Embrace an optimistic outlook to enhance your adaptability and resilience. Focus on the positives and enjoy the good things your new home offers.
- Reframe challenges as unique opportunities for growth and learning.
- Reserve some time to do things that bring you joy and feed your soul, grounding you in your new environment.

STAGE THREE: HOME SICKNESS

"Without the rain, there would be no rainbow."
-Gilbert K Chesterton

When you move to a new country, it's natural to start missing everything from home, big and small. You miss your family, friends, favorite foods, familiar activities, and the comforts you no longer have. Sometimes, you may question your decision: "Why did I move here? What was I thinking?" Feelings of anxiety, frustration, and overwhelm can become frequent companions.

This realization hit me hard one weekend night in Collierville, Tennessee, a few months after we moved there. My husband and I were lying in bed on a Saturday night simply because all the local restaurants and bars had already closed. We would never be home in Mexico on Saturday nights—unless we hosted a lively gathering.

Then, close to midnight, the phone rang. It was my cousin, calling from his wedding, telling me how much he missed us being there. He passed the phone to every member of my large extended family, each sharing how much they loved and missed us, wishing we were with them. In the background, I could hear music, laughter, and the familiar hum of people enjoying each other's company—everyone was having a blast. Meanwhile, here we were, just the two of us in bed, missing out on the celebration.

Being away from my family for these moments was and still is one of the most complex parts of living abroad. I felt a deep sense of loneliness, missing the closeness, laughter, and connection that family brings. That night, I lay awake, questioning my decision. Why had I given up so much for what felt so little at that moment? Why had I left behind so much happiness, family, vibrant social life, great weather, and comfort only to feel this disconnect? Was this the right choice? Everything felt completely different from what I was used to and wasn't what I had anticipated.

Back home, I had everything I could want: an amazing and supportive family, great friends, lively late-night restaurants and bars, outstanding food and service, weekend gatherings, a job I loved, and easy communication with everyone I cared about. That night, it felt like I had left all of that behind. Nostalgia and homesickness hit me hard—very hard.

But here's some good news: nothing lasts forever, and this challenging phase is no exception. That night was the worst of it. The following months were tough, but I gradually overcame those feelings. By the time we moved to Belgium, I had learned so much about adapting that this phase of homesickness only lasted two weeks instead of the months it took the first time I moved.

This phase might pass and never return, or it might come back in a much gentler form. After twenty-five years of living abroad, I still miss my family and friends and have days of homesickness, especially when I can't be there for special occasions. But those days are fewer, they pass quickly, and they're never as intense as that night.

A beautiful realization is that whenever I return home, it's like stepping into a timeless embrace. The love, warmth, and connection are as strong as ever, welcoming me wholeheartedly. Living abroad has taught me to cherish every moment with loved ones and reinforce that distance can never diminish those bonds. I've learned never to take these precious ties or anything for granted.

How to get the best of it

- Learn to let things go.
- Avoid comparing your hometown with your new place.
- Keep in mind the reasons you moved.
- Remember that this phase will pass.
- Allow yourself to feel your emotions. If you need to cry, cry. If you need to call your family, call them. If you need to leave the house and run like crazy, do it. If you want to eat an entire box of chocolates, resist the urge—you'll regret it the next day. But indulge in some. Do whatever makes your soul feel better, then get up and move forward.
- Look for ways to connect with people at work, school, or through expat groups. You might find a page on social media or at church.
- Don't wait too long to open your doors. Meet your neighbors, colleagues, and the parents of your child's friends, and invite them over for coffee or dinner.
- Make a list of the things you like about your new place and keep it nearby. You can read it whenever you need a reminder.
- Look at the bucket list you made during the honeymoon phase and try to do something from it.
- Focus on finding the positives in your new situation.
- Look for daily doses of joy. This may be my best advice: make time daily for activities that bring you joy and happiness. It may be hard to find the time, but this is a game-changer.

STAGE FOUR: ACCEPTANCE, ADJUSTMENT AND INTEGRATION

"It is not the strongest species that survive, not the most intelligent,
but the most responsive to change."
-Charles Darwin

A significant shift begins after weeks, or perhaps even months, navigating the ups and downs of a new culture, language, and environment. The initial hurdles—understanding local customs, finding your way, and making friends—slowly transform into everyday ease, signaling the arrival of a phase of genuine satisfaction and contentment.

As you comfortably communicate in a new language, cultivate friendships, and create a cozy, personalized space, every accomplishment, whether big or small, brings a sense of comfort and fulfillment. You've learned where to find your favorite ingredients, adapted your cooking, picked up new hobbies, reached some goals, and established routines that add structure and ground you in your new environment. Perhaps you have even explored some exciting new places, which add a spark to each day and bring purpose to your journey.

The quicker this phase arrives, the more effortless and rewarding the experience of adapting becomes.

The turning point came for me when I overcame the learning curve at work, reached a new level of language fluency, and found a wonderful group of friends. Being accepted into a master's program felt like a significant milestone in my integration.

I started dedicating more time to what made me feel truly happy—traveling, socializing, and pursuing my passions. I checked off my bucket list experiences, learned to paint, cooked Thai food, and snow skiing for the first time—things that might have been harder to do back home in Mexico.

In these moments, I knew my decision to move was right. The sacrifices felt worthwhile, and the enthusiasm and motivation that initially led me to embark on this journey returned stronger than ever. I had finally reached a place where this foreign country felt like home. Although I knew there would be more challenges ahead, I felt ready to face them, seeing each as an opportunity for growth and learning. The journey to this phase is often challenging, but once here, it's a rewarding affirmation of resilience, adaptability, and personal development.

How to get the best of it

- Spend quality time with friends, whether exploring the city, sharing a meal, or attending local events together.
- Embrace experiences unique to your new location—opportunities you may not have had back home. For example, try snowboarding if you're from Brazil and moved to Sweden, or explore scuba diving in Australia if you're from Algeria.
- Keep growing by learning new skills or deepening your knowledge through classes, hobbies, or personal projects.
- Design your space to be warm and inviting, a true reflection of your style and comfort, making it a welcoming retreat.
- Explore your new surroundings, travel, and immerse yourself in the nearby landscapes, neighborhoods, and cultures that make your new area unique.
- Join local initiatives, volunteer, and participate in community events. It's a great way to connect with others and make a positive difference.
- Prioritize well-being, ensure you and your family are happy and healthy, taking time for self-care and family activities that enrich everyone's quality of life.

KEY TAKEAWAYS

- **The Adjustment Process:** Encapsulates the emotional highs and lows most people experience during significant life transitions, particularly when moving abroad. It's a path marked by growth, challenge, and discovery moments.
- **It has four stages:** Honeymoon, Cultural Shock (or frustration), Home Sickness and Acceptance, Adjustment, and Integration.

CHAPTER 11

Spread your wings without guilt

"People who lack the clarity, courage, or determination to follow their dreams will often find ways to discourage yours. Live your truth, and don't ever stop!"
- Steve Maraboli

One aspect rarely discussed when moving abroad is the guilt that expats may face. As humans, we care about the feelings of others, and it's natural to question if the decision to move was the right one. Guilt, a moral emotion, arises when someone believes they have compromised their standards or violated moral norms, taking significant responsibility.[67]

I am blessed with the most amazing parents—caring, loving, independent, cheerful, kind, generous, patient, fair, active, fun, encouraging, supportive, hardworking, and responsible. They have always put our family's well-being first, offering unwavering love and support. Besides their love, one of their greatest gifts was the confidence and independence to pursue my dreams. They provided me with the wings to fly, even if it meant I would fly far from them. Despite the distance, they share in my happiness, even when it means not seeing me as often as they would like.

I remember calling my mom on my daughter's first day of kindergarten, sharing my mixed emotions—sadness, joy, and pride. I wanted to slow down the time; my daughter was growing up in the blink of an eye, but she was extremely excited about her new school and friends; as soon as she saw her new classroom, she hugged and kissed me and went straight to her class without looking back. No fuzz, no crying, no hanging up on my leg. Just a happy little girl growing up into an independent girl.

That day, my mom shared something I didn't know: she secretly cried when I was packing to move out before getting married. She had the same bittersweet feeling I felt for my daughter's milestone, only magnified by knowing I would no longer live under the same roof. I had never noticed her sadness at the time; she had hidden it well, prioritizing my joy and excitement. She was overjoyed to see me marry a good man and start my own life, even if it meant her heart ached a little as I left the nest.

When we decided to move abroad, it was also difficult for my parents to see me go. Yet, they supported me wholeheartedly, recognizing the incredible opportunity it represented. Instead of burdening me with guilt, they encouraged me to pursue my dreams. Isn't that what parents ultimately want for their children? To see them forge their paths and lead happy, fulfilling lives?

Of course, the move came with its sadness. I knew my parents would miss me deeply, especially when we couldn't spend every vacation together in Mexico or when my children couldn't grow up as close to their grandparents, cousins, and extended family as I did. I felt the weight of not being there for family events, like weddings, funerals, graduations, or birthdays, and missing out on moments like seeing my nieces and nephews grow up. In those moments, I wished with all my heart to be in two places at once. It's not easy, and I won't sugarcoat that. But deep down, I knew I was making the best decision I could, given the circumstances. Thanks to the unwavering support of my parents and family, my guilt never consumed me.

Unfortunately, not everyone has the same support system. A friend of mine had always dreamed of studying for her MBA in England. She worked hard, maintained stellar grades, and earned a scholarship to her dream college. Her family had known about her aspirations for years, and her mom had been incredibly supportive. But after her mom passed away, when she was finally accepted, her brother told her that their grieving father would be devastated if she left, implying her absence could harm his already fragile state. Torn between her ambition and her family's well-being, she gave up her dream.

Her dad and brother would indeed have felt the pain of her absence, and things would have been more challenging for them without her. But what about her aspirations? Wouldn't it have been possible to celebrate her achievement and support her while maintaining close contact? Couldn't they have found ways to make it work for everyone, balancing her pursuit of success with continued connection?

Supporting her dreams and maintaining a strong bond could have provided a more balanced and healthier solution. Caring about others' feelings and practicing empathy is essential, but not to the extent that you sacrifice your own life and happiness to meet others' expectations. Please others at the expense of your fulfillment isn't sustainable, and you may resent it sooner or later. Living authentically means finding harmony between caring for those we love and staying true to ourselves.

EXPAT'S GUILT

Guilt is a feeling that can pounce on us each and every time an occasion calls us home...and we don't go."

—*Jessica Scott-Reid*

In some cultures and families, as discussed in Chapter 6, saying no to your parents or leaving your community is seen as unacceptable, even if it means giving up your dreams, aspirations, happiness, opportunities, or prosperity. Choosing a path that leads away from the family is often perceived as abandonment or selfishness—putting your desires above the needs and emotions of those who raised you. The expectation is to stay close, care for one another, and uphold the cycle of support. After all, they took care of you as a child or at pivotal moments in your life, and now, it's considered your turn to look after them.

These cultural and familial expectations can create immense, sometimes unspoken, pressure. You love your family and don't want to disappoint them. You want to be near them and share in the important moments, but you also yearn to chase your dreams and forge your path.

For many expats, this struggle leads to feelings of sadness and, in some cases, guilt for leaving family and friends behind. As humans, we care deeply for our loved ones and strive to make them proud. It's painful when those cherished, shared moments are missed.

Deciding to move abroad and leaving behind family, friends, memories, and traditions are among the most difficult choices. It's a leap into the unknown, away from everything familiar and beloved. No one, or at least no one I know, makes this decision mindlessly.

People move for valid, often good reasons: to provide better for their families, feel safe, pursue a lifelong dream, access education or work unavailable in their home country, achieve significant personal or professional milestones, take advantage of unique opportunities, find a place that energizes and uplifts them, for health, or to be with a partner who lives abroad. Rarely, if ever, is the decision made to forsake family bonds. So why do we feel guilty?

Guilt often arises from cultural norms or the reactions of loved ones. I have friends who feel profound guilt and pain for moving far from their families, not because it was the wrong choice but because, in their culture, living apart from family is rare. Sometimes, guilt is heightened by remarks that linger: "I'm getting older and sick, and you're not here to care for me." "When I'm going to die, you won't be here." "I dreamed of enjoying my grandchildren nearby, but now they live so far away." "You're robbing me of those precious moments." "You missed your cousin's wedding—after all the time you spent together before, how could you be so ungrateful?" "You'd rather be somewhere else for Christmas than spend time with your family."

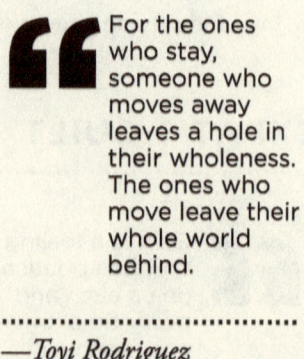

For the ones who stay, someone who moves away leaves a hole in their wholeness. The ones who move leave their whole world behind.

—Toyi Rodriguez

These words, often spoken from a place of love and longing, can intensify the emotional burden of an expat already balancing ambition and loyalty to loved ones. Most expats don't move to turn their backs on family; they do it to embrace life's opportunities and challenges, and often because studying or working abroad would allow them to be in a better position to look after their families back home.

Your family and friends form your support system, built on mutual sacrifice and care. You've always been there for one another, looking out and fulfilling your roles within this close-knit circle. When someone leaves, it disrupts the balance of the group. Why? Because everyone must adjust to a change they didn't choose or want. Such changes can bring discomfort, disillusionment, fear, and uncertainty.

Directly or indirectly, they may make you feel selfish, but in reality, it reflects their own emotions and fears. Alternatively, you might feel guilt or greed due to past experiences, comments, values, or beliefs shaping your thinking. But wouldn't anyone who truly loves you want to celebrate your successes, see your dreams come true, and witness your happiness?

If you decide to move abroad or have already made the leap to pursue your dreams, why is it so difficult for them to accept and share your joy? Many expats face this harsh reality: the tension between following their aspirations and grappling with the disappointment or resistance of those they hold dear.

Feeling sad and missing loved ones when you leave is entirely natural. It's normal to wish you could be there for special occasions—birthdays, weddings, funerals, and those priceless moments watching children grow up. It's equally normal to long for the ability to be in two places at once, balancing the care of a family member back home with fulfilling obligations in your new life. But while these emotions are understandable, don't let guilt or unrealistic expectations hold you back from embracing the opportunities in front of you.

Guilt can be a helpful emotion when it fosters reflection, leads to balanced conclusions, and inspires thoughtful actions. However, beyond that, guilt becomes a burden rather than a guide. No one should be consumed by guilt, especially given the complexities and challenges that come with such significant life transitions. Your journey is about growth, resilience, and creating a fulfilling life—not being trapped by the weight of expectations.

TYPES OF EXPAT GUILTS

Guilt is both a cognitive and an emotional experience that occurs when a person realizes that they have violated a moral standard and is responsible for that violation. A guilty conscience results from thoughts that we have not lived up to our ideal self.[68] Accurately or not, guilt is a feeling of having done wrong or failed in an obligation.

Guilt for not being present

This is perhaps the most common form of guilt expats experience. You feel deep remorse for not being there when someone needs you, knowing you can't help from afar. You miss family gatherings, cherished traditions, and those simple, meaningful daily activities like walking with your mom, cooking with your dad, spending Sundays with your siblings and parents, or watching football games together. There may even be guilt when you explore new destinations instead of going home for the holidays.

Guilt can also arise from no longer being able to perform specific tasks you once handled, like driving your parents to doctor's appointments, helping them with technology issues, or taking your niece to soccer practice on Tuesdays. The thought of them facing these challenges without your help and the worry that there might not be anyone to take over those responsibilities can deepen these feelings of guilt. It's a powerful mix of longing and responsibility that weighs on the heart, reminding you of the sacrifices in pursuing your path.

Guilt for not meeting family or societal expectations

Expectations aren't inherently wrong; we all have them, and it's natural to hold them. The issue arises when you try to live up to other's expectations and seek their approval, sacrificing your own needs and letting them control your life.

Expectations are predetermined ideas of what should happen in an uncertain future. While they can help us make decisions, they may not always be realistic or suitable for you. They might not align with your desires, dreams, beliefs, values, skills, abilities, or talents.

Expectations are based on people's experiences, opinions, and values, which may differ from yours. Living by others' expectations when they contradict your own is exhausting and draining. It's impossible to please everyone, and trying to do so will leave you feeling unfulfilled.

For instance, if you aspire to become a doctor but there are no medical schools where you live, moving abroad may be your only option to pursue your dreams. However, your family might expect you to stay close, work at the family business, join weekly dinners, or care for their cat when traveling. Meeting both their expectations and your own will be impossible.

The guilt of not meeting family or societal expectations stems from disappointing people you love by not fulfilling what they anticipated. It's essential to recognize that while their expectations are based on their experiences and values, your path should be guided by your aspirations and principles.

Toxic guilt

Toxic guilt is feeling responsible for others' feelings, afraid of hurting them, or worried that your decision will make them unhappy. Experiencing guilt because your family feels sad, abandoned, disappointed, or angry when you leave can lead to misery and burnout. Although you influence the feelings of others, just as they influence yours, each person is ultimately responsible for their happiness, emotions, and responses to someone else's choices.

When you prioritize others' happiness over your own and neglect your well-being, it can lead to anxiety, resentment, and exhaustion. This dynamic is often linked to emotional projection in psychology, where individuals attribute their unacceptable feelings or impulses to someone else to avoid confronting them[69]. This can result in unhealthy relationship patterns, including insecure attachment, resentment, anger, victimization, exhaustion, and anxiety.

It's good to be empathetic, care for others, and be willing to make others happy. But carrying other's feelings on your shoulders is a significant burden.

Guilt for taking something important from others

This type of guilt arises when you feel your decisions have negatively impacted those you care about. For instance, moving abroad with your family can create several challenging scenarios:

Spousal Sacrifices: If your spouse quits their job to accompany you and cannot find a fulfilling career in the new location, you might feel guilty for disrupting their professional life.

Children's Struggles: If your children miss their friends and their familiar school environment, they may cry because they don't understand the new language or haven't made new friends yet. They may also miss family interactions with cousins, grandparents, and relatives.

Lost Opportunities: Feeling like you are depriving your family of valuable interactions and experiences with extended family or traditions back home.

This guilt can make you question whether you made the right decision for your family.

Guilt of your privileges

This guilt stems from the privileges and advantages you enjoy that your family or those back home may not have. It might manifest when you earn a significantly higher salary than someone doing the same job in your home country or when you're able to maintain a higher standard of living, live in a more spacious or luxurious home, and have the means to travel and experience things that would be considered unattainable back home. This contrast can create a sense of discomfort as you become keenly aware of the disparities and begin to question the fairness of it all.

Financial Disparities: You may feel guilty for having financial stability while your family struggles with economic hardships. This can make it difficult to fully enjoy your privileges, knowing the sacrifices your family makes.

Safety and Security: Living in a safer environment can also contribute to guilt. You might be able to walk safely at night, let your kids ride their bikes to school without adult supervision, and not need an alarm system at home. Meanwhile, your family might live in areas plagued by violence and insecurity.

Access to Experiences: You might have access to new experiences, travel opportunities, and a higher quality of life, while your family and friends back home lack these opportunities. This disparity can make you feel like an outsider and can strain relationships.

Perceived Privilege and Belonging: In some cultures, your higher standard of living might be seen as an undeserved privilege, making you feel like you don't belong to your original group. You might be perceived as wealthy while your family and friends struggle financially, leading to feelings of isolation and alienation.

Family and friends may come to expect you to align your life with theirs by assisting financially, doing things such as paying their bills, inviting them on vacations, finding them jobs, or stepping in to solve their problems. While the desire to help those you care about is natural and commendable, it's essential to recognize a delicate balance between being supportive and being taken for granted.

The pressure to meet these expectations can be intense, driven by love, loyalty, and a sense of duty. However, it's important to set healthy boundaries to ensure your kindness doesn't become an obligation that erodes your well-being or financial stability. Being generous should be an act of choice, not a burden imposed by others' assumptions or dependence.

Feeling that you're betraying your country

When you move to another country, it's natural to adopt new traditions, celebrate different holidays, try new clothing styles, savor unfamiliar foods, and even pick up language nuances, sometimes altering your accent along the way. However, when you return home, these changes may be met with comments or opinions that imply embracing aspects of a new culture is somehow a betrayal of your own. Such remarks, whether made jokingly or with underlying judgment, can leave you feeling like an outsider or even a traitor to your roots.

It's important to remember that integrating parts of a new culture is a natural and enriching part of living abroad. It doesn't mean abandoning or diminishing your original culture; it signifies broadening your experiences and perspective, enriching your life in ways that combine the best of both worlds.

Don't let others make you feel less connected to your homeland simply because you live abroad or incorporate new traditions into your life.

The guilt of not seizing the opportunity of living abroad

It's a common misconception to view life in another country as an extended vacation filled with endless adventure and leisure. However, the reality is often far different. Daily life abroad still includes working, cooking, caring for children, and juggling many other responsibilities. It can be even more challenging than life at home because everything—customs, systems, and basic interactions—is different.

As time goes by, if you find that you haven't met all your initial goals or fulfilled those ambitious aspirations, whether it's learning the new language fluently, traveling as much as you intended, forging close networks with locals, or contributing through volunteer work—you may feel a sense of guilt. This guilt stems from the belief that you're not fully taking advantage of your time abroad or living up to the idealized version of the experience you once envisioned.[70]

DEALING WITH EXPAT-GUILT

Dealing with expat guilt can be difficult, particularly when you've just moved abroad and are still building a support system. The good news is, you're not alone. Most expats experience some level of guilt or shame at some point during their journey. It's crucial to put things in perspective and show yourself compassion as you navigate this new chapter. Here are some tips to help ease the weight of expat guilt:

Acknowledge your guilt

Why do you feel guilty? Are you doing something wrong, or is it that others don't like your decision? Why are your family and friends unwilling to see you go? Are you internalizing what's expected of you? Determine if you did something wrong. Knowing the cause of guilt can help you resolve the problem.

Feeling guilt is a natural part of any significant life change. Understanding why you feel that way can help you work through these emotions more healthily than any other emotion.

The first thing to do is accept guilt and then reflect on it. Determine if you have irrational responsibility, feel guilty for no reason, if your guilt is proportionate to the situation, and if there is something you can do to minimize it. Start noticing when you are catering to the needs of others and neglecting your own needs and desires.

Sometimes, you don't have an option, you don't have control over it, or you're assuming responsibilities that don't belong to you. In these cases, you may feel irrational guilt. Do a reality check and determine if your guilt is reasonable or not.

Pay attention to what you think and feel; don't believe everything your mind says. Question your thoughts: are they realistic? Is this thought based on emotion or facts? What's the worst thing that could happen?[71] What's the best thing that could happen? Is this black-and-white, or are there some shades of gray? Is this accurate?

Again, reflect on it, and don't let the guilt take control of your life and decisions.

Be clear about your reasons

First, you must know well why you're moving abroad. List any reasons for moving abroad and how each will benefit you and others, now and in the future. When you're clear about your motives to move, you can stay focused on the positive instead of losing track when a negative emotion hits.

It helps to document your feelings, options, decisions, and the possible outcomes of each scenario. For example, if you have to choose between option a) Stay home and option b) Move abroad, ask yourself:

- How would you feel about choosing A over B?
- What makes you think choosing A is a better option than B?
- What are the consequences and benefits of choosing A?
- What would be the outcome of selecting A in the following years?

Repeat this process for option B to weigh your choices comprehensively. Once you have decided, embrace your opportunities, enjoy what you're doing right now, and consider the paybacks and benefits ahead of you. Reframe any negative thoughts with encouraging and positive ones.

Take time to appreciate the good things in your life and be thankful for what you have.

Don't buy guilt trips.

Take a practical approach. Why are your family and friends reluctant to see you go? Simply because they'll miss you. No matter how much we wish otherwise, people might comment on our decisions, and this may trigger feelings of guilt. Understand that when someone expresses guilt, it often masks love and indicates unmet expectations in the relationship. They talk through guilt trips when they don't know how to express the real issue .[72]

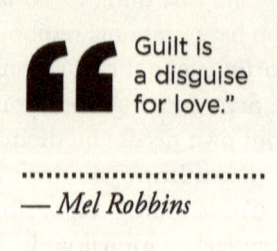

Guilt is a disguise for love."

— *Mel Robbins*

Guilt can indeed be a complex emotion, often intertwined with feelings of love and care. When someone feels guilty, it might be because they believe they've let down someone they care about, reflecting their deep emotional investment in the relationship.

To maintain positive relationships, we must communicate our emotional needs without sacrificing our wants and desires. Asking for understanding from those who might not fully comprehend the situation can help alleviate any feelings of guilt and create stronger bonds moving forward.

When loved ones express guilt:

1. Create emotional distance: Knowledge that guilt is not about you but the person making you feel guilty. When you start feeling guilty, stop! And create some emotional distance.

2. Address it and re-direct it to talk about the real issue: You address it by talking about the real problem. Tell them this: "Instead of complaining about me not being there to take you to your doctor appointments or visit you at the hospital when you get sick. Could you please say what you mean? Which is that you love me, and you would miss me, and you're terrified to be alone at the hospital, and you'd like to find ways not to feel alone there or find more ways to spend more time together."[73]

Love won't change

Recognize that moving away doesn't mean you've stopped loving or caring for those you left behind. You can hold deep, unwavering love for your family and friends while choosing what is best for your growth and well-being. It's possible to honor your needs and aspirations without diminishing your love for those back home.

Reassure your loved ones by expressing how much they mean to you and reminding them that distance won't change your feelings or bond. Let them know they remain vital to your life, even if you're miles apart. While they may not initially agree with or like your decision, it's important to remember that true love endures and transcends physical presence.

Lots of communication

Understanding your feelings, opinions, wants, and needs is crucial. Find the right time to communicate them clearly and often with anyone affected by the move and whom you consider worth talking to. Let them know how you feel and why you want to move abroad. Explain the benefits you see for yourself—and potentially for them—by taking this once-in-a-lifetime opportunity to feel fulfilled and happier.

Also, share how you might feel about missing the chance to study, get a better job, travel, utilize your talents and skills, and improve personally and professionally. Would you feel resentful, limited, unhappy, frustrated, or depressed if your hard work didn't pay off?

Allow them to express their emotions, fears, and worries, and listen to understand their perspectives. This will help resolve problems and misunderstandings and create the best action plan possible. The goal is to have better, healthier, and more fulfilling relationships with your family, ensuring that no one has to sacrifice their well-being to accommodate another's wishes.

Involve them in planning

If you're taking your family with you (spouse, children), ask yourself: Am I doing what you think is best for them? Write down your reasons. Perhaps your child might be sad because they would miss their friends or are worried because they don't speak the new language. But they will be in a safer place, have better access to education, enjoy a higher quality of life, or have better access to medical assistance. Discuss it with them peacefully, and if possible, involve everyone affected by the move.

Open and frequent communication is essential when preparing to move abroad. Share your reasons for moving and the benefits you foresee. This transparency helps family members to understand your motivations and feel included in decision-making. Involve your family in the planning stages of the move to create a sense of teamwork and ease the transition. Here are some ways to do that:

- Research and learn about the new country's culture, language, schools, and healthcare as a family. This shared research reduces anxiety by turning the unknown into an exciting discovery.
- Include your family's input when making significant decisions, such as selecting a neighborhood, schools, or local activities. Valuing their opinions helps everyone feel included and invested in the move.
- Work together on a moving checklist that covers all essential tasks, from packing and paperwork to setting up utilities and furnishing the new home. This structured approach keeps everyone on track and involved in the process.
- Explore your new city together, seek out favorite spots, discover local parks, restaurants, and entertainment, and join community clubs, sports teams, or social groups to cultivate a shared sense of belonging.
- Give them something to look forward to. Find activities or experiences in the new location that your family can get excited about—such as visiting a local attraction, trying a unique cuisine, or planning a family day out. This gives everyone a positive milestone to anticipate and makes the transition more rewarding.

Involving your family at every stage creates a supportive and engaged environment that helps everyone adjust and build excitement for this new chapter.

Create a plan

Develop a reasonable, realistic, and detailed plan based on your discussions with the family members staying behind and those moving with you. Sharing this plan, if you believe it would be helpful, can alleviate anxieties and set clear expectations. It should address the concerns raised during conversations and outline how you intend to stay in contact and provide support. Include details on visitation and communication plans and how you'll stay involved in family milestones and celebrations, virtually or in person.

If those staying behind are children, elders, disabled individuals, or anyone with a condition that prevents independence, talk to other family members, friends, and relatives to arrange support. Inform them who will take over the chores you used to do and how you will continue to support their needs and address their problems. You might realize that physical presence isn't necessary to show your support. It may be more about redefining roles and redistributing, delegating, or sharing responsibilities more equitably among those involved.

Caring for ill, disabled, or elderly relatives from abroad poses many practical, communication, timing, and logistical challenges. Therefore, creating a support network that can handle emergencies, provide care, and keep you informed of health and other vital issues is essential. If possible, meet the doctor before you leave or via videoconference, and keep an emergency contact handy.

Delegate responsibilities. If other family members can help, divide responsibilities to cover everything needed, such as finding nursing care, cooking and cleaning, buying medicines, providing transportation, or scheduling and attending doctor appointments

This approach reduces their feelings of abandonment or neglect and helps them feel heard, cared for, and supported by you, even from afar. While you may not be able to solve all their problems, you aren't abandoning them either.

Remember that despite all your plans and efforts to care for their needs, there may be times when you feel sad and helpless about not being there and not knowing what is happening as those who are present do. Find peace in knowing you're doing the best you can.

Make the best of your time together

When you visit, call, or video call, treasure every moment. Here are some ways to make the most of your time together:

- Find out how they would like to spend time with you when you visit. Do they want to show you a special place, cook together, watch a movie or a soccer game, or look at old pictures and share stories?
- Let them know what you would like to do as well. This mutual exchange of wishes ensures that both parties are heard and valued.

- While it may not be possible to do everything, knowing each other's wishes allows you to plan meaningful activities for both of you. With a little effort and goodwill, you can create memorable experiences together.
- Be fully present in person or on a call. Listen actively, engage in the conversation, and maximize your time together.
- Take photos, make videos, or journal your time together. These mementos will be precious reminders of the moments you shared.
- Call them spontaneously, but it is also helpful to schedule days and times that work for you and them to have a more extended and intentional conversation instead of rushing a conversation because someone is busy or due to different time zones.

Set healthy boundaries

Setting boundaries can be challenging and intimidating, especially if you grew up in a family where saying no or having a different opinion from your parents or elders was unacceptable. However, establishing boundaries doesn't mean you don't respect or care for others' opinions or feelings, are trying to control others, or are being unkind.

Setting boundaries means communicating and protecting your values, needs, and well-being. It involves setting limits and standards for how you want to be treated and what you can and cannot tolerate.

Communicate your boundaries lovingly and respectfully but firmly. For example:

- If they call you multiple times a day out of longing, gently let them know that you're busy with work and can only talk during designated times, like after work or during breaks.
- Vacation Plans: If they expect you to spend all your vacation time with them but wish to explore new places, be upfront and clear about your plans and intentions. Assure them you value your time together but must balance it with your desires.
- If they anticipate more financial support than you can afford or feel is fair, explain your financial limitations honestly. Emphasize that while you're happy to help within your means, you must manage your budget responsibly.
- If they want to visit you for extended periods, like the entire summer, but you have plans with your spouse or other commitments, kindly express your preferences and provide a schedule that works for everyone.
- Address hurtful comments. If they make remarks that trigger uncomfortable, sad, hurt, or angry feelings whenever you call or visit, let them

know how their words impact you. Be honest about the emotional effect and ask for their understanding. If things don't change despite your efforts, consider keeping some distance or limiting contact to protect your mental and emotional well-being.

Practical tips for setting boundaries

- Clearly articulate your boundaries and why they are important to you[74].
- Use "I" statements. Communicate your feelings and needs without placing blame or criticizing others. This approach encourages understanding and reduces defensiveness. For example, say, "I need some time alone to recharge after work," rather than, "You always overwhelm me when I get home."
- Be consistent; maintain and reinforce your boundaries regularly to ensure they are respected.
- Choose guilt over resentment. It's a powerful way to take control of your life and prioritize your well-being instead of living with mounting anxiety, frustration, and resentment.
- Stand by your boundaries even if others push back or resist. It's okay to say no and protect your personal space and needs[75].
- If setting and maintaining boundaries becomes difficult, don't hesitate to seek help from a therapist or counselor. Professional guidance can provide tools and strategies to navigate boundary-setting effectively and maintain your emotional health[76].

Healthy boundaries help maintain strong, positive, respectful, and fulfilling relationships. They ensure that interactions are respectful and supportive, preventing resentment and burnout.

Let go
Acknowledge any negative thoughts and emotions and reframe them with something positive. Loss, saying goodbye, and not being close to loved ones are all painful experiences. However, it's essential to let go of these emotions that hold you back and focus on the next steps to accomplish your goals and enjoy your life abroad.

Remember, you are responsible for your happiness, not others. Thinking otherwise can be overwhelming. Find peace in knowing that you are doing everything possible to make the transition easier for everyone without sacrificing your well-being.

Acknowledge and reframe your negative thoughts and emotions by focusing on the opportunities and growth your move will bring. Focus on your goals and steps needed to achieve your aspirations abroad. This will help you stay positive and motivated.

Letting go isn't about giving up or thinking negatively of others; it's about releasing attachment to outcomes and eliminating the need for validation[77]. Once you make a conscious decision, own it and move forward without looking back or second-guessing yourself.

Don't live by other's expectations of you

It's normal for people who love and care about you to express their concerns, expectations, and opinions. This may be their way of saying, "I love you," "I want the best for you," or "I would like to spend more time with you." Similarly, it's natural to care for the people you love and to consider their opinions. While their input and perspectives can be beneficial, it doesn't mean you must meet their expectations or please everyone at the expense of your well-being.

Take responsibility for your feelings, expectations, and actions. Remember that someone else's expectations of you are theirs, not yours. They may not align with your values or be your best choice. Identify what's important to you, who you are, and what you want to achieve. Stay true to yourself and make decisions that align with your values and beliefs.

Let go of living up to others' expectations and live by your own. Listen to your inner voice: Does it feel right or good? Does it make you happy, sad, anxious, or angry? Does this match your beliefs, values, standards, wants, and desires? Use your inner voice as a guide.

Accept that you cannot change other people, that you are not entirely responsible for someone else's happiness, and that holding them to an unrealistic standard will make you miserable. Even with their best intentions, their expectations are based on their experiences, opinions, and values. No one knows you better than yourself. Understand your feelings, opinions, wants, and needs. Find the right time to communicate with them effectively and speak your truth.

Connect with others around you

Seek out expat communities, as they can be invaluable for emotional and practical support. These communities are often filled with people who understand the challenges and emotions of living abroad. They can offer insights, advice, and shared experiences to help you navigate the process and feel less alone. See Chapter #12 for more on finding and engaging with supportive groups.

Take care of yourself

Give yourself time to process your emotions and engage in relaxing activities, such as reading a book, connecting with nature, practicing deep breathing, listening to music, chatting with a friend, or treating yourself to a massage. Prioritizing downtime helps you recharge mentally and emotionally.

Also, reserve time for activities you enjoy, whether indulging in a hobby, participating in a sport, trying something new, or volunteering. Life shouldn't revolve solely around work or taking care of others. Without making time for what brings you joy; you miss out on the full potential of your experience. Strive for a balance between work, others, and yourself. This doesn't require hours daily—even just a few minutes dedicated to yourself can make a significant difference.

Adjusting to a new environment comes with a steep learning curve, encompassing everything from new work practices to navigating daily life. It's essential to allow yourself time to learn and adapt while also giving yourself permission to rest and recharge. While this is easier said than done, learning and adaptation become more challenging when running empty.

Modify your expectations. Some people mistakenly view moving abroad as akin to an extended vacation, forgetting that everyday responsibilities like work, chores, and life obligations still apply. This misconception can lead to frustration when they don't immediately accomplish all the fun plans they envisioned. Don't be disheartened if you can't do it all right away. As you settle into your new home and work, these opportunities will come with time.

Practice self-compassion, be patient, and allow yourself to move at your own pace without guilt. Adjusting to a new life and environment is an ongoing process, and it's okay if everything doesn't fall into place immediately. Treat yourself with kindness as you navigate your new reality.

KEY TAKEAWAYS

- Reflect on your guilt by identifying its source and determining whether it's rational or based on inaccurate thoughts.
- Embrace your decision by focusing on the benefits of moving abroad and how it aligns with your goals and values.
- Find balance and ways to meet your needs and pursue your dreams while staying close to loved ones back home.
- Set healthy boundaries to maintain respectful and fulfilling relationships.

- Prioritize self-care, practice self-compassion, and recognize that following your dreams doesn't mean neglecting your loved ones.
- Make the most of your time together, whether in person or virtually, and let go of guilt by acknowledging your right to pursue a fulfilling life.
- Strive to live a life that is meaningful and fulfilling to you!

CHAPTER 12

Find your tribe

*"If you want to walk fast, walk alone. But if you want
to walk far, walk together."*
- Ratan Tata[78]

Building a solid support system is the key to enjoying life in a new place and truly making it feel like home. Moving to a new country can be isolating, especially if you're far from family and familiar surroundings. Friends create a sense of belonging and a connection to a community, helping to stave off feelings of loneliness.

Friends are not just companions. They are essential to our emotional, mental, and even physical well-being. They provide a safe space to express your feelings, fears, and joys. Their empathy, understanding, and unwavering support during tough times are truly invaluable. A strong support network can help you navigate the emotional rollercoaster of living abroad, whether dealing with culture shock, homesickness, or daily challenges.

Friends, especially those who are locals or have lived in the country longer, play a pivotal role in your cultural adaptation. Their insights and support can significantly ease the transition, helping you better understand and navigate the cultural nuances, traditions, and social norms or improve your language skills. These relationships provide emotional support, practical advice, and insights, making professional and personal adjustments smoother.

BLIND DATE

Blind dates aren't just for romantic encounters; they can also lead to lifelong friendships. I met Lety, my best friend in Belgium, on a blind date. She and her family moved to Brussels around the same time my husband and I relocated to Mechelen.

A few weeks after we arrived in Belgium, our realtor called to ask if she could share my contact information with another client of hers—a fellow Mexican woman who had also recently moved to Belgium. The following day, Lety reached out. We introduced ourselves over the phone and talked for over 80 minutes. By the end of the call, she invited me over for coffee at her house. Later that week, I took a taxi for an hour-long ride to meet her. With no social media back then, I couldn't look her up or get an idea of who she was—I was walking into this meeting completely blind.

Imagining someone based solely on their voice is tricky and often misleading. When we finally met, Lety was nothing like I had pictured—she was younger, more relaxed, incredibly kind, and even more social than I had expected.

We sat down for coffee and talked for hours as if we were old friends catching up after years apart. From that day forward, we became inseparable, and our husbands quickly became friends as well. It may sound cliché, but when you live far from your family, your friends become your family. While friends can feel like family even when you're near home, the bond formed with friends while living abroad is uniquely powerful. These are the people you turn to for everything.

As the months passed, we began meeting new people and expanding our social circle. We shared countless gatherings, traveled together, and supported one another through life's challenges. You lean on your friends for the kind of support you would usually seek from family members when living abroad. For instance, when Lety was in the hospital delivering her baby, her oldest daughter stayed with me at my house, and I took care of her until they allowed visitors at the hospital.

Friendships are forged under unique conditions and often develop into deep, lifelong bonds that feel as warm and secure as family ties. After Belgium, they moved to Panama, and we went to the USA. We reunited with Lety and her family two years ago after nearly fifteen years apart. It felt like no time had passed—the love, connection, and closeness were just as strong, even though we don't talk as frequently as we once did.

Tips to find friends on blind dates:

Leverage technology to find and connect with potential friends in your new country. Several apps and websites are designed to meet people and build social circles. Here are some popular ones to try:

- **Meetup:** Perfect for finding new friends who share your specific interests. Whether you enjoy painting, cooking, reading, or a particular sport, Meetup connects you with groups where you can enjoy your hobbies with like-minded people. I have used this App to connect with other writers in my city, and it helps; they gather frequently, and we write together for a couple of hours while having a coffee.
- **Hey! Vina:** Often referred to as "Tinder for (Girl) Friends," this app is designed for women looking to make friends. It aims to empower women by helping them connect with others who share similar interests and values.
- **Atleto:** Are you looking for a marathon partner, gym buddy, or tennis or basketball opponent? Atleto connects you with people who share your sports and fitness interests.
- **Nextdoor:** This is ideal for people who have just moved into a new neighborhood and want to make friends. It's a private social network for you and your neighbors designed to connect with your local community. I also use Nextdoor to connect with neighbors, and once, they helped me find my lost cat.
- **Peanut:** This is highly recommended for moms who feel lonely and want to connect with other moms who understand what they're going through. Peanut connects women from pregnancy through motherhood, offering support and friendship.
- **Friender:** This "friends only" app is designed to help you meet new people with similar interests. It's not a dating app—its sole purpose is to help you build friendships.
- **Bumble BFF:** If you're looking to build one-on-one friendships, Bumble BFF is a great tool. It's like the friendship version of a dating app, where you can match people who share similar interests and values.
- **Internations:** Specifically tailored for expats, Internations is a global community where you can connect with others in your area who are navigating similar experiences. They often organize social events and activities that make meeting new people easy.
- **Facebook Groups:** Join local groups for expats or special interest communities in your area. These groups often share events, recommendations, and meet-up opportunities.

Begin by having a conversation over the phone with your prospective friend. This initial chat allows you to get a sense of their personality, hear their voice, and learn about their background and interests. It creates an opportunity for light, natural conversation and sets a comfortable foundation before meeting in person. Starting with a phone call can also help ease initial nervousness, making your first face-to-face meeting feel more familiar and relaxed.

Approach the conversation with an open mind and heart. Openness invites genuine connection and helps build trust right from the start.

Take the risk and step out of your comfort zone. While leaping to meet someone new can be intimidating, it often leads to lasting friendships.

Plan something enjoyable and exciting for both of you. From your phone conversations, you've already learned about their interests, likes, and dislikes, so use that knowledge to create a fun first meeting.

Be yourself; authenticity fosters deeper and lasting relationships.

MAKING FRIENDS AT WORK OR SCHOOL

Making friends at work or school can be one of the most natural and effective ways to expand your social circle in a new place. When my husband and I moved to Memphis, we worked full-time for the same company. Due to our busy schedules, we had limited opportunities to meet people outside of work, so our social circle primarily consisted of coworkers and people connected to them.

Tips for making friends at work:

- Introduce yourself and engage in light conversation. A simple greeting can open the door to a new friendship.
- Participate in company events, picnics, games, and holiday parties. These gatherings are great opportunities to meet people in a relaxed setting.
- A simple and effective way to start a conversation is to ask a coworker for recommendations on nearby restaurants, shops, or local events or attractions. This shows interest in their opinion and opens the door for a casual follow-up invitation. After they suggest a place, invite them to join you for an event, lunch, or a drink after work. If you're more comfortable in a group setting, consider inviting a few colleagues along to ease any first-time nerves. Group outings can be a relaxed way to get to know each other better, creating a natural atmosphere for conversation and connection without the pressure of one-on-one interaction.
- Eat lunch away from your desk. Joining others in the cafeteria or a nearby café is a great way to get to know your coworkers better.
- Volunteering for company initiatives or small acts of kindness can help you connect with others and create positive relationships.

MEET YOUR NEIGHBORS

Knowing your neighbors is one of the simplest yet most effective ways to build a sense of home and community. Creating these connections can help you feel more settled and secure in your surroundings, giving you a feeling of belonging.

My husband and I have moved nine times in twenty years and have always met our neighbors. Some have become close friends, while others have remained familiar and friendly faces. Knowing our neighbors has provided a sense of support, community, and comfort that's been invaluable as we've adjusted to each new home.

Our relationships with our neighbors have gone beyond simple greetings—we've genuinely looked out for each other, creating a strong sense of community. We've helped one another with everyday tasks like mowing the lawn, taking out the trash, and picking up mail when one of us was away. During my pregnancy, when my husband was traveling, our neighbors kindly shoveled our driveway after a snowfall. We've borrowed tools, shared supplies, and even relied on each other for childcare in emergencies.

They've recommended trusted babysitters, service providers, and the best local shops, and they've looked after our home while we traveled. We've always reciprocated and appreciated the mutual support.

In one of our U.S. neighborhoods, most families had children close in age to ours, so the kids often played outside together, riding scooters, tricycles, and bikes. We knew there were always a few adults nearby to keep an eye on them, allowing us to take a break, cook dinner, or take work calls without interrupting the kids' fun. We lived in a cozy cul-de-sac with our next-door German friends. Our kids, so close in age, spent hours playing together on the street. Many evenings, the kids enjoyed their popsicles or juice while the adults would unwind by trading Heinekens for Coronas, sharing laughs and stories as the sun went down.

The homeowners' association hosted biannual gatherings in the last two neighborhoods—perfect for getting to know each other. The neighborhood kids would play while the adults mingled, and then we all joined for family activities.

Most places we've lived in have had welcoming neighbors who introduced themselves. However, when we moved to Belgium, no one reached out initially, so I decided to take the first step and introduce myself. As they say, "If the mountain will not come to Mohammed, Mohammed must go to the mountain."[79] I'm so glad I did—our neighbors were incredibly kind and welcoming. The next-door neighbor introduced me to other ladies on the block, many of whom were older than my parents, and they graciously invited me to their tea parties and elaborate, multi-course dinners, which are very much in the Belgian tradition.

I treasure those tea parties, experiences I had only seen in films. At 27, I was moving through life at full speed, eager to do everything and absorb as much as possible. These gatherings provided a peaceful contrast to my fast-paced lifestyle, a chance to slow down, enjoy the moment, and embrace the art of being fully present. It was a gentle reminder to pause and relax.

Sitting with these extraordinary ladies—sipping tea, enjoying artfully prepared appetizers and desserts at a beautifully set table with fresh flowers, on a cozy patio with soft music in the background, and immersed in warm conversation—felt like a serene retreat, almost like meditation or a day at the spa. In those moments, time seemed to pause; there was no rush, no worries, only the pleasure of being fully present, savoring the surroundings and the company. It was mindfulness at its finest.

Dinners in Belgium were far more than just a culinary experience; they were a cultural celebration. In Belgian culture, as in many others, food holds a deep significance. Belgian meals are designed to bring family and friends together, creating a space for a leisurely and delicious dining experience that reflects their pride in their cuisine. Mealtime in Belgium is almost sacred, connecting with others and strengthening relationships—it's never about business.

Our dinners with Belgian neighbors often lasted five hours, featuring multiple courses—sometimes as many as twelve—each thoughtfully paired with a different wine. These extended meals were a true reflection of Belgian hospitality and tradition. No wonder they lasted so long; I might have been tipsy at most of them without the pace and structure!

Each course was served on a different plate with the appropriate silverware, so for a ten-course dinner, each person used ten dishes, ten to twenty pieces of silverware, and several glasses—one for each type of wine, plus one for water. Coffee was served after dessert, not with it, and it was usually without milk or sugar. Dining with them was an incredible cultural experience.

Beyond the meals, our neighbors were incredibly welcoming, kind, and helpful. They were probably my closest connection to Belgian culture. Thanks to them, I had firsthand experiences with the locals, learned insider tips about Belgium and Europe, discovered their traditions, tasted their food, and found the best local restaurants and places to visit. Even though I had to take the first step in introducing myself, it was worth it!

Tips for meeting your neighbors:

- Greet people with warm and friendly smiles. It's a simple yet powerful way to foster a sense of community with your neighbors.
- Spend time outdoors; staying inside won't help you meet new people. Visit common areas, take walks, and spend time in community spaces like parks, gyms, clubhouses, or pools. Or try working in your front yard—this can naturally increase your chances of connecting with neighbors and sparking conversations.
- Show interest in your neighbors by asking about the area, local restaurants, events, activities, or service companies. It's a great way to start conversations and gather helpful information.
- Offer to help, be proactive, and lend a hand if your neighbor needs it. Acts of kindness, like mowing their lawn, shoveling snow, or picking up their mail when they're away, can go a long way in establishing yourself as a friendly and helpful neighbor.
- Ask for a small favor, like borrowing a cup of sugar. Most people enjoy helping others; small requests can help build a positive relationship.
- Visit local spots such as coffee shops, flower shops, or restaurants regularly. Becoming a familiar face in the neighborhood can help you connect with neighbors and local business owners.
- Share a treat. Bring some goodies, fresh tomatoes from your garden, or a small souvenir from your hometown. A thoughtful gesture like this can leave a lasting impression.
- Invite your neighbors for coffee, beer, or even a small gathering. Before extending an invitation, be mindful of cultural differences. For example, do not offer alcohol to a Muslim or pork to a Jew.
- Intentionally Make a point to bump into your neighbors and start a casual conversation. Try to catch them when they're not in a hurry, allowing the chat to feel natural and unforced.

OTHER WAYS TO MAKE FRIENDS ABROAD

Making new friends takes time and effort. Here are some additional ways to expand your social circle:

- Participate in activities you enjoy, such as book clubs, hiking, or cooking classes. Museums and cultural sites often host events where you can meet individuals with similar interests.

- Participate in festivals, fairs, and community gatherings. Professional networking events and industry meetups or casual venues like farmers' markets, libraries, and book signings offer easy opportunities for conversation.
- Volunteer to a cause you care about, such as shelters, food banks, or environmental projects.
- If faith is important to you, join services, study groups, or retreats and build a supportive community.

Building meaningful connections abroad

For some, meeting new people and forming strong friendships is a natural and seamless part of life. For others, the process can feel daunting, requiring more time, effort, and the courage to step beyond their comfort zones. Yet, at our core, we are all social beings—wired for connection and belonging. Building relationships isn't just a choice; it's essential to being human. These connections enrich our lives, providing support, joy, and a sense of purpose that shapes our experiences and well-being.

I've gathered valuable tips to help you become likable and cultivate meaningful friendships.[80]

Overcome Social Anxiety

Experiencing negative thoughts in social situations, like "I'll embarrass myself" or "people won't like me," is common. However, you can counter these thoughts with more positive and realistic perspectives. Remember that everyone makes mistakes, and those moments are part of being human. Most people are often too preoccupied with their concerns to focus on judging others.

Shifting your mindset to understand that social interactions are about connection, not perfection, can ease your anxiety. Embrace the idea that imperfections make you relatable and that authenticity is more appealing than trying to be flawless. Recognize that genuine conversations and small acts of kindness often leave a lasting positive impression, not the fear-driven worries you imagine.

Create Opportunities for Connection

Invite someone to do something low-key, like visiting a museum, hiking, or having a quiet dinner. These activities allow for meaningful interaction without the pressure of constant conversation. If you're comfortable, consider hosting a small gathering, such as a dinner party or casual get-together. Inviting people into your home creates a welcoming environment.

Large social gatherings can be daunting if you're an introvert or prefer smaller, more intimate settings. Instead of diving into these overwhelming environments, focus on one-on-one interactions without the pressure of a crowd.

Maintain a Positive Attitude

Be a source of encouragement, support, and motivation by celebrating others' successes and cheering them on. This approach acts as a powerful magnet, drawing people to you effortlessly. Cultivate the art of uplifting those around you by acknowledging their strengths and offering sincere, positive, and constructive feedback. Your positive energy can transform the atmosphere, creating a space where people feel valued, inspired, and eager to connect, making you someone they want to have in their circle.

Show Sincere Interest and Listen Actively

Ask open-ended questions to encourage deeper conversation and invite others to share their lives, interests, passions, and goals. This approach demonstrates genuine interest and opens the door to meaningful dialogue. Be fully present in the moment—set aside distractions like your phone or laptop—and take the time to respond thoughtfully to what others are saying. Your attentiveness and engagement will make others feel valued and respected, helping to foster a stronger connection.

Start slowly and observe how they respond. Please pay close attention to their answers and body language. Do they seem comfortable and engaged in the conversation? Are they maintaining eye contact, or are they looking around? Are their responses brief or detailed? Consider slowing down or shifting the topic if you notice signs of discomfort or disengagement, such as short answers or wandering attention. You don't want to come across as intrusive. However, if they appear to enjoy the conversation, continue building on your established rapport.

Pay close attention when others speak and show your engagement through gestures such as nodding, maintaining eye contact, and offering thoughtful responses. Be mindful of cultural differences in body language and communication styles. Practicing active listening signals that you care, fosters trust and connection. Offer unwavering support and take the time to understand others' needs, feelings, and perspectives. Consistently demonstrate compassion and understanding.

Be Approachable

Being approachable means exuding warmth, friendliness, and openness, making you easy to talk to and inviting to others. Approachable people naturally draw others in by creating a sense of comfort and trust through welcoming body language, expressions, and tone.

Maintain an open and relaxed posture, using gestures such as a genuine smile, eye contact, and an attentive presence to show you're receptive to interaction. Avoid crossed arms and face the person you're speaking to for a more engaging connection. While these universal gestures signal warmth, be mindful of cultural differences, as certain behaviors may be interpreted differently. By projecting approachability, you make it easier for others to reach out, fostering the groundwork for deeper and more meaningful relationships.

Speak with calmness, clarity, and respect. Your tone sets the stage for how your words are received, so ensure it conveys warmth and understanding. Use humor thoughtfully, being mindful of cultural sensitivities to ensure it's appropriate and well-received. The right balance of tone and humor can ease tension, foster connection, and enhance communication, but it's crucial to approach it with awareness and consideration.

Extend kindness and be proactive in offering help, whether providing directions, holding a door, or sharing helpful information. Additionally, offering sincere compliments when appropriate—acknowledging others' efforts or achievements brightens their day and strengthens your relationships. Take the first step and introduce yourself, especially in social settings where people are unfamiliar with one another. Initiating conversation shows confidence and helps everyone break the ice.

Use their name. Incorporating someone's name into conversation adds a personal touch and demonstrates genuine interest.

Embrace Authenticity

Authenticity is the cornerstone of building genuine friendships. When you stay true to yourself, you naturally attract others who appreciate and connect with the real you. People are drawn to those who are confident in their skin, as it creates a sense of trust and comfort. By sharing a bit of your true self— thoughts, experiences, and vulnerabilities—you invite others to do the same.

Understand Others' Perspectives

Approach conversations with an open mind and empathy, resisting the urge to judge or dismiss others' viewpoints. Recognize that people come from different backgrounds and experiences, which shape their perspectives. Respect these differences rather than seeing them as obstacles. Reflect on your beliefs and biases that might color your interpretation of others' perspectives, and express compassion and understanding even if you don't fully agree with their viewpoint.[81]

Learn about their culture and understand what is appropriate and what isn't in your new environment. Conduct some research beforehand and immerse yourself in your new home's culture, politics, and language. Stay informed by following local news.

Be Patient and Persistent

Building new friendships takes time, effort, and patience. Don't expect them to match the depth of lifelong bonds right away. In many cases, friends in a foreign country become like family—but that doesn't happen overnight. Avoid rushing or forcing connections; stay open, approachable, and consistent. The strongest friendships grow naturally over time.

Use Icebreakers

Breaking the ice can make it easier to start conversations. Here are some effective icebreakers:

- **Compliments:** A well-placed compliment can foster a positive connection.
- **Thoughtful Jokes:** Use humor, but ensure it's appropriate for the new culture.
- **Open-Ended Questions:** Ask questions like, "What do you enjoy doing in your free time?" "What is your favorite restaurant around?" or "What's the best place you've traveled to?" to encourage conversation and learn more about the other person.

THE FRIENDS YOU NEED TO HAVE WHEN YOU LIVE ABROAD

When living abroad, having a diverse and supportive network of friends can significantly impact your experience. Here are the types of friends you should consider having when you live abroad:

The Local Friend

A local friend can help you understand your new home's culture, language, and social norms. They offer insider knowledge about the area, assist with navigating local customs, traditions, food, and places you can visit, and provide a deeper connection to the local community.

The Fellow Expat Friend

An expat friend understands the challenges of living in a foreign country because they're going through the same thing. They can offer empathy, practical advice, and share experiences. They provide a sense of camaraderie, support, and shared understanding, making it easier to cope with the ups and downs of expat life.

The Mentor or Guide
This person could be a local or an experienced expat who has lived in the country for a long time. They can offer valuable advice and insights on navigating life's personal and professional aspects abroad. They help you avoid common pitfalls, provide guidance on integrating into the culture, and offer advice on everything from legal matters to everyday challenges.

A mentor is someone with whom you feel completely safe asking all kinds of questions as you navigate and learn how things work. They are a guiding presence that offers wisdom and provides a nonjudgmental space where your learning and development are genuinely supported.

The Language Buddy
Learning the local language is crucial for deeper integration and daily communication. A language buddy can help you practice and improve your language skills in a relaxed, informal setting.

The Social Connector
A social connector knows many people and enjoys bringing others together. They can help you expand your social circle and invite you to events, gatherings, and activities, helping you meet new people and feel more connected to the community.

The Activity Partner
Having someone with whom you can share hobbies and activities makes your time abroad more enjoyable. Whether exploring the city, hiking or attending cultural events, an activity partner adds fun to your routine.

The Supportive Listener
Living abroad can be an emotional rollercoaster, filled with challenges, uncertainties, and triumphs. Having a supportive listener by your side is invaluable. This person offers a judgment-free space to share your struggles, fears, and successes openly. They listen with empathy and understanding, providing the emotional support you need to process your experiences. Their presence helps you navigate the complexities of life in a new country, ensuring you stay mentally healthy and emotionally balanced.

The Professional Ally

A professional ally who understands the local work culture is invaluable. They can offer insights and advice on how to navigate the professional landscape. They assist with networking, offer career advice, and help you adapt to the workplace culture, making your professional transition smoother.

The Emergency Contact

It is crucial to have someone you can rely on during an emergency, whether it's a medical issue, legal matter, or personal crisis. If you find yourself in an emergency abroad without a trusted contact, make it a priority to familiarize yourself with local emergency numbers for police, fire, and medical assistance as soon as you arrive.

Your country's embassy or consulate can assist in various emergencies, such as finding medical care or legal support. Most embassies maintain a 24/7 emergency contact number for citizens in distress.

Local healthcare facilities, pharmacists, hotel staff, landlords or rental hosts, insurance providers, expatriate community groups, churches, local authorities, or neighbors can also be valuable sources of support.

Always remember that most people, even strangers, are compassionate and willing to help. Never hesitate to ask for assistance when needed, you might be pleasantly surprised by the kindness and readiness to help that exists all around you. The world is full of compassionate individuals, and you are never alone!

The Long-Distance Old Friend

Staying connected with friends from home is invaluable as you adapt to your new environment. These friends know you deeply, offering a comforting connection that helps you maintain ties to your roots. They've shared your joys, made you laugh, comforted you in times of sadness, and provided that essential sense of safety we all crave. Even as you embrace new experiences, they remain a significant part of your life, grounding you with unwavering support and familiarity. Their presence, even from afar, continues to be a source of strength and warmth as you navigate your new surroundings.

***

You don't need a large circle of friends to meet all your social needs; many friendships can naturally fulfill multiple roles. For instance, a local friend might be a mentor, a language partner, and an activity companion.

While connecting with people who share your language, beliefs, and traditions is comforting and rewarding, try not to confine yourself solely to familiar circles. Expanding your friendships to include those from diverse backgrounds can significantly broaden your worldview and unexpectedly enrich your life.

It might seem like there are a lot of rules, but trust me, it's not that difficult. Our brains are naturally wired to connect, so this is something already within us. To connect with others effortlessly, you only need three key things:

Be open to new friendships and actively seek or create opportunities to meet people.

Show genuine interest and practice active listening with empathy and kindness.

Be authentic.

KEY TAKEAWAYS

....

- Build a strong support network as soon as possible. Friends foster a sense of community and belonging, helping to combat loneliness when living abroad and making life more enjoyable.
- Diversify your friendships and reach beyond people who share your language and traditions.
- Be proactive, take the initiative to introduce yourself, participate in local events, and use technology to connect with others.
- Have reliable emergency contacts, and remember, you're never alone!
- Strive to be the kind of friend you would want to have.
- Be authentic.

CHAPTER 13

Language barrier

*"To learn a language is to have one more window f
rom which to look at the world."*
—Chinese Proverb

C ommunication is one of our most fundamental needs, a skill we begin developing from birth. It allows us to connect with others, express our needs and thoughts, form relationships, and navigate the world's complexities. It is essential for both being understood and understanding those around us.

However, finding yourself in a place where you cannot speak or understand the language can be deeply frustrating and limiting. The inability to communicate effectively can restrict your interactions, hinder opportunities, and amplify feelings of isolation. This chapter is born from my journey, as I firmly believe that facing the language barrier has been the most challenging aspect of my life as an expat—and overcoming it has proven to be the most rewarding.

The language barrier is widely recognized as one of the most challenging tasks of living in a foreign country. It is often the primary source of worry and frustration among expats. While the benefits of being multilingual are well-documented, I have seen many individuals become so overwhelmed by the fear of communication struggles that they retreat into solitude or are immobilized by anxiety. This fear can quickly spiral into a cycle of isolation, leading to feelings of depression and heightened stress, further deepening the sense of disconnection from the world around them.

Some are convinced that learning a new language is too hard or impossible, so avoid the effort altogether. They remain within their comfort zone, confined to a circle of friends who speak their native language, missing the rich experience of truly integrating into the new culture.

People from all backgrounds, including highly accomplished individuals, often share how tough and stressful it is to navigate daily life while struggling to communicate in a new language. Everyday situations become sources of frustration: missing critical points during meetings, battling to be understood due to an accent, ordering food at a restaurant only to receive the wrong dish, or spending an exhausting amount of time explaining a destination to a taxi driver. However, it doesn't have to be this way.

If any of this resonates with you, know that this chapter is written with you in mind. I understand the challenges because I have been through them and know firsthand how disheartening they can be. But I am here to reassure you—you are not alone in this struggle.

I will share my experiences, the mistakes I made, the lessons I learned, and the strategies that ultimately worked for me. I hope these insights will make your language-learning journey smoother and more enjoyable.

MY JOURNEY TO LANGUAGES

The joy of language learning

My fascination with languages began at an early age, inspired by my uncle, Fernando Rodriguez, and his family; he was the founder and first director of Mexico's Philharmonic Orchestra. His career took him around the world, and often, he was accompanied by his mother, Cuquita, my grand aunt.

Cuquita always brought me unique and intriguing gifts from different countries, but what I loved most were the captivating stories she shared about her travels. I would sit, mesmerized, imagining how incredible it would be to journey across the world, discovering new places and meeting people while speaking to them in their native languages.

Adding to my curiosity, Fernando's wife was French, so my cousins spoke Spanish and French. French became their secret code, a language they would switch to when they wanted to keep their conversations private from the rest of us. This sparked an intense desire to learn other languages, not just to communicate with people from different countries but also to unlock the "secret code" my cousins used.

Determined to learn English, I begged my parents to send me abroad, believing it was the only way to master the language. At 16, a close family friend, Nelson, and his wife, Mindy, invited me to spend the summer with them at their home in Louisville, Kentucky. At that time, my English was limited to a handful of basic words and phrases—"yes," "no," "please," "thank you," and the like. We all knew this was an incredible opportunity for me to learn, and with the reassurance that I would be in good hands, my parents agreed.

Nelson and Mindy traveled to Mexico to accompany me back to Louisville, likely concerned that my limited English skills might result in me boarding a plane to the wrong destination or missing my flight altogether. When we arrived in Louisville, I was greeted with an exciting surprise—a limousine waiting to whisk us away from the airport. It was my first time in a limousine, and I felt like a celebrity as we toured downtown Louisville for over an hour.

As Nelson and Mindy pointed out various skyscrapers and landmarks, I tried desperately to understand their enthusiastic explanations, but the language barrier was too great. The only words I could muster were, "Oh! Beautiful," and "Thank you." Despite my limited participation, they seemed content, and I enjoyed the ride, even though I missed most of the commentary.

In those first weeks, we communicated mostly through gestures and body language, with very few words exchanged. They spoke little to no Spanish, and my English was just as limited. However, as time passed, I began picking up more words and phrases, gradually gaining the ability to communicate with the new friends I made.

One of the most rewarding experiences was volunteering at Mindy's preschool. By the end of the first month, I was able to teach a group of children how to make piñatas from scratch—using balloons, newspaper, tissue paper, and engrudo, a homemade glue made from flour and water. I explained the entire process, from cutting the paper into different shapes to the meaning and traditions of piñatas in Mexican culture, all in English. I was incredibly proud of myself.

By the end of that summer, I could understand the news, movies, songs, and everyday conversations, and I communicated in English without relying on gestures. Learning English not only allowed me to connect with various people and make new friends, but it also enabled me to enjoy my summer abroad fully.

The experience was so enjoyable and rewarding that upon returning to Mexico, I eagerly enrolled in Italian and German lessons, excited to further explore the world of languages.

What helped

- **Motivation:** I understood that learning English would benefit me academically, help me secure a better job in the future, make travel more enjoyable and accessible, allow me to communicate with people beyond Spanish speakers, and enable me to understand my favorite songs and watch movies without subtitles. This kept me driven to continue learning.

- **Enjoyment**: The learning process was both fun and rewarding. As I became more fluent, making friends became easier, leading to more social invitations and opportunities to do things I enjoyed.
- **Language** Immersion: I was fully immersed in English, with no other option but to speak and listen to it constantly. The radio, TV, and everything around me were in English, with very few people speaking Spanish. This immersion is an excellent way to learn any language.
- **Observing and Listening**: I spent much time listening to others and closely watching how they formed words, focusing on their lips and mouths to imitate the sounds. Over time, these sounds and words became more familiar, making it easier for me to speak and understand.

From confidence to crisis

I thought my English was reasonably good until we moved to Memphis, and I started working in customer support for North America. When I initially saw the job listing mentioning "North America," I assumed it included Mexico. However, I quickly discovered that "North America" in this context meant "English-speaking America," specifically the USA and Canada. This meant no Spanish breaks—everything was in English, all the time.

During my training, I had to disassemble and reassemble a real engine—almost as tall as I was—like a giant puzzle. I had to learn the names and functions of parts like crankshafts, manifolds, flywheels, and cylinder liners—terms I wasn't even familiar with in Spanish. Daily, I was bombarded with automotive terminology and technical terms, making conversations increasingly challenging.

Having an informal chat with friends in English is one thing but participating in business meetings where professionalism and precision are expected is an entirely different challenge. In casual conversations, missing a few words wasn't a big deal; I could still understand the general idea without knowing every term. However, missing a single detail was not an option in a work environment. My job relied on complete comprehension, and I was determined to perform at my best.

Answering the phone became a daily struggle, people spoke so fast it felt like they were talking at the speed of light. They used idioms and slang I'd never heard before, and there were so many different accents, all without helpful cues of body language. Every conversation required intense concentration, and I found myself not only learning the technical skills for my job but also expanding my vocabulary and improving my grammar to keep up.

The challenge extended beyond the workplace. Everywhere I went—the grocery store, the doctor's office, the dentist, even just walking down the street—I constantly encountered new terms and concepts. My grocery shopping trips became mini language lessons, often requiring me to translate most of my shopping list or rely on my trusty English-Spanish dictionary (this was before smartphones). Sometimes, I had to describe what I was looking for, like saying, "It's an herb used for cooking pasta," only to be directed to something similar but not quite right. Other times, even when I knew the word, my pronunciation didn't help. A typical exchange at the supermarket might go like this:

– "Where can I find Wo-chess-ter-shire sauce?"
– "What?"
– "Wer-ches-ter sauce."
– "Lady, I'm sorry, but I can't understand you."
– "It's a brownish sauce in a brown glass bottle with a yellow label, used to marinate meats."
– "Oh! Worcestershire sauce?"
– "Yes, that's the one!" (I still struggle with pronunciation).

Every conversation demanded my full attention, and my brain was in overdrive, trying to absorb all this new information. Many days, I came home with a headache, feeling drained and exhausted from thinking in English all day. It felt like my brain was about to explode.

But it wasn't just the language; moving to a new place meant learning many new things. I had to get accustomed to my new job, study for the driving test, navigate a new city while avoiding unsafe areas, learn to cook on an electric stove instead of the gas range I was used to in Mexico, and figure out where to find the ingredients I needed for cooking. All the daily aspects of life differed from what I was used to back home.

My social life also took a hit. The language barrier kept me from truly connecting with friends. No one got my jokes, sarcasm, or humor, and I didn't get theirs. I couldn't speak as quickly as I did in Spanish, and miscommunications were common. When our English-speaking friends invited us to dinner or a party, I dreaded it. I prayed they wouldn't ask me something I couldn't understand or that I wouldn't embarrass myself with my broken English.

My confidence in learning something new evaporated for the first time in my life. As a (recovering) perfectionist, not being able to communicate and understand as I did in my native language was devastating. I became my worst critic, constantly beating myself up for not remembering a word, being unable to express a thought clearly, or not understanding every single word in a conversation. I wanted to be professional at work, but instead, I felt like a child trying to talk to adults, which was neither fun nor acceptable.

I fell into the perfectionist trap of all or nothing. I didn't want to speak at all if I couldn't speak perfectly. Speaking English, once something I enjoyed, became a source of stress. I started associating English with anxiety and began avoiding it whenever possible. I surrounded myself with people I could communicate with easily, avoided unnecessary conversations with non-Spanish speakers, and resorted to watching the news in Spanish and movies with subtitles.

I didn't want to be judged, seem ignorant, or unintelligent, so I withdrew whenever possible, desperately clinging to my comfort zone. I'm not proud of how I thought or behaved during this time—in fact, I'm ashamed of it—but I share this in the hope that it might help someone in a similar situation avoid making the same mistakes.

Over time, I understood that my fear of not performing well due to my English skills, struggling to communicate effectively, or being judged by others was mainly in my mind. When I received performance evaluations, customer and coworkers' feedback was positive.

Language learning errors

So, what changed? Why did speaking another language transition from being enjoyable to becoming a source of stress? What truly held me back?

- **Unrealistic Goals:** Without realizing it, I was making steady progress—adding new words to my vocabulary, getting accustomed to different accents, and becoming more fluent. However, I wasn't advancing as quickly as I had hoped. The pace I expected was unrealistic, discouraging me from continuing.

- **Not Breaking Down the Big Goal:** I aimed for fluency, perfect grammar, and mastery of all the vocabulary I needed for daily life and work. But I didn't focus on the progress I was making along the way. Instead of taking it step by step, I fixated on the end goal, making the journey feel overwhelming.

- **Perfectionism:** Learning a language takes time, and mistakes are an inevitable part of the process. Just as we must learn to walk before we can run, we stumble many times before we master a new skill. If we refuse to step out of our comfort zone, we'll remain stuck, never progressing beyond the basics. Making mistakes means we're trying, and they're unavoidable if we genuinely want to learn.

- **Comparing Myself to Others:** I unconsciously compared my English to that of my husband and other bilinguals without considering factors like how long they had studied or how often they practiced to master it. When learning a new language, the only comparison that matters is between your past self and your current self.

- **Negative Self-Talk:** I was incredibly impatient and focused solely on my mistakes. Every time I struggled to understand something, every little error, every time I had to ask someone to repeat themselves, or whenever someone kindly corrected me, I was my own worst critic. No one else judged me as harshly as I judged myself.

Tip: It's crucial to find ways to encourage yourself, focusing on your efforts and progress rather than dwelling on your mistakes.

Breaking barriers

Over time, I finally overcame my fear of embarrassment when speaking English. I realized that I had been my biggest obstacle, holding myself back and missing out on countless opportunities—to connect with incredible people, enjoy social gatherings, learn new things, excel in my career, and unlock countless possibilities.

Determined to break free from these self-imposed limitations, I consciously tried to engage more with non-Spanish speakers. I started a cooking club, joined various groups, and spent more time with friends who didn't speak Spanish.

One day, my American friend Kate invited me for a walk. Since I love exercising and being outdoors, I eagerly agreed. Soon, we started walking together twice a week, and without even realizing it, my English skills improved. My vocabulary grew, and I began speaking more fluently and confidently.

These walks were the perfect combination: I was getting exercise, unwinding, receiving invaluable parenting advice, and chatting with a great friend—all while improving my English. Kate was the ideal conversation partner—patient, articulate, and free of excessive idioms. She gently helped me find the right words and would tactfully correct and rephrase my sentences when needed. She became the best English conversation buddy I could have hoped for.

This experience taught me that language learning can be effective and enjoyable when paired with activities I love.

Before long, another opportunity came my way. I had always dreamed of writing a book, but I knew my English wasn't at the level needed to tackle such a project alone. So, I reached out to Brooke, a friend who is a writer and editor, to see if she would help me with editing.

To my surprise, she didn't just agree to offer tips; she invited me to join her writers' club. When she mentioned that the group was made up entirely of native English speakers, accomplished authors, and seasoned writers, I felt thrilled and nervous. It felt like the excitement of opening a Christmas present as a child and the jitters of the first day at school.

This was an incredible opportunity. For someone whose writing experience had mostly been limited to college essays and letters to my grandmother, the chance to write a book—while receiving feedback from talented writers and improving my English writing skills—was priceless.

I knew the journey wouldn't be easy. It would require effort, dedication, and a willingness to push myself. I had to contribute meaningfully, step out of my comfort zone, and embrace the mistakes I was bound to make along the way.

This time, however, I approached it with more realistic goals. I was prepared to embrace mistakes as part of the process and learn from them, improving with each chapter. I didn't compare myself to the other writers—that would only have discouraged me, given their extensive experience.

Instead, I had developed a method, system, and schedule that worked for me, and I was highly motivated to succeed. This new mindset was my key to rediscovering the joy and confidence I once had in speaking English and using it to pursue my dreams.

What helped

- **Discovering My Motivation**: I identified compelling reasons to improve my English: to build deeper, more meaningful connections with my American friends, express my ideas more clearly, perform better at work, travel more comfortably, and meet new people. Above all, my greatest source of motivation has been writing this book. It fuels my drive, pushing me forward with purpose and determination.
- **Having a Learning Partner:** I surrounded myself with supportive individuals who encouraged me to improve thoughtfully and constructively, making the learning process more enjoyable and effective.
- **Finding a Method and System That Work for Me:** I committed to writing for at least eight hrs. weekly, using tools to refine my spelling and grammar. I also set reading goals and now read more than ever before. Joining a writers' club has been instrumental in helping me improve and address my mistakes.
- **Making It Fun:** I've rekindled my enjoyment of learning by incorporating activities I love, such as listening to music and podcasts, writing, reading, and participating in clubs that align with my interests. These activities not only help me improve but also make the process enjoyable.

From stress to success

Belgium has three official languages: Dutch, French, and German. We lived in the Flemish region, where Dutch is the primary language. A few weeks after we moved, I began taking Dutch lessons but soon stopped when I realized that English was sufficient for communication there.

Instead, I switched to French and started with the basics. Before long, I could ask for directions and understand the answers, order meals at restaurants, greet people, hold simple conversations, and follow the main ideas of movies in French, even if I didn't catch every detail.

Learning French was a completely different experience from the stressful time I went through while learning English in Memphis. I approached it with a relaxed mindset, more confidence, and self-encouragement this time. Rather than criticizing myself for not speaking perfectly, I celebrated every small step forward.

I acknowledged my progress each time I:

- Ordered at a restaurant without resorting to pointing at the menu.
- Asked for directions and successfully followed them to reach my destination.
- Watched a movie and understood it without needing subtitles.
- Held a five-minute conversation in French.
- Read a page and comprehend 60-80% of the content.

By celebrating each small achievement, I found renewed motivation to keep studying and practicing, making the learning process far more enjoyable and rewarding.

What helped

- **No rush, but clear goals:** I had no urgent need to learn the language—there was no pressure from work or necessity for communication. I pursued it purely for the joy of learning. However, I still set clear goals to track my progress, ensuring I had milestones to work toward.
- **Celebrating small achievements:** Recognizing and celebrating small victories was crucial, especially when the overall task felt daunting. These incremental successes built my confidence and steadily moved me closer to my larger goal.

Lessons from a polyglot

While studying Italian, my teacher gave me a unique opportunity to assist at an International Medical Congress in my hometown of San Luis Potosí. My role was to help Italian-speaking attendees navigate the registration process, understand the facilities, manage schedules, and address other logistical questions.

The congress was a prestigious event that drew doctors and psychologists from around the globe. Presentations were conducted in five or six different languages, each simultaneously translated into four or five others through headphones for the audience. The diversity and scale of the event were awe-inspiring, but what truly captured my attention was one of the translators, Carlos Lomeli.

Carlos left a lasting impression on me. He spoke six or seven languages fluently and possessed an extraordinary ability to switch seamlessly between them. During breaks, I watched in amazement as he engaged effortlessly with groups of doctors who each spoke different languages. He would converse in German with one, shift to French with another, and continue switching languages fluidly, connecting with nearly everyone around him.

I was in awe of his linguistic skills and how naturally he transitioned between languages. Intrigued by his abilities, I approached him to ask how he had learned so many languages. His response was even more astonishing.

Carlos explained that he had never spent more than a week in any countries where these languages were spoken, nor had he attended formal language classes. His learning method was entirely self-taught: he watched foreign films repeatedly, imitating the sounds and mouth movements until he could recite entire phrases. He then used dictionaries and books to expand his vocabulary and fine-tune his grammar. Isn't that incredible?

This encounter changed the way I thought about language learning. It showed me that passion, persistence, and creative methods can overcome traditional barriers.

TIPS FOR LEARNING A NEW LANGUAGE

Learning a new language is something we all can achieve, but it doesn't happen overnight. It requires time, effort, making plenty of mistakes, and consistent practice. The language acquisition requires commitment, strategic effort, and an open mindset. This chapter will outline the key steps and techniques that helped me on my language-learning journey and can guide you to learn a new language effectively.

Find a method you enjoy

Finding a learning method that suits you is crucial. A balanced mix of enjoyable techniques can enhance your skills and make the journey of language learning fun and engaging.

- **Language Software:** Many software programs are designed to teach new languages through images, conjugations, grammar, and pronunciation. These tools are excellent for building a solid foundation.
- **Watch Movies:** Watching films in your target language is a fun way to learn idioms and expand your vocabulary. Pause and repeat phrases to practice your pronunciation and gain confidence.
- **Language Apps:** Mobile apps like Duolingo, Rosetta Stone, and Babbel are convenient tools that allow you to practice anytime, anywhere, or explore other language-learning apps, and you'll discover a wide range of options that cater to different learning levels and preferences
- **Games:** Learning through games can make the language acquisition process effective but also fun and engaging. From digital flashcards to crossword puzzles and classic games like Hangman, countless interactive language games are available online or as mobile apps. These games challenge your vocabulary, grammar, and comprehension skills while keeping the learning process light and enjoyable. Search for "language games in (specific language)."
- **Listen to Radio or Podcasts:** Immerse yourself in the target language by listening to radio stations or podcasts, even if you don't understand much. Over time, your brain will acclimate to the new sounds, and you'll start picking up words.
- **Find a Language** Partner: A friend, coworker, or stranger can help you practice your new language. Don't be afraid to ask for help—you might be surprised how many people are willing to assist you. Set up regular meetings to practice together.
- **Join a Conversation or Interest Club:** If you have a hobby, such as cooking, consider joining a club where you can practice your new language while learning something new. The same applies to interests like running, painting, reading, or any other activity.
- **Language Classes or a Tutor:** Investing in professional instruction is always a wise choice. A qualified teacher or tutor can provide structured learning and personalized feedback, helping you progress more effectively.
- **Self-study:** Use grammar books and a dictionary to refine your skills. This approach allows you to focus on specific areas for improvement.

- **Read:** Reading books in your target language is an excellent way to enhance grammar and vocabulary. Start with simple texts and gradually move on to more complex material.
- **Spaced Repetition:** A highly effective learning technique involves repeatedly reviewing learned material at increasing intervals. Revisiting words, sentences, and concepts over time reinforces memory and makes it easier to retain new information. Spaced repetition is a powerful tool for language learning, helping you build a strong and lasting command of the language. Some software programs that utilize spaced repetition algorithms to enhance language learning are available.

How Spaced Repetition Works:

1. When you first encounter new information, such as a vocabulary word or a grammar rule, you begin by learning it and attempting to understand its meaning and usage.

2. Instead of reviewing this information frequently in a short time (which often leads to quick forgetting), spaced repetition systems (SRS) schedule reviews at increasing intervals. For example:

- After the first exposure, you might review the material after one day.
- The following review could be scheduled for three days later.
- Then a week later, and so on.

3. Spaced repetition systems often adapt based on your performance. If you recall the information quickly, the interval before the following review increases. If you struggle, the interval is shortened. This adaptive approach ensures that you focus more on material that needs reinforcement.[82]

Practical tips for success

Immerse Yourself in the Language

Dive into listening and speaking from the start. Don't wait until your skills feel perfect—immerse yourself in the language as much as possible daily. Seize every opportunity to learn new words, whether you're working out, commuting, or waiting for an appointment. Seek out conversations with anyone willing to practice with you. When the process feels overwhelming, shift from active learning (such as studying grammar or vocabulary) to passive learning, like listening to music, watching TV shows, or tuning into podcasts in the target language. Even if you don't fully understand, simply hearing the language helps train your brain to recognize patterns and sounds. Push your mind to think and respond in the target language as much as possible.

Listen Actively
Developing strong listening skills is essential for effective language learning. The more you listen, the more familiar your brain becomes with words, phrases, and intonation, making it easier to understand and speak. Dedicate time to focused listening activities, such as listening to native speakers on the radio or watching videos with varied accents.

Practice Speaking
Regular speaking is vital for reinforcing new vocabulary, improving pronunciation, and building fluency. Engage in conversations with locals at the supermarket, neighbors, and friends, or even practice speaking to yourself. Speaking aloud regularly helps reinforce new vocabulary, improve pronunciation, and build fluency.

Imitate Sounds and Movements
Mimicking the sounds, facial expressions, and mouth movements of native speakers can significantly improve your pronunciation and make your speech sound more natural. Familiarize yourself with the phonetic alphabet and learn how each sound is produced within the mouth. This method helps fine-tune your accent and makes your speech more authentic.

Learn the Most Common Words
Focus on learning the top 500-1,000 word families (lemmas). According to BBC News, learning just 800 of English's most frequently used lemmas enables you to understand 75% of everyday language. Native speakers know 15,000 to 20,000 lemmas, but starting with the most common will help you communicate effectively much faster. Concentrate on colloquial topics and frequently used phrases.[83]

Visualize New Vocabulary
Visualizing the words you're learning can help you connect concepts and improve memorization. This mental imagery makes it easier to recall words when you need them.

Embrace Mistakes
Expect to make mistakes and use them as learning opportunities. Avoid the

desire for perfection and the fear of judgment—especially self-judgment. You can't become fluent without putting yourself out there, so embrace your errors and keep talking.

Find Your Motivation
Clearly define why you want to learn a new language. List the benefits and how they align with your personal goals. This motivation will drive you forward, especially when learning is challenging.

Create a Consistent Schedule
Commit to dedicating as many hours daily to studying and practicing the language. Regular, focused practice is key, whether for 30 minutes or several hours. Consistency is essential for building and retaining language skills, as frequent exposure helps reinforce what you've learned and accelerates your progress.

Set Realistic Goals:M
Break down your long-term language goals into smaller, specific, and measurable objectives. This approach keeps you motivated and prevents you from feeling overwhelmed.

Test Yourself Regularly
Make a habit of taking practice tests through online platforms, study guides, or standardized language proficiency exams. Regular self-assessment helps you stay on track by highlighting your strengths and pinpointing areas that need improvement; it also reinforces what you've learned and provides a clear measure of progress.

Make Learning Fun
Incorporate activities you enjoy into your language practice. Whether you watch movies, play games, or join a conversation club, learning becomes faster and more effective when having fun. Allow yourself the time to learn, be patient with the process, and, above all, enjoy the journey.

KEY TAKEAWAYS
....
- Be patient and embrace the process, allowing yourself to make mistakes without self-judgment.
- Relax and immerse yourself in the language by listening, speaking, writing, and mimicking how others communicate.

- Choose enjoyable learning methods that suit your personality, such as classes, apps, books, podcasts, or engaging with native speakers.
- Set clear, achievable goals with a structured plan, starting with basic phrases and building gradually.
- Celebrate small victories, acknowledge your progress, and make learning fun while staying motivated to improve.

CHAPTER 14

Wanderlust

"The best gift you could have given her was
a lifetime of adventures."
-Louis Carrol - Alice in Wonderland

Wanderlust, a term derived from the German words "wandern" (to hike) and "lust" (desire), [84]encapsulates a profound and often unexplainable craving to explore the world. It is more than just a simple desire to travel; it is an insatiable yearning to experience new places, cultures, and perspectives.

Wanderlust is rooted in our natural curiosity and thirst for adventure. This drive to explore the unknown isn't just a modern trend; it's a throwback to our ancestors, who ventured beyond familiar paths to secure better survival, find new resources, and create opportunities that benefited their whole communities.

Today, while survival doesn't depend on discovering new lands, that same spirit fuels our desire for new experiences. Travel isn't just a fun getaway for those with wanderlust. It's a way of life. It pushes us to seek the road less traveled, choosing unique and authentic experiences over typical tourist spots. These journeys open our eyes to new cultures, languages, and ways of thinking, break down stereotypes, challenge what we know, and broaden our perspective.

Travel is more than ticking destinations off a list—it's a journey of discovery. Experiencing different cultures challenges our beliefs, encourages self-reflection, and often leads to personal growth. It can spark new passions, reveal unexpected career opportunities, and reshape our perspective in ways we never imagined.

MY ADVENTURE SOUL

Ever since I was a little girl, I've had an insatiable curiosity about exploring new places and meeting different people. This wanderlust led my husband and me to move to the United States. I wanted the experience of living and working in another country, learning a new language, and connecting with people from diverse backgrounds. It wasn't that I didn't love my life in Mexico—I did—but I craved the adventure of seeing more of the world.

Jose Luis and I got married in June 2000, and before our first anniversary, we moved to Collierville, Tennessee, in April 2001. We both signed new job offers and planned to stay for just two years. The plan was simple: gain valuable international experience and then return to our beloved Mexico.

But two years turned into three, then three became four, and before we knew it, the years kept adding up. Staying longer hadn't been part of our original plan. We hadn't anticipated moving to Belgium after those two years, becoming U.S. citizens seven years later, having our children born here, or living outside of Mexico for over 20 years. My mother-in-law, who counted down the days during those first two years, was probably the most unprepared for this unexpected change. Whenever we called, she would say, "Only 14 more months," or "Just 65 more days." To this day, she's probably still disappointed that we didn't return when our first work visas expired.

Two years after moving to the U.S., I applied for a position in human resources. Although my background was in marketing, sales, customer service, import/export, customs, and supply chain management—where I even implemented the software for inventory and sales—I had zero experience in HR. However, being a people person at heart, I was drawn to working with individuals' skills and talents and connecting people to the right tasks. The HR job seemed the perfect fit, offering the chance to work in a new area and learn something exciting. The team was fantastic, and my future boss was friendly, funny, and enthusiastic. Every conversation with him was a delight.

I passed the final round of interviews and became the top candidate. The job was practically mine—99% certain. All that was left was formalizing the offer, and I would sign on in just a few days. I was beyond excited and couldn't wait to start. But life had other plans. That evening, my husband came home with news of his own: he had been offered a promotion that required us to move to Belgium.

I had only visited Belgium once on vacation and knew little about living there, but I had already fallen in love with Europe. Before Jose Luis could finish explaining, my adventured soul took over. I interrupted him and said, "That's amazing! When do we move?"

Surprised, he asked, "But what about your new job? And the house we just bought?"

I replied, "I can find a similar job when we return, and there will always be homes for sale. But living in Belgium? That's a once-in-a-lifetime opportunity like an extended three-year honeymoon!"

Slightly amused, he said, "Are you aware this isn't a vacation, right? I'll be working there."

"Yes," I laughed, "but I know there will be holidays, weekends, and breaks when we can travel."

And so, in April 2003, we moved to Belgium.

***

Natalie, our intercultural consultant, was one of the first people we met in Belgium. She was Belgian but had spent several years as an expat near New York. During one of our conversations, I asked her which place she liked most in the U.S. She said New York but admitted she hadn't explored many other cities. Curious, I wondered why.

She explained that when she announced she was moving near New York, family and friends made plans to visit—and, naturally, they all wanted to explore the city with a familiar face.

"You'll see," she said. "Your family and friends will want to visit you, and they'll all want to see the same places—Paris, Brussels, London, Venice. But unfortunately, this won't leave you with enough time or money to discover other places."

"Not over my dead body!" I thought. I was determined to explore Europe beyond the typical tourist hotspots and make it so appealing that our guests would join us in visiting those hidden gems off the beaten path. And that's precisely what we did.

I always advise my clients to explore their new country fully, not just revisit the same places over and over. Returning to your favorite spots is fine, but don't limit yourself. Broaden your horizons and take in all that your new home has to offer.

A JOURNEY OF WANDERLUST AND NEW BEGINNINGS

I was on a mission to squeeze every ounce of experience out of our three years in Europe. My goal was simple: discover, visit, and learn as much as possible.

My passion for travel started early. When I was just 12 years old, I landed my first job at Viajes Montiel, a travel agency owned by friends of my mom. It was supposed to be a simple summer gig, with tasks like making photocopies and organizing brochures. But by the end of the summer, I was booking flights, arranging hotels, answering customer calls, and earning a significant amount in commissions! I loved flipping through those brochures, imagining myself in the stunning places depicted—churches, temples, palaces, beaches, mosques, castles, deserts, and wildlife. The detailed itineraries filled me with excitement and wanderlust.

Fast-forward to our time in Belgium. I decided to channel that same energy and enthusiasm into creating a little travel agency. I bought a giant map of Europe and hung it in my office, marking all the places we visited with pins. I started collecting travel guides—first for Belgium and neighboring countries like Germany, France, and the Netherlands—then expanded to cover most of Europe.

I wasn't content with flipping through guidebooks. I made a list of top-notch travel websites—National Geographic, Conde Nast, Lonely Planet, Michelin Guide, and visitor centers from each country. I searched the internet for the best food, music, history, art festivals, key events, and the optimal times to visit each destination. I even downloaded the UNESCO World Heritage list and became well-versed in low-cost airlines, train routes, and the best travel methods across Europe.

But the real treasure trove of travel tips came from talking to people. I made it a point to ask everyone I met about their favorite places. This wasn't your typical "What's your favorite city?" conversation—no, I dug deeper. My questions were more like:

- What are the most memorable or favorite places you've ever visited? Which destinations were the most exotic, charming, or thrilling, and what made them special?
- Which small town, hidden gem, or off-the-beaten-path spot had that unique magic or charm that left a lasting impression?
- Which city stands out for its stunning architecture, captivating atmosphere, or culinary treasures?
- Which beach has given you the most serene, vibrant, or picturesque experience?
- Which travel websites or apps do you rely on to find the best deals and up-to-date information?
- And how about your local favorites? Which spots nearby are worth recommending for their charm, character, or hidden magic?

I compiled all this information into a master Excel list, with columns for the town or city, country, sightseeing highlights, must-try foods, festivals or events, essential websites, the best times to visit, notes, and priority level.

Then, I prioritized each destination from 1 to 5. The 1s were must-visit places before our third year ended, while the 5s were exciting but not critical. I highlighted the spots we'd visited as we traveled, keeping track of our adventures.

To make our travels even more exciting for our guests, I prepared detailed information, costs, itineraries, and pictures for each destination—just like a professional travel agent. I listened to their plans, considered the places they wanted to see, and tailored three different itinerary options for them to choose from. Each option had a unique route, cities, sightseeing suggestions, and even included websites for further research.

Sometimes, due to my husband's work or my classes, we couldn't accompany our guests for their entire trip. When that happened, we'd join them later or catch up with them before or after visiting certain places.

Over those three years, my parents, brothers, sister-in-law, cousins, Jose Luis's best friend and his wife, my best friend and her sister, friends from Memphis, my uncle Damaso and his family, and various other friends and coworkers came to visit us. I crafted personalized itineraries for each group, rarely repeating a city—and it worked like a charm.

I became an expert at finding incredible travel deals. Executive five-star hotels on weekends for 20-50 Euros per night when the weekday rates were over 180 Euros. Airplane tickets to Italy, Spain, or Turkey for 20-40 Euros. I traveled with my husband, friends, family, classmates, and even alone. Some adventures were quick day trips, while others FLEXIBLE into two-week vacations. I seized every opportunity to explore, no matter how big or small. Each journey was a chance to discover something new and make unforgettable memories.

Traveling from Brussels to Paris was a breeze—just 1 hour and 20 minutes on the Thalys high-speed train, with tickets as low as 25 Euros if booked in advance. We could be in Paris for breakfast, spend the day exploring, and return to Belgium after dinner without needing a hotel. Despite Paris being so close and affordable, we only visited it a handful of times. I aimed to avoid repeating destinations and explore as many new places as possible.

Thanks to this strategy, I visited over 121 cities while my husband explored 69 (not including his work trips), spanning 23 countries during our three years in Belgium. It did require a significant amount of mileage, time, and money. We used nearly every day off and invested much of our income into these adventures. But every single penny and second spent on planning and traveling was worth it. The experiences, memories, and discoveries were priceless; I would do it again without hesitation.

Despite my husband's demanding work schedule and my MBA studies, we managed to balance work, school, and travel. Plus, without children at the time, we could move around freely. The company even adjusted his two-week vacation to the four-week European standard, doubling the days we had initially expected.

Ultimately, I was right—it was an extended three-year honeymoon!

I'm not sharing this to brag about our travels. My main goal is to inspire you to embrace your time living abroad fully. Travel, explore, and discover as much as you can. Keep a list of places you'd like to visit or things you want to do so you're ready with options and a clear idea of where to go or what to do when the opportunity arises.

You don't need to go to these extremes or do what I did for a memorable experience; many may find it intimidating and overwhelming. The key is to do what feels right for you. Ultimately, the goal is to enhance your enjoyment of life abroad, not to add more stress. Focus on what brings you joy and fulfillment and let that guide your journey.

Travel requires time and money, but you can save a lot by learning where and when to look for promotions. Join frequent travel programs, use your credit card to earn free hotel nights or flights, check low-cost airlines, avoid peak seasons, opt for the chef's tasting menu instead of à la carte, pack only the essentials to avoid extra baggage fees, and travel with friends to split expenses.

Money comes and goes, but the memories of a great trip last forever. And trust me, there's nothing better than looking back and saying, "Wow, what a wonderful time we had—we couldn't have done it better."

You don't have to travel far to be a traveler—explore your city by discovering new places, visiting a coffee shop you've never tried, exploring a park, browsing a library, or wandering through a museum. This will help you appreciate and enjoy your surroundings even more.

Be a traveler, not a tourist

Travel is full of surprises; some of the best experiences often come from the most unexpected places. Coconut isn't usually my top choice for ice cream, but the best ice cream I ever had was, surprisingly, coconut. My husband and I were visiting Chiang Mai, Thailand, and every day, as we made our way from the hotel to the Buddhist temples, the market, or downtown, we noticed a long line of locals waiting for ice cream from a street vendor.

The first time we passed by, I said to my husband, "It must be amazing. I want to try it later when the line gets shorter." He just shrugged it off. But on our way back, the line was longer, and the same thing happened the following days.

The vendors were a charming Thai couple with a simple setup—a big steel box, a small tent attached to a bicycle, coconuts hanging from the tent, and four buckets full of fresh mangos on the ground. Everything looked modest but spotless. They washed their hands frequently, the woman handled the money, and the man served the treats.

Our guide had already warned me about eating street food after she saw me indulging at the floating markets. "Be careful," she said. "Yes, it's clean, but the food here has different bacteria than you're used to back home. It could make you sick."

But I couldn't resist. The temptation was too strong, so I lined up behind the endless queue of locals. In a sarcastic tone, my husband asked, "Are you sure you want an E. coli ice cream?" I just laughed. It looked too good to care. He opted for a fancy coffee shop across the street and ordered a Dolce de Leche Häagen-Dazs while I patiently waited for my street treat.

When it was finally my turn, I was served what turned out to be the best ice cream I've ever had. The man scooped the creamy coconut goodness into half a freshly cut coconut shell. The ice cream was rich and sweet but perfectly balanced, with tiny roasted coconut flakes for texture. He topped it with small pieces of freshly cut Okay Rong Damnoen mango—a sweet, extra-juicy variety—and something crunchy that I couldn't quite identify, but I was sure it wasn't E. coli. It was incredibly fresh and full of flavor, and the combination of ingredients was exquisite!

When traveling, always go where the locals go. Skip the international chains and fast-food franchises. Instead, dive into regional dishes and local eateries. Listen to the locals' recommendations on places, food, events, and hidden gems. They often hold the best-kept secrets.

As the renowned celebrity chef Andrew Zimmern wisely said, "Be a traveler, not a tourist."[85] Travelers immerse themselves in the essence of the people and places they visit, gaining a richer, more authentic experience.

Traveling broadens your horizons, making you a better person by exposing you to new cultures, ideas, traditions, foods, and ways of life. It enriches your mind and soul, making you wealthier in knowledge and wisdom. Travel has transformed my life, opened my eyes, and sparked my creativity in ways I never imagined.

How to be an authentic traveler:

- Familiarize yourself with the local history, culture, and language basics to deepen your experience.
- Engage and immerse yourself in the culture, interact with locals—they offer insights that no guidebook ever could—savor local flavors, listen to their music, and live like a resident by exploring less touristy spots and using local transportation (whenever is safe).
- Be Flexible and Open-Minded: Be spontaneous, respect local traditions, adapt to changes, and be open to new experiences and different perspectives.
- Embrace the Unexpected: Don't worry too much—sometimes the best memories come from taking a chance.
- Show respect for the local religion, culture, and traditions. Avoid judgments and appreciate their uniqueness.
- Don't worry too much about things like "E. coli ice cream"—sometimes, taking a chance leads to the best memories or flavors.

TRAVELING WITH CHILDREN

We couldn't have visited all those cities if we'd had children then, but now that we do, our travel style has changed. We move at a slower pace, but the rewards are just as gratifying, if not more so.

We started traveling with our kids when they were just two months old. Our first trip was to Mexico to introduce them to the family, and we haven't stopped exploring ever since. Traveling with these little adventurers has been a joy. Their curiosity is boundless, and seeing the world through their tiny eyes is magical. Everything is extraordinary to them, and their energy and sense of wonder are contagious. They ask the most insightful questions, often leading to learning moments for all of us.

Discovering new places as a family has always been a beautiful adventure. Whether it's watching them feel the sand between their toes, laughing as they jump in the waves, or seeing how they interact with art in a museum, the experience is constantly enriching. Their ability to notice details and read facial expressions often surpasses that of adults, making each experience even more enjoyable.

One of our most unforgettable family journeys was our European adventure in the summer of 2019. Andrea was 13, and Luis was 10. We visited

London, Paris, Interlaken, Zurich, Lucerne, Colmar, and Strasbourg. I was a bit worried about how jet lag and the time zone differences would affect the kids, but they surprised me in the best ways possible. They weren't cranky, adjusted to the new schedule on the first day, walked more than six miles a day, and remained interested and engaged for five hours at the British Museum and more than six hours at the Louvre. The best part? Not a single complaint.

How do a kid and a teenager enjoy two museums for that long?

Like many other museums, attractions, and national parks worldwide, the British Museum offers maps, coloring pages, passports, and other activities designed especially for children. Everything is explained in a fun, easy-to-understand way, making the experience enjoyable for kids and surprisingly helpful for adults, too.

The Louvre offers an interactive guide that looks like a smartphone, complete with GPS, maps of the galleries, photos, background music, and explanations you can listen to or read while exploring the art. In both museums, we let the children take the lead. We asked for their help in finding specific galleries or pieces of art, and they guided us using the maps provided by the museums. For them, it was like a scavenger hunt or an adventure, and they felt a sense of accomplishment every time they found something.

My favorite part was watching them—their focus, their creativity, and how much they were absorbing.

By the end of the day, when they started to get tired, their creativity was at its peak. Both love photography, so they took hundreds of beautiful pictures and created hilarious videos. In one of the videos, they narrated a story using three different paintings, making it seem like the characters were talking to each other. They made me pay closer attention to the paintings' gestures, expressions, and landscapes, and their stories made perfect sense.

Another video featured a woman intently studying a Greek sculpture of a handsome, strong man. The sculpture's eyes seemed to be looking back at her, so the kids created a boomerang video of the sculpture gazing at her while she closely examined it. The statue said, "Why are you looking at me that way? We're all naked here!"

Seeing the details they observed and the thoughtful questions they asked was impressive. These interactions helped us adults learn even more as we tried to provide them with accurate answers. Their innocence encouraged us to reflect on our world and choices, while their curiosity opened our eyes to new perspectives.

Children can be the best teachers and travel companions—just let them be themselves.

Tips for enjoying family vacations:

- Plan around their needs, consider sleeping, meals, and breaks for play when scheduling your day.
- Pack smart; bring essentials, comfort items, and snacks to keep them happy and comfortable.
- Make it fun and get creative to keep them entertained and engaged during the trip.
- Choose child-friendly options, and ensure your accommodations and activities suit children.
- Review safety plans, teach them what to do if they get lost, and consider using a GPS tracker.
- To minimize waiting times, buy entry tickets in advance, pre-check at airports, and use fast passes when available.
- Don't rush them unless you're about to miss your flight.

KEY TAKEAWAYS

- Wanderlust is a deep, insatiable desire to explore the world, rooted in curiosity about the unknown and a craving for new experiences.
- It's a path to personal growth through exposure to different cultures, languages, and perspectives. It can lead to introspection, reshaping beliefs, values, and life goals.
- Seize unexpected opportunities.
- Engage with locals; seeking their insights can lead to discovering hidden gems and authentic experiences. Immerse into the local culture.
- Travel with children; they may slow the pace but add joy and wonder, offering a different, equally rewarding experience.

CHAPTER 15

The grass is greener

"Comparison is the thief of joy."
-Theodore Roosevelt[86]

Humans have an instinct to compare. We're constantly searching for improvement; sometimes, comparisons help us evaluate different options, motivate us to make positive changes, and advance our lives. However, constant comparisons can also make us miserable.

For ex-pats, this may be one of the biggest causes of unhappiness. The more they negatively compare their current location or life with their previous one, the more frustration they feel. I often hear clients say things like, "The food doesn't taste the same," "The weather was better in my home country," or "I don't like the culture here."

These comparisons focus on the best aspects of their past experiences while highlighting the worst of the new ones. This selective memory often leads to dissatisfaction, as they forget the annoying things they disliked before and instead focus on what they've lost rather than what they've gained. Suddenly, things they once took for granted in their native countries become essential in their new environment.

To some degree, we all fall into this trap, whether consciously or unconsciously.

I'm happy living where I am, but I've also compared Mexico and the U.S., Columbus and Carmel, and Belgium with Mexico and the U.S. I still do it, but rarely and only briefly, which makes all the difference.

When we moved from Mexico to the U.S., I compared my social life, closeness to my family, warmth of the people, weather, domestic help, food, social life, and culture with what I didn't have in the U.S. This is a common yet unproductive way to compare two places. Comparing one country's negatives with another's positives is neither objective nor fair, leading to unhappiness.

You inevitably lose something with every move or change but also gain. After all, why would you move in the first place? Focusing on what you've achieved rather than lost will make your life much easier.

Several people have asked me how I could find joy living in a place they didn't consider appealing. My response is simple: I shifted my mindset and focused on the positives quickly; instead of dwelling on what I was missing, I began to appreciate the unique aspects of my new environment and found ways to turn the things I didn't initially like into sources of enjoyment.

For instance, it's easy to agree that a sunny, warm day is generally more enjoyable than a cloudy, dark, rainy one. In San Luis Potosí, Mexico, most days were filled with bright, clear skies, while in Mechelen, Belgium, the weather was often the opposite—gray and rainy. Naturally, I missed the sunshine and the chance to wear summer dresses, which is entirely understandable!

If I had spent all my time focusing on the gloomy weather in Mechelen, I would have been miserable for over 300 days a year. Instead, I redirected my attention to the beautiful architecture, the countless excellent restaurants, the creative fashion, the rich and diverse culture, the ease of travel, and all the other beautiful aspects of life there.

I'm not a fan of constant rain, but my passion for photography allowed me to see it in a new light. Some of my favorite photos capture the stunning reflections of city lights on wet pavements at night, revealing a hidden beauty in the rain. Although I'm not keen on carrying umbrellas, I have a soft spot for stylish raincoats. So, I indulged in a few chic ones and found unexpected joy in wearing them, turning rainy days into something to look forward to. Whenever I grumbled about the weather, I quickly reminded myself that the lush greenery around me was a beautiful gift of that rain.

Not only did I distract my mind with the beauty around me in Belgium, but I also learned to enjoy something I didn't like—rain—by associating it with positive experiences, like wearing my favorite raincoat, taking beautiful pictures, or enjoying the landscape.

Life often challenges our comfort and stability, and we encounter moments when we must decide how to respond. In these moments, we face three fundamental choices: accept the situation, work to change it, or leave it behind. This chapter explores these three powerful options—accept, change, or leave—and how they can guide you in navigating life's challenges.

Before we proceed, let's take a moment to read a fragment of the Serenity Prayer—a timeless piece of wisdom that speaks to life's complexities. This prayer encapsulates the core themes of this chapter: letting go, embracing change, and liberating ourselves from the burdens that circumstances can place upon us.

Serenity Prayer

God grant me the serenity.
To accept the things I cannot change,
Courage to change the things I can,
And wisdom to know the difference.

Living one day at a time.
Enjoying one moment at a time.
Accepting hardships as the pathway to peace.
Taking, as He did, this sinful world....

-Reinhold Niebuhr-[87]

ACCEPT

Acceptance is the cornerstone of all change and the first step toward moving forward. The opposite of acceptance is resistance. Over time, resistance can lead to sadness, depression, irritability, anxiety, and resentment. But why do we resist, criticize, or try to change things we cannot control? The answer lies in our natural reaction to unpleasant situations—most of us respond with resistance or avoidance, which only worsens the problem.

You may think that the grass is greener on the other side. But before you jump to conclusions, ask yourself: Why am I here in the first place? Were there good reasons for my decision? Did I choose to be here, or was it out of necessity? Could I return to where I came from, and if so, how would my life be different now?

Be objective in your self-reflection. After answering these questions honestly, consider whether the grass is greener on the other side or if you only see part of the picture. If you conclude that life might be better elsewhere but must stay where you are due to factors like work, political circumstances, or marriage, the best approach is to practice radical acceptance

> " I can't change the direction of the wind, but I can adjust my sails to always reach my destination."
>
> — *Jimmy Dean*

until your situation can change.

Radical acceptance

Radical acceptance is a concept rooted in mindfulness and dialectical behavior therapy (DBT), popularized by psychologist Marsha Linehan. It involves fully accepting reality as it is, without resistance, judgment, or attempts to change it. Radical acceptance doesn't mean you approve of or agree with the situation; it means acknowledging the present moment and the circumstances you find yourself in, even if they are difficult or painful.[88]

The "radical" part of radical acceptance refers to its depth and completeness. It's about fully embracing reality without clinging to how things "should" be or wishing they were different. By practicing radical acceptance, you reduce the suffering from fighting against reality and instead find peace and clarity in facing the truth of your situation.

Accept your new reality as it is, with all its advantages and drawbacks. Appreciate the positives and recognize the challenges or difficulties you face. Fully immerse yourself in the present moment and let go of the past.

Remember, no perfect country, flawless city, or ideal home exists. I'm not perfect. You're not perfect. No one is perfect. Yet, there is profound beauty in that imperfection.

Acceptance doesn't mean surrendering to circumstances, giving up, or letting go of your goals and dreams. It means acknowledging where you are and allowing unwanted experiences to pass without attaching negativity, judgment, or resistance. Acceptance is about being fully present and recognizing reality as it is.

The sooner you accept your situation, understand that perfection is an illusion, and start focusing on the positives around you—finding joy in the small things—the more accessible and less painful your adaptation will be.

I had to embrace my reality: My family was far away, my social life wasn't as vibrant, I wasn't fluent in English, and the weather limited the outdoor activities I once loved. The food tasted different, and many of the ingredients I needed for cooking were hard to find. Domestic help and other services were also much more expensive than back home. Many aspects were beyond my control, and I needed to accept them and move forward, finding new ways to create joy and fulfillment in my new environment.

Ways to cultivate acceptance

Notice your resistance and question your patterns

When encountering something difficult or undesirable, pay close attention to your thoughts, emotions, and behaviors. Do you notice feelings of frustration, anger, or denial? Do you wish things were different, or are you trying to change something beyond your control?

Once you've identified your resistance, the next step is to question your patterns. This can be a liberating process. Ask yourself why you are resisting. What are you trying to avoid or protect yourself from? Is your resistance helping you or only adding to your distress? By exploring these questions, you can understand the underlying fears, beliefs, or expectations fueling your resistance.

Often, resistance to reality stems from unrealistic expectations about how life should be. Reflect on whether your expectations are adding to your suffering. Adjusting your expectations to align with reality can be an empowering step that helps you fully accept your situation.

Acknowledge your reality
Identify the aspects of your situation that are beyond your control. Accepting these uncontrollable factors is crucial for practicing acceptance.

Cultivate mindfulness
Engage in mindfulness practices that keep you grounded in the present moment. This can involve deep breathing, meditation, or simply paying attention to your thoughts and feelings without judgment. Mindfulness helps you stay aware of your reality without becoming overwhelmed by it.

Practice self-compassion
Be kind and compassionate with yourself as you practice radical acceptance. Recognize that it's okay to feel pain, disappointment, or frustration. Allow yourself to experience these emotions without judgment, and treat yourself with the kindness you would offer a friend in a similar situation.

Embrace gratitude
By developing a habit of focusing on the positive aspects of your life, even during challenging times. Practicing gratitude has a significant impact on mental and emotional well-being. It can help alleviate stress, anxiety, and symptoms of depression while fostering resilience and enhancing your ability to cope with adversity.

Use affirmations
Incorporate affirmations into your daily routine to reinforce radical acceptance. Phrases like "I accept this moment as it is," "I cannot change the past, but I can influence my future," or "I am at peace with what is" can be powerful tools in developing a mindset of acceptance.

Seek support if needed

Radical acceptance can be challenging, especially in tough situations. Don't hesitate to seek support from a therapist, counselor, priest, pastor, or support group to help you navigate the process.

I won't sugarcoat it—accepting reality can be challenging, especially when it doesn't meet your expectations. Know that this struggle is completely normal. The key is not to dwell in denial, comparison, or past regrets, as these will only bring more pain. Instead, choose to let go. Remember, resisting what it is doesn't change the reality—it only holds you back from finding peace and moving forward.

CHANGE

Now comes the exciting part—the moment when you have the power to create change and transform what you don't like. This phase takes courage because change isn't easy; it demands effort, discipline, and a willingness to step outside your comfort zone. However, with determination and persistence, you can reshape what you dislike and grow through the process.

So, what steps did I take? First, I enrolled in English lessons to build my language skills, which opened up new opportunities for connection and confidence. Then, I explored new hobbies to bring joy and fulfillment into my daily life and discovered indoor exercise methods to stay active and maintain my well-being. To keep a sense of home in my new environment, I asked family and friends who traveled to Mexico to bring back cherished ingredients, and whenever I had the chance to visit Mexico, I stocked up on items that reminded me of my roots.

To further integrate into my new surroundings, we began inviting people over and fostering new friendships, creating a sense of community that made all the difference. These changes took time—there were moments of doubt, and patience was key—but they were worth every effort. Each small step added up, leading to a life that felt more like my own, full of comfort, connection, and growth.

> Change is painful, but nothing is as painful as staying stuck somewhere you don't belong."

— *Mandy Hale*

What steps can you take today to create positive change in your life? Remember, it starts with small actions and a willingness to embrace the journey. Are you ready to step out of your comfort zone and transform what you don't like into something you love? The power is in your hands—what will you do with it?

How to implement changes

Identify what needs to change
Take time to assess your current situation and identify what needs to change. Is it a habit, mindset, relationship, or aspect of your environment? Understanding the root of your dissatisfaction is the first step.

Believe in yourself
This is essential to achieving your goals. Don't let impostor syndrome chip away at your confidence or stop you from moving forward. Release anything that holds you back. Thoughts like "I'm too old to learn a language," "I'm too young for that job," or "I'm not good at _____" are limiting beliefs that will keep you stuck unless you challenge them. Please pay close attention to your inner dialogue and shift it to one that empowers you.

Yes, it may be challenging. Yes, it may take time, effort, and resilience. You may stumble along the way, but that's okay—you can always pick yourself up and keep pushing forward. Remember, you've got this! Trust yourself, and don't let self-doubt or negative thoughts prevent you from reaching your potential.

Know that there is always someone out there who has faced similar "limitations" and has still reached the goals you aspire to achieve. Let their journey inspire you and remind you that it's possible. Most importantly, focus on everything you've already accomplished, the obstacles you've overcome, the skills you've developed, and the strength you've shown. Recognize your progress, and let it fuel your belief in what you can achieve.

Find fulfillment
Change should lead you toward a more enriched and satisfying life. Take a moment to recognize the potential benefits of changing and visualize how your life could improve. Imagine the confidence and opportunities that would come with speaking and understanding the local language, earning that sought-after certification, or securing the job you've always wanted. Now, compare the sense of pride and accomplishment you would feel after achieving these goals to how you feel now.

Understanding the "why" behind your goals is crucial. Be crystal clear about your motivations, and ensure they align with your values and what you genuinely care about. The journey becomes more meaningful when your goals resonate with your core beliefs and passions. The vision of your desired outcome should be powerful enough to inspire and energize you, driving you to put in the hard work and perseverance needed to achieve it. Let that vision be your compass, guiding you toward lasting fulfillment.

Develop an Action Plan

To create an effective action plan, you must first understand the steps required to achieve your objectives. What's the most effective approach to reach your goal? Do you know the specific steps you need to take? What challenges might arise, and what resources will you need? Before you begin, gather as much information as possible. Without a clear understanding of the process, it's easy to get lost and risk failure.

If you're unsure of the steps involved, seek help. Consult a professional in the field, or join a group or community related to your goal, where others can guide you in the right direction.

For example, if you want to learn a new language but don't know where to start, look for language tutors or classes. If you're going to run a marathon for the first time, research the necessary steps online, buy a book, or hire a trainer. Understanding the process is crucial for achieving success.

Change requires structure. Identify the actions, activities, materials, schedules, and support systems that will work for you and determine which ones won't.

Break it down

Break it down into smaller, manageable steps. Unrealistic goals can be overwhelming, leading to frustration and lacking motivation. For instance, if you aim to learn a new language in just two months while working from 8 a.m. to 6 p.m., picking up Children from school, cooking, cleaning, handling other chores, and spending time with your family. You may only have a few hours per week to study. Under these circumstances, learning a new language in such a short time frame isn't a realistic goal.

Break big goals into smaller,

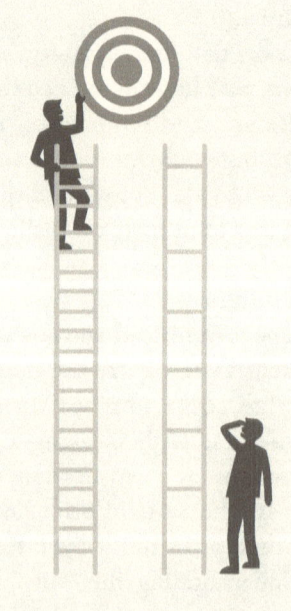

Figure 13: Smaller Steps

manageable steps to make them more achievable. Take it one day at a time, one step at a time.

Set S.M.A.R.T. Goals

George T. Doran introduced the "S.M.A.R.T. goals" concept in his 1981 paper, "There's a S.M.A.R.T. Way to Write Management's Goals and Objectives." In his article, Doran emphasized the significance of setting Specific, Measurable, Achievable, Relevant, and Time-bound goals. This framework has since gained widespread popularity in personal development and business management.[89]

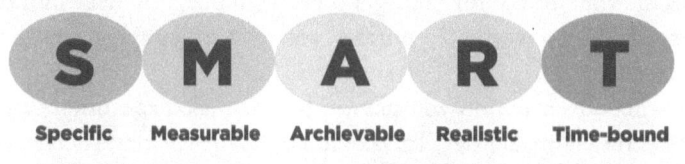

Figure 14: SMART Goals

Specific

Your goal should be clear and detailed. Ask yourself: What exactly do I want to accomplish? Why is it important? Who will be involved? Where and when do I want to achieve it? What resources do I have, and what do I still need? The more specific you are, the better.

For example, instead of saying, "I want to learn English in one year," be more precise: "I want to read a book in English and only need to look up fewer than two words per page. I want to be able to answer the phone, understand the conversation, and engage in a 30-minute discussion in English." Or "I want to go to a restaurant and be able to order without pointing at the menu."

Measurable

It's crucial to measure your progress. Determine your deadline and the criteria you'll use to evaluate your success. Use specific indicators like time, quantity, percentage, money, or other measurable outcomes. For instance, "I want to score above 90 on my TOEFL test."

Achievable

Set goals that are ambitious yet realistic. Break them into smaller, actionable steps and develop a strategy to achieve them. For example, "I'm going to study for two hours, five days a week. I aim to pass my English tests on the first attempt each time."

Relevant

Ensure that your goal is meaningful and aligns with your desires. It should be something that matters to you and contributes to your objectives. For example, "Learning English will help me make friends, secure a job, and communicate effectively at school.
"

Time-bound

Set a specific time frame for your goal. For instance, "By next month, I will have learned 50 new words, 20 phrases, and 10 verb conjugations, and I will pass my test."

Set a schedule; when do you plan to begin? Pick a meaningful start date and mark it on your calendar. This could be a symbolic day, such as your birthday, New Year's Day, or the start of a new month or week. Choosing a fresh start helps you visualize the "new you" compared to the "old you."

Next, block out specific days and times to work on your goal. This will increase your commitment and make it easier to achieve your objectives. Additionally, set a monthly reminder to check in on your progress.

Prioritize and Simplify

First, focus on the most impactful changes. Determine which steps will have the most significant positive effect and start with those.

Moving to a new country involves navigating many changes: adjusting to a new job, improving language skills, learning to navigate the local systems, finding doctors, schools, and hairdressers, understanding the culture, mastering traffic rules, and much more. The list can seem endless.

Everything might seem important, but not everything truly is.

It's crucial to prioritize. Identify your top three priorities for the week, and focus on one goal at a time. Start with the most critical task before moving on to the others.

Natte, a Brazilian friend of mine married to a Swede, temporarily moved to the U.S. for a three-year stay. From the outset, Natte consciously decided not to focus on learning English, even though it was what most people expected her to do. Her reasoning was straightforward: it simply wasn't a priority for her.

Natte already spoke Swedish, Portuguese, and Spanish and had a full schedule. She wanted to dedicate her time to what truly mattered to her: traveling, hosting gatherings with friends, and pursuing her passions in baking, cooking, gardening, fashion, and other personal interests that would enrich her life when she returned to Sweden.

She was realistic about her circumstances. Why should she commit time and energy to learning English? Her visa didn't allow her to work, and her husband was there to translate for medical or administrative appointments when needed. Without children navigating school-related communications and equipped with an AI translator for emergencies, Natte saw little benefit in investing in English, especially since she wasn't planning to stay in the U.S. long-term.

The only compelling reason might have been to make English-speaking friends. However, by the time she became fluent, it would almost be time to return to Sweden. Natte already had a strong circle of friends.

I admire Natte's thoughtful approach. Effectively prioritizing goals takes significant self-awareness, realistic expectations, and unwavering focus. She accomplished what was important to her by staying committed to her path and not getting sidetracked by external pressures or others' expectations.

The lesson here is powerful: Focus on what truly supports your goals and intentions and commit to those pursuits wholeheartedly.

Make It Enjoyable
Many procrastinate when they don't enjoy the activity or the process. Let's be honest—studying English for several hours straight isn't exactly fun. However, you can find ways to make it more engaging by incorporating fun elements.

If you enjoy movies, try watching one without subtitles and focus on following the dialogue or practicing pronunciation. You can do the same with music, listening to songs and trying to understand the lyrics. Or listen to a podcast while you go for a run. You might also study in your favorite coffee shop or practice with a friend. (see more in chapter #13). While there will inevitably be times when you need to sit down and study traditionally, you can complement this with more enjoyable learning methods.

Recognize Your Progress
Find a way to track your progress regularly. Without consistent tracking, it's easy to feel stagnant, quickly leading to frustration and loss of motivation. Staying consistent is essential for making meaningful, lasting change. Keep moving forward, even when progress isn't immediately visible—the steady steps make all the difference over time.

Take my experience with writing this book as an example. I've poured countless hours into this project for the past two years. Sometimes, it feels overwhelming and endless when I think about all the remaining tasks: finishing chapters, finding an editor, deciding on a title, designing the cover, and connecting with publishers and printers. It can be daunting.

However, when I take a moment to reflect on what I've already accomplished—over 85,000 words written and hitting my monthly writing goals for most of the journey—I feel a renewed sense of motivation. This progress reassures me that I'm steadily moving toward the finish line. Regularly acknowledging these milestones helps me stay energized and confident that I'm on the right path.

Make It Rewarding

When tackling significant changes—like learning a new language, earning a promotion, or immersing yourself in a new culture—don't wait until you've reached the end to reward yourself.

Break down the big goal into smaller steps, and celebrate each achievement. Celebrating even small victories triggers a release of "happy" chemicals in the brain, reinforcing feelings of success. This keeps your mindset positive, your motivation high, and your self-esteem growing.[90]

Rewards can be as simple as treating yourself to your favorite snack or drink after each English lesson. This way, you start associating learning with something positive, like enjoying a smoothie or a coffee.

As you hit intermediate milestones, such as advancing from level 1 to level 2, celebrate with something more unique, like a night out with someone you enjoy spending time with. For larger goals, consider treating yourself to a trip, a party, or buying something you've long wanted. Choose rewards that genuinely resonate with you and bring you joy.

Remember, most people struggle to stick with more painful activities than rewarding, so ensure your journey is filled with meaningful and enjoyable incentives.

Surround Yourself with the Right People

Seek out individuals who inspire, challenge, and uplift you. Connect with those who have already achieved the goals you aspire to and can share their journey with you. Learn from their experiences—how they overcame challenges, planned for success, and used strategies to reach their objectives.

Recognize the Benefits of the Outcome

Focus on the benefits of your progress to strengthen your commitment to change. For instance, studying and learning grammar rules might not be enjoyable, but noticing how it improves your communication, helps you make new friends, or enables you to understand the news on the radio can reinforce your dedication to studying.

Embrace a positive mindset that views change as an opportunity for growth rather than a threat. As Tony Robbins wisely said, "The purpose of a goal is not to achieve it but to become the person you grow into along the way."[91]

Cultivate Patience
Understand that meaningful change takes time. Be patient with yourself and the process, recognizing that transformation doesn't happen overnight.

Practice. Practice. Practice!
Repetition makes progress and increases the probability of success.

LEAVE

If you are deeply unsatisfied with your current situation and cannot accept or change it, you have only two options: leave or stay and continue feeling unhappy. Deciding to leave is significant and complex, so it's essential to assess whether relocating to where "the grass is greener" is realistic.

Start by considering the potential consequences. How feasible is moving back or relocating to a new place entirely? Weigh the benefits against the sacrifices you'd have to make. Would it be easier to leave than to try accepting or changing your current reality? Most importantly, would leaving genuinely make you happier in the long run?

Consider various scenarios. Perhaps you left a beautiful country because of war, insecurity, or political reasons, yet you still feel that life was better there. Could you return, and if so, would you be willing to sacrifice the peace and stability you currently have for what you miss?

Or perhaps you married someone from another country, moved there, and started a family, but now long for life in your own country. Is your partner willing to make the move with you? Would they be able to find a job there? What would be the implications for your children, lifestyle, and future?

Alternatively, you might have relocated for work but now find the new country challenging. Can you return and find employment back home? Would you prefer to be unemployed in your familiar environment rather than employed in a place that feels foreign or unsatisfactory?

These scenarios demand careful thought and consideration. Weigh the pros and cons and evaluate your emotional and practical needs. Ultimately, the choice should be guided by where your heart and mind align, whether that means staying and finding ways to make peace with your situation or making the brave decision to leave for a better, more fulfilling path.

FINAL THOUGHTS

We all dream of finding that perfect place where everything aligns, our desires are fulfilled, and life feels complete. But the reality is that such a place doesn't exist. Making decisions can be daunting, especially when no obvious answer exists. However, it's essential to remember that you always have choices: accept, change, or leave. Whatever you decide, steer clear of the fourth option—remaining stuck or unhappy—because that's the most complex and painful path.

If you're feeling disappointed, down, or lost, take a moment to pause and reflect. I hope you find clarity, wisdom, and courage to make the decision that's truly best for you.

The first step toward any meaningful change is awareness. Recognizing where you stand and understanding the factors at play is vital before you can act. Awareness lays the foundation for every step that follows, whether it involves improving your current situation, shifting your mindset, or pursuing a goal. It allows you to identify what is within your control and what isn't, guiding you toward making informed decisions and setting the stage for real progress.

Why does the grass often seem greener on the other side? While some elements may be out of your control (such as location, sun exposure, or soil quality), there are steps you can take to make your grass greener and thrive where you are. Are you ready to put in the effort to nurture your growth?

- **Water it more often:** Cultivate a positive mindset, practice mindfulness, express gratitude, and seek the good in your life.
- **Remove the weeds:** Eliminate negative thoughts and comparisons, break bad habits, and release denial or resistance.
- **Fertilize it:** Take proactive steps such as meeting new people, learning a new language, immersing yourself in the local culture, or obtaining the licenses or certifications needed to advance your career.

Remember, good things take time. Don't be discouraged if reaching your goals takes months or even years. Every action you take and every step forward brings you closer to your goal.

Lastly, meaningful change often requires building new habits and routines. Many people wish to change but struggle with how or where to start. Start small with intentional steps, and the path will become more apparent as you move forward. Stay committed to your journey, knowing that each step is progress toward the life you deserve, no matter how small.

KEY TAKEAWAYS

- When confronted with life's challenges, the notion that every problem has three possible solutions — accept it, change it, or leave it — is a powerful guiding principle for empowerment and growth.
- Acceptance demands that we embrace reality, even when it's uncomfortable or far from what we had hoped for.
- Radical acceptance involves letting go of what you can't control.
- Change calls for action, determination, and the willingness to step out of our comfort zone to create a better reality whenever possible.
- Leave involves letting go of what no longer serves us and moving forward with clarity and purpose.

CHAPTER 16

When in rome, do as The romans do... or not

"Adapt what is useful, reject what is useless,
and add what is specifically your own."
— Bruce Lee

One of my grandfather's golden rules was, *"In the country you visit, do as they do."* This resembles the well-known saying, *"When in Rome, do as the Romans do."* In other words, when you find yourself in a foreign land, it's wise to follow the local traditions, rules, and customs. By eating, dressing, behaving, and acting as the locals do, you can blend in more quickly and avoid unintentionally offending anyone. After all, as a visitor, it's respectful to adhere to their code of conduct.

I've always thought this was sound advice. Not only is it polite and helps you stay out of trouble in a foreign country, but it also allows you to fully immerse yourself in the new culture and gain more from the experience. It enables better interactions with locals and makes life abroad much smoother.

However, a part of me has always tended to challenge the rules. Don't get me wrong—I follow most rules, but I also question them. I must be convinced that following a rule is better than breaking it. So, I've asked myself: What if doing what the locals do goes against your core values? What if it puts your life in danger, causes you to lose authenticity, or harms yourself or others? In such cases, I believe it's better to be a rule-breaker.

If you can't find a solid and valid reason not to try something new, go for it whenever possible. Step out of your comfort zone and face your fears. These new experiences will enrich your life the most. But never do something that compromises your well-being or values.

ADAPTING TO NEW ENVIRONMENTS

At its core, the phrase "When in Rome, do as the Romans do" encourages us to respect and adopt the customs of the place we visit or inhabit. This approach demonstrates respect for the local culture and allows us to experience life from a different perspective.

One of the most significant benefits of adapting to new environments is deepening our cultural awareness. When we take the time to learn about and participate in the customs of others, we gain insights into their values, beliefs, and worldviews. This cultural immersion can challenge preconceived notions and broaden our worldview. For instance, a traveler who adopts local customs—such as participating in a traditional festival or learning a few phrases in the local language—often feels welcomed and appreciated by the community.

Adaptability is not just about cultural sensitivity but also a key factor in personal and professional success. We expand our capabilities and resilience by embracing new ways of thinking and doing. Adapting to a new environment—learning a new language, adjusting to a different work culture, or navigating unfamiliar social norms—can be daunting. However, overcoming these challenges strengthens our adaptability muscles and builds confidence in our ability to handle change. Over time, we become more open-minded, resourceful, and versatile individuals.

However, adaptation does not mean abandoning our identity or mindlessly conforming to every new situation. True adaptability involves finding a balance between respecting the new environment and staying true to our core values and beliefs. It is about being flexible without losing our sense of self. In this sense, the wisdom of "When in Rome, do as the Romans do" is not about conformity but about harmony—about finding ways to coexist and thrive within different cultural and social frameworks.

EATING WITH YOUR HANDS

In my family, the rules of etiquette were non-negotiable, especially for my mom. Table manners weren't the exception. She drilled the correct placement of forks, knives, spoons, glasses, napkins, and plates into us. We had special utensils for everything—fish, meat, dessert—you name it. And heaven help you if you dared put your elbows on the table! She taught us where to sit if we were the host and to ask if we were the guests. There were rules upon rules, and using your hands to eat was generally a big no-no—unless you were eating tacos, pizza, hamburgers, or maybe a few appetizers.

So, you can imagine my inner turmoil when I found myself in an authentic Indian restaurant during a trip to Asia. I'd always loved Indian food, but until then, I had only tried it in American restaurants. This time, I was in a non-tourist area, surrounded by Indians who knew what authentic Indian cuisine was all about. I asked for recommendations and ended up in a packed restaurant where I was likely the only non-Indian person present. The aroma of spices was fantastic, and everyone around me seemed to be in a state of food bliss.

I didn't know the names of any of the dishes, so I asked for the house's specialty. Here's where things got interesting. The food was served on a banana leaf instead of a plate, and I was brought curry-marinated chicken, white Basmati rice, three different kinds of sauces, and Naan bread. Noticeably absent? Utensils.

As I glanced around, I realized everyone was eating with their right hand, using their fingers as makeshift spoons. Now, eating pizza or a taco with your hands is one thing, but tackling wet curry and rice with just your fingers? It's an art. Eating a taco without dropping the ingredients out requires some skills, but my taco-eating skills were useless here. Eating wet food with your fingers is another level.

But I wouldn't let my concerns about messy fingers ruin the experience. I dug in—literally—using my fingers and bread to scoop up the food. At first, it felt strange, a mix of excitement and rebellion. This would be considered inappropriate table manners back home. In Mexico, or most Western countries, this kind of manners would earn you the label of someone with terrible etiquette, or worse, as a "disgusting eater." Yet here, not only was it accepted—it was expected. It was liberating to break free from Western dining etiquette and enjoy the food.

Of course, not all restaurants in India follow this practice. Many modern establishments provide utensils—except for knives, as is common in many Asian countries since the food is typically prepared in bite-sized portions. Additionally, different regions have their unique dining customs. However, in more traditional settings, eating with your hands is a cultural norm that enhances the sensory experience of a meal.

Have you ever closely observed a baby eating? Well, I felt like one (in a good way), a little child, amazed by the feeling of touching and discovering new sensations through my fingertips. Exploring food with all their senses and tasting the food's temperature, texture, and consistency. It connected me better with the food and the present moment.

Eating with your hands engages all your senses in the meal. You can smell the rich spices more vividly and appreciate the vibrant colors of the curry, rice, sauces, and bread, all beautifully contrasted against the bright green banana leaf. Before reaching your mouth, you feel each bite's warmth, texture, and consistency. And as you savor each morsel, you can hear the subtle crunchiness in your mouth. It was an entirely new way of experiencing food that made the meal taste even better.

I broke the etiquette rules I was raised with and embraced the local customs. It might not look fancy by Western standards, but the food tasted better this way. Sometimes, to truly enjoy life—and food—you have to be willing to get your hands dirty.

THE SPA EXPERIENCE

Living in Belgium, I searched for the perfect wedding anniversary gift for my husband. As someone who values experiences over material possessions, I wanted to find something unique.

Belgium is renowned for its spas; interestingly, the term "spa" originated from Spa, located in the Province of Liège. In the 14th century, this town became famous for its curative thermal spring waters. "Spa" derives from the Latin spargere, meaning sprinkle or moisten.

What could be better for a wedding anniversary than a couple's massage in a spa located in Spa?

I searched for the best spas in Belgium and found one that looked extraordinary. The exterior resembled a castle, and the interior boasted pristine facilities, including saunas, thermal pools of varying temperatures, ice pools, Jacuzzis, and steam rooms. It felt like a place out of a fairytale.

Without hesitation, I booked a couple's package, which included a welcome glass of champagne and appetizers, a one-hour couples massage, and unlimited time at the spa. I was thrilled to have found the perfect anniversary gift and couldn't wait to experience it.

On the day of our appointment, we woke up early and headed to the spa, arriving a few hours before our massage to make the most of the facilities. Upon our arrival, we were greeted by our concierge, who, as promised, welcomed us with a glass of champagne and beautifully arranged appetizers. She invited us to relax in the lounge area, where she pointed out the locations of the lockers, massage rooms, bathrooms, showers, and other amenities and explained the procedure and our massage schedule.

After we enjoyed our champagne and appetizers, the hostess returned with two bathrobes on a neatly arranged tray. "Here are your bathrobes," she said. You can head to the changing room, undress, leave your belongings in the lockers, and enjoy the facilities at your leisure. Bathrobes are required only in the lounge area. I'll pick you up here ten minutes before your massage appointment to escort you."

Wait, what? Did she say "undress"? I assumed she meant to change into a bathing suit. Sensing my confusion, she added, "Bathing suits or other clothing are prohibited in the spa. Bathrobes are only for drying off or wearing while eating or drinking."

I looked at my husband in disbelief. Somehow, I had missed the fact that this was a nude spa! A mixed-gender spa!

Having grown up in a conservative family with strict beliefs about modesty, the idea of being naked in front of strangers, especially men, was shocking to me. My upbringing had ingrained the notion that exposing too much skin was inappropriate, even provocative. Being naked in front of anyone other than your spouse was considered almost immoral in my culture.

But here we were. I had spent significant money on this experience, driven nearly two hours, and it was our wedding anniversary gift. I didn't want to miss out, but the thought of being naked in front of strangers was nerve-wracking.

After discussing it with my husband, we decided to try it. We were already there, after all. We could always retreat to the lounge area and wait for our massage if we felt uncomfortable.

At that moment, I desperately needed more champagne! But instead, I headed to the changing area and undressed. The pool seemed like the best place to start, as the water would at least partially cover my naked body. As I walked toward the pool, I became hyper-aware of my body. Had I shaved properly? Was I too pale? Did my belly show too much? Was it in good shape? It felt incredibly awkward to walk naked into the common area, surrounded by other naked people. I consciously tried to resist the urge to cover myself with my hands. I felt so awkwardly exposed.

Finally, I gathered the courage to enter the pool and tried the sauna, steam room, and various pools. The first 10 to 15 minutes were the toughest. But gradually, I began to feel more comfortable in my skin. Why? Because no one else seemed to care. The other guests were accustomed to nudity in these settings and saw it as entirely natural.

No one stared, harassed, or made anyone feel uncomfortable. Not the nervous newcomers like us, not the young, fit individuals, and not the older or less conventionally attractive ones. Everyone was respectful, minding their own business and relaxing. After all, that's what a spa is for, right?

As I started to relax, I found myself enjoying the experience. I loved how the water, steam, sun, and air felt directly on my skin.

I began to question why we create such taboos around nudity. Why do some cultures make people feel so ashamed of their bodies? Why do we fear showing our imperfections? Why is it acceptable for the young to expose some of their skin, but not the elderly? Why do humans, in many societies, feel shame or discomfort about their nudity despite being born naked? How do gender dynamics influence societal attitudes toward nudity, and why is female nudity often more heavily policed than male nudity?

Clothing was initially created out of necessity, designed to protect us from the harshness of the elements—keeping us warm in the cold, shielding us from the sun, and offering protection from the environment. Over time, clothing evolved beyond mere functionality to become a powerful tool for self-expression, allowing individuals to convey their identity, social status, cultural background, and personal style. However, the role of clothing in society has become far more complex, influenced by taboos, marketing, and religious beliefs, which have all significantly shaped how we view and use clothing today.

This experience challenged my perspective. I'm glad it was an unforgettable and worthwhile experience in a safe, respectful, and controlled environment—a naturist spa. It's important to note that not all nudity-focused places are the same. Some nudist beaches or resorts cater more to hedonistic pursuits, where people go for sexual pleasure. Naturist places, on the other hand, have strict codes of conduct to ensure everyone feels comfortable (e.g., no photography, staring, or sexual activity).

I left the spa feeling like a different person.

I felt refreshed, confident, and rejuvenated—not just because of the splendid massage but because I had stepped out of my comfort zone. I confronted my fear of being naked in front of strangers and, in doing so, changed the way I view nudity. From that day on, I began to see nudity as something natural.

This experience transformed me. I became more confident in my skin, more accepting and loving my body as it is, and less judgmental about others' bodies. I started to shed the taboos around nudity that had been instilled in me.

This openness to nudity isn't just for spas or beaches. It extends to mixed-gender locker rooms, doctor's offices, and other everyday settings.

When I visited my gynecologist there, he said, "Okay, undress and lie on the table." I hesitated, expecting him to leave the room or hand me a robe, as is customary in other cultures. But nope—he just sat there, waiting. So, nervously and awkwardly, I started undressing, lay on the table, and tried to act like this was normal. He quickly checked, said everything was fine, and casually returned to his desk as if nothing had happened.

In Mexico, doctors step out and give you a robe. In the U.S., it's the same, but when they come back, they usually bring a nurse—probably to ensure you don't sue them for unprofessional touching.

Very few people know this story. I never imagined I would share it so openly, much less write about it in a book. My parents, family, and friends are unaware of it. Why? Perhaps because I fear their reaction—their disappointment, judgment, or lack of approval. Or maybe because I don't want to hear the lecture that would inevitably follow.

I'm sharing this now because this experience liberated me from the beliefs imposed on me—beliefs passed down through generations. I'm sharing it to emphasize the importance of being open-minded and learning to see things from new perspectives. This doesn't mean you have to agree or take the same path but rather recognize that other perspectives are equally valid. It's also essential to emphasize the importance of questioning your beliefs—not determining whether they are right or wrong, but exploring their deeper reasons.

Ask yourself: Do I hold these beliefs because they resonate with me or because someone else told me this is what I should believe? Am I convinced of their truth, or have I accepted them without reflection? This introspection can lead to a richer understanding of yourself and the world, empowering you to live more authentically.

By embracing nudity in that spa, I neither harmed anyone, put my life at risk, nor compromised my core values. Yes, it was very uncomfortable, but it was also profoundly freeing. It was incredible to witness how others interacted with nudity in such a natural, non-judgmental way, devoid of any morbid curiosity.

Now, I can already picture my mom, mother-in-law, and a few friends widening their eyes in sheer disbelief as they read this. But in my defense, I was following my grandfather's sage advice: "When in Rome, do as the Romans do." The only problem? He forgot to include the fine print about the exceptions! So, here's to living a little, stepping out of your comfort zone, and realizing that sometimes, the best experiences come from embracing the unexpected—even if it means dropping more than inhibitions!

WHEN IN ROME? NOT ALWAYS

While "When in Rome, do as the Romans do" can foster cultural understanding and respect, there are times when following the crowd can lead to compromising your values and engaging in unethical or harmful practices. In such situations, it's crucial to remember that not all customs are worth adopting, and sometimes, standing firm in your principles is the best course of action.

For example, find yourself in a business environment where cutting corners or engaging in dishonest practices is the norm. It might be usual to falsify reports, inflate numbers and bravery, and engage in unethical practices to achieve targets or secure deals. Even if everyone around you seems to be doing it, participating in such behavior can lead to legal consequences, damage your professional reputation, conflict with your ethics, and affect your self-respect. In this case, it's essential to uphold your integrity and refuse to engage in practices that compromise your values, even if it means standing out or facing peer pressure.

Another example is if you're traveling in a region where animal cruelty is part of traditional entertainment, such as bullfighting in some countries. Even though it's a local custom and has cultural significance, participating in or supporting such events might go against your ethical beliefs about the treatment of animals. In this case, it's imperative to stand by your values rather than just following the local customs, as doing so could contribute to practices that you fundamentally disagree with.

***

Similarly, there are moments in everyday life when standing up for what you believe in is essential, even when it means going against familiar traditions or the expectations of those around you.

I'm proud of my daughter for stepping up and speaking out. She was spending time with her cousins, and they began making racially charged jokes. As I've mentioned before, in Mexico, humor often covers everything, including ourselves, and it's usually not meant to offend—so people are typically not easily offended or inclined to take it personally. Everyone laughed except for my daughter. With a steady voice, she said, "Hey, I know it might not have been your intention, but jokes like that can be hurtful and perpetuate negative stereotypes. Please stop."

A moment of tension filled the room. For her cousins, it was just "harmless fun." One of them responded, "Why are you so upset? The joke isn't even about you. Don't be so serious." Without missing a beat, she replied, "It doesn't have to be about me for me to stand against it. Humor doesn't need to come at the expense of others, even if they aren't here. We should always show respect."

I couldn't be prouder of her for standing by her values and speaking up, even when it meant going against the crowd. In these situations, it's essential to remember your core values and the principles that guide your actions. Upholding your integrity, even in the face of pressure to conform, not only preserves your moral compass but also sets a positive example for others.

Ultimately, "When in Rome, do as the Romans do" should be taken cautiously. While respecting cultural differences and adapting where appropriate, it's equally important to recognize when a local practice conflicts with your ethical standards. In those moments, staying true to your values is the right choice, ensuring that your actions align with your integrity and the broader principles of justice and fairness.

LIKE IT OR NOT: LOCAL CUSTOMS AND LAW

Sometimes, while traveling or living abroad, you may come across customs, traditions, or laws significantly different from what you're accustomed to—and occasionally, you might not even agree with them. However, it's often wiser to follow these practices for your safety and to show respect for the local culture, even if they feel unfamiliar or uncomfortable.

Understanding how local people expect you to behave and recognizing their daily practices is essential to fitting in and avoiding potential problems. There are two main types: enforced laws and unspoken codes of conduct.

Enforced laws are the rules you must obey to avoid legal consequences such as fines or imprisonment. For example, in Iraq, women are expected to cover their entire bodies in public. In Singapore, chewing gum is banned, and blowing bubbles on the street can get you fined. Swearing in the U.A.E. is illegal and can lead to severe penalties. In Rome, dog owners are required by law to walk their pets daily, and in Japan, dancing in most public venues after midnight is prohibited. While these laws might seem excessive or unnecessary based on cultural norms, ignoring them can put your safety, freedom, or finances at risk.

Non-spoken codes of conduct are behaviors that, while not legally enforced, are expected by locals and can make your interactions smoother and more pleasant. Adapting to local customs—such as practicing the local greeting, removing your shoes when entering someone's home, being mindful of your voice volume and personal space, and avoiding offensive gestures or actions can help you connect with the culture and avoid misunderstandings.

In many cases, actions that seem harmless in your culture, like chewing gum, wearing a summer dress, or making eye contact, can be interpreted differently in another country. To ensure a safe and respectful experience, it's often wise to follow local rules and customs, even when they differ from what you believe or are accustomed to.

STAYING TRUE TO YOUR VALUES

How do you balance honoring traditions and cultural expectations while staying true to your values? How do you determine when to challenge the norms that have shaped your identity, even if it means standing alone?

Navigating different cultures, environments, and social situations often requires a delicate balance between staying true to one's authentic self and adapting to the expectations and norms of one's surroundings. By staying true to your authentic self and embracing the adaptive self, you can navigate different environments with confidence, integrity, and respect.[92]

Adaptive self

All humans need to feel loved, accepted, connected, and have a sense of belonging. To fulfill these needs, we often develop an adaptive self—a version of ourselves that helps us navigate challenging situations and adjust to different environments by aligning with a group's or society's expectations and norms.

This aspect of your personality allows you to fit in, connect with others, and navigate the complexities of social interactions. Adaptation is essential for building relationships, finding common ground, and succeeding in various contexts—whether in a foreign country, a new job, or a different social circle.

The adaptive self acts as a shield, protecting us from rejection and judgment. It follows the rules, conforms to societal norms, and represents who we think we should be rather than who we indeed are.

While adaptation is often necessary, it comes with the risk of losing touch with your authentic self. When you constantly adapt to fit in, you may compromise your values or suppress your true feelings and beliefs. The key is to adapt in a way that allows you to engage with the world around you while still holding onto your core identity.

Authentic self

The authentic self is the core of who you are— your values, beliefs, personality, the things that genuinely make you happy, and desires that define your identity (Chapter #1). It's the part of you that remains constant, regardless of external influences. Being in touch with your authentic self means understanding your principles and what you stand for, even when pressured to conform. It's the self that feels real, confident, and whole. The one who confronts fears steps out of their comfort zone and explores new and unfamiliar experiences with courage.

Fitting in
Is becoming who you think you need to be in order to be accepted.
Belonging
Is being your authentic self and knowing that no matter what happens, you belong to you.

....

— *Brene Brown*

Staying true to your authentic self is crucial for maintaining integrity and self-respect. It allows you to decide based on what genuinely matters to you rather than simply following the crowd or succumbing to external expectations. However, staying rooted in your authentic self can sometimes be challenging in a world where we are constantly exposed to different cultures, ideologies, and social norms.

When we betray our authentic selves to gain acceptance from society, we often feel resentment, sadness, and anger. This disconnect between who we are and who we present ourselves to be can lead to inner conflict.

Finding balance

Exposing ourselves to a new culture allows us to question our beliefs, values, and emotions, helping us connect more deeply with our authentic selves. Yet, there's a risk of trying too hard to fit into a new culture, leading to losing touch with who we are. This can create a sense of not belonging anywhere—neither in your home culture nor the new one.

The challenge lies in finding the right balance between authenticity and adaptability. This balance is not about sacrificing one for the other but integrating both aspects to enrich your experience and personal growth. Here are some strategies to help you achieve this balance:

Know Your Non-Negotiables

Identify the values and beliefs fundamental to your identity and non-negotiable in any situation. It would be best never to compromise these aspects of your authentic self, regardless of external pressures. Knowing your non-negotiables allows you to navigate different environments confidently without losing your sense of self.

Adapt Without Losing Integrity

Adaptation doesn't mean abandoning your principles. Instead, find ways to align your authentic self with the expectations of your surroundings. For example, suppose you value honesty but find yourself in a culture where direct communication is frowned upon. In that case, you can still maintain integrity by being truthful in a respectful and culturally appropriate manner.

Practice Cultural Sensitivity

Understanding and respecting the customs and norms of different cultures doesn't mean you have to adopt them entirely. You can engage with new cultures in a way that honors their traditions while staying true to your values. Cultural sensitivity involves listening, learning, and finding common ground rather than simply conforming or rejecting what's unfamiliar.

Reflect and Recalibrate

Regular self-reflection is crucial for maintaining authenticity and adaptability. Assess whether your actions align with your true self and whether your adaptations enhance or diminish your sense of identity. If you are straying too far from your authentic self, recalibrate and realign your actions with your core values.

Embrace the Dynamic Self

Recognize that your identity is not static but dynamic, capable of evolving and growing through new experiences. The balance between your authentic and adaptive selves is not a fixed point but a fluid process that changes over time. Embracing this dynamic nature allows you to remain open to growth while staying grounded in who you are.

Prepare to Be Vulnerable

Being honest with yourself and those around you requires vulnerability as you express your thoughts and feelings, show your imperfections, and potentially disappoint those with different views.

***

The ideal balance lies in being true to yourself while embracing the best aspects of the cultures you encounter and letting go of outdated patterns and beliefs that no longer serve you. In other words, "do as the Romans do" when it aligns with your values, beliefs, and goals, but remain authentic when local customs conflict with who you are. If staying true to yourself puts you at risk, prioritize your safety, consider relocating to a safer environment, or become a catalyst for change, fully aware of the risks involved.

Ultimately, the goal is not just to fit into your old or new society but to foster a sense of belonging. It's about embracing your authenticity and adaptability, building a life that reflects who you are while staying deeply engaged with the world. Living authentically allows your core identity to guide your actions as you adapt to new experiences. It's about being open to learning and evolving while staying anchored to the values that define you.

Balancing your authentic and adaptive selves doesn't mean choosing one over the other; it's about integrating both to create a life that resonates with your true nature while remaining responsive to the world. This balance allows you to cultivate meaningful relationships, discover purpose, and find fulfillment. Living authentically enriches your life and inspires others, fostering a culture of honesty, trust, and respect.

Embracing your true self challenges outdated norms and encourages others to do the same, shaping a world that values diversity, inclusivity, and genuine self-expression.

KEY TAKEAWAYS

- Adaptive self is the aspect of your personality that allows you to fit in, connect with others, and navigate the complexities of social interactions.
- Authentic self is the core of who you are—your values, beliefs, personality, the things that genuinely make you happy, and desires that define your identity.
- True adaptability involves balancing respect for new environments while staying true to one's core values and beliefs.
- Over-adapting to new cultures can lead to losing touch with one's authentic self and feeling disconnected from home and new cultures.
- Living authentically and embracing diversity helps challenge societal norms and inspires others, fostering a more compassionate and inclusive world.

"True belonging doesn't require you to change who you are; it requires you to be who you are."[93]

EPILOGUE/CONCLUSION

Living abroad or immersing yourself in other cultures is not just about external exploration—it's a deeply personal, transformative journey that begins with understanding yourself. As the captain of your voyage, it's essential to know your values, beliefs, and biases, which allows for a more profound understanding of others. Each of us views the world uniquely, and by learning to see through different cultural lenses, we can connect, communicate, and empathize more effectively. This process leads to personal growth, helping you shed limiting beliefs and adopt new values that align with your authentic self.

In the end, by embracing the diversity of other cultures, you learn more about the world and who you indeed are. It's a journey of constant transformation, allowing you to evolve into a more open-minded and genuine version of yourself, enriching your personal and professional life.

ACKNOWLEDGMENTS

Writing Global Citizen has been an extraordinary journey of growth and reflection, and I am deeply grateful to everyone who has walked this path with me.

To my husband, Jose Luis, my lifelong adventure companion, thank you for standing beside me through every twist and turn, sharing dreams, challenges, and triumphs. Andrea and Luis, you are the greatest teachers I could ask for, showing me patience, resilience, and how to see the world with curiosity, kindness, and hope.

To my parents, Jorge and Toyi, my greatest cheerleaders, your unwavering belief in me, encouragement, and boundless pride have been the foundation of everything I've achieved. You've taught me the power of self-belief, persistence, and determination, and I will always treasure your love and support.

To my brothers, Paco and Jorge, you've been my constant best friends, bringing humor, camaraderie, and unwavering support into my life. To my brothers' families, my cousins, uncles, aunts, nieces, nephews, and my grandparents, both present and those who are no longer with us. I have always said I'm the luckiest to be part of this family, and it is what I treasure most in this world. Your love and encouragement have carried me forward every step of the way.

Thanks to Nelson and Mindy Worden for welcoming me into their home and giving me my first unforgettable experience living abroad. Thanks for your kindness and generosity.

To my talented writing club friends—Brooke Manning, William Johnson, Christy Hubbard, and Rudy Lopes, your invaluable feedback, patience, and support helped bring this book to life. It wouldn't have been possible without your guidance.

To my friends and colleagues worldwide, thank you for challenging my thinking and inspiring me to grow. Each of you has played a unique role in shaping this book. I am incredibly grateful to those who believed in my dream, cheered me on, and directly contributed: Francisco Olguin, William Johnson, Monica Chavez, Adriana Ugarte, Maria Guadalupe Castañeda, Luis De Alba, Andrea De Alba, Jose Luis De Alba, Ariadna Fergadis, Jorge Diaz Barajas, and Adriana Brito. Your support was invaluable in designing, reviewing, or sharing resources. To my clients, you were the spark that ignited this project. Your stories, challenges, and triumphs inspired every word.

To my readers, you are the heart of this book. Your curiosity, openness, and enthusiasm for global citizenship have been my guiding light. Thank you for embracing this journey and believing in the power of connection across cultures.

To all who have helped along the way—the authors and sources who have informed my work—I have done my best to credit you fully.

Finally, to all the angels I have encountered on my journey, those who have shown me that this world is brimming with kindness and compassion. Your light has guided me and continues to inspire my belief in the beauty of humanity.

This book exists because of all of you. Thank you from the bottom of my heart.

BIBLIOGRAPHY

Chapter 1

1 Tylor, Edward. *Culture Definition.* Primitive Culture. Vol 1. New York: J.P. Putnam's Son. Adapted from: 1871

2 **Iceberg Culture:** Hall, Edward T, *Beyond Culture.* **Anchor Books.** 1977.

3 "I am not who I think I am; I am not who you think I am; I am who I think you think I am.": Cooley, Charles Horton 1902.

4 **Bias.** "a prejudice in favor of or against one thing, person, or group compared with another, usually in a way considered unfair.": The Oxford Diccionary.

5 There are 188 known cognitive biases that impact our thinking and actions.: Desjardins, Jeff. Every Single Cognitive Bias in One Infographic (visualcapitalist.com). 2021. https://www.visualcapitalist.com/every-single-cognitive-bias/#google_vignette

6 **Understanding Cognitive Biases:** Linus. *"Behavioral Finance: Understanding How Psychology Affects Investing"* - Dollarscaler. 2024. https://dollarscaler.com/behavioral-finance-understanding-how-psychology-affects-investing/

7 **The History of the White Wedding Dress:** Forrest, Kim. *"The (Surprising!) History of the White Wedding Dress.".* 2019. https://www.weddingwire.com/wedding-ideas/white-wedding-dress-history

8 **A Natural History of the Wedding Dress:** Brennan, Summer. *"A Natural History of the Wedding Dress".* - JSTOR Daily. 2017. https://daily.jstor.org/a-natural-history-of-the-wedding-dress/

Chapter 4

9 Numerous scholars have explored the concept of time in relation to different cultures. Ideas are drawn from their work, then modified through my

experiences and adapted based on my observations:

Hall, Edward T.: examined the contrast between monochronic (linear) and polychronic (cyclical) time orientations.

Hofstede, Geert: analyzed long-term versus short-term orientation as part of his cultural dimensions theory, emphasizing how societies plan for the future or focus on immediate results.

Trompenaars, Fons: differentiated between sequential and synchronic time orientations.

Lewis, Richard: categorized cultures into linear-active, multi-active, and re-active time orientations, offering insights into how various societies approach time management and relationships.

Hall, Edward T. *The Dance of Life: The Other Dimension of Time.* Knopf Doubleday Publishing Group. 1984.

Hofstede, Geert. *Cultures and Organizations – Software of the Mind.* McGraw-Hill. "Chapter 7: Yesterday, Now or Later". 2010.

Trompenaars, Fons. Hampden-Turner, Charles. *Riding the Waves of Culture: Understanding Diversity in Global Business.* Nicholas Brealey Publishing. 2020.

Lewis, Richard D. *When Cultures Collide: Leading Across Cultures.* 4th Edition Paperback. **Nicholas Brealey.** 2018.

[10] **India Train.** 22 million passengers daily: Sun, Shangliao. "Passenger traffic in railways across India from financial year 2010 to 2022. Indian railway passenger traffic FY 2010-2022". Statista. 2023. https://www.statista.com/statistics/726386/india-railway-passenger-traffic/

[11] **Muhurtha is a science of timing based on Vedic (Hindu) astronomy:** "Muhurat in Panchang". AstroYogi. 2024. https://www.astroyogi.com/panchang/muhurat

And "Muhurta Shastra - The Science of Auspicious Timing" The Divine India. 2024. https://www.thedivineindia.com/muhurta-shastra-the-science-of-auspicious-timing/7561#:~:text=Muhurta%20Shastra%2C%20also%20known%20as%20the%20science%20of,%22time%2C%22%20while%20%22shastra%22%20refers%20to%20%22science%22%20or%20%22knowledge.%22

[12] **Abhijit Muhurat, an auspicious 48-minute window:** Astrobix. "Abhijit Muhurat and its Importance | Astrological Aspect Behind the Abhijit Muhurta" 2024. https://astrobix.com/astroblog/1194-abhijit-muhurat-and-its-importance-astrological-aspect-behind-the-abhijit-muhurta.html

[13] Kamen, Robert Mark. *The Karate Kid* Film. Director: John G. Avildsen. Writer: Robert Mark Kamen. Columbia Pictures. 1984.

[14] "**Nemawashi** (根回し) is a Japanese gardening term that translates to

"turning the roots." Before transplanting a plant, gardeners give special attention to each portion of the roots, loosening them gradually before relocating them to ensure healthy growth. Rushing this process could kill the tree.: "NE-MAWASHI - JAPANESE CONSENSUS BUILDING
Why is an Understanding of "Nemawashi" Important?". Cultural Savy. https://www.culturalsavvy.com/japan_Nemawashi.htm#:~:text=Nemawashi%20is%20a%20Japanese%20term%20that%20translates%20to,individually%20digging%20each%20portion%20of%20the%20root%20system.

[15] **What is Nemawashi?:** Clifford, Joe. "What is Nemawashi? Toyota Production System Guide". Toyota UK Magazine. 2024. https://mag.toyota.co.uk/nemawashi-toyota-production-system/

Chapter 5

[16] "World Inequality Database." Gini Index. WorldBank.org (worldbank.org). 2023. https://data.worldbank.org/indicator/SI.POV.GINI?most_recent_year_desc=false
[17] **The order in which business cards are exchanged in Japan is also crucial.** Matsuoka, Tomoko. "Japan Business Card Etiquette: What to Know and Do." Mailmate. 2023. https://mailmate.jp/blog/introductions-japanese-clients
[18] **Japanese business card will list the company name first.** Laura. "Complete Guide to Japanese Business Card Etiquette." Yougo Japan. https://yougojapan.com/japanese-business-card-etiquette/
[19] **England Birth Oder.** "British royal family line of succession: Who's who." CNN. 2022https://www.cnn.com/2022/09/08/world/royal-family-line-of-succession/index.html
[20] **Succession to the Saudi Arabian throne.** Wikipidia.
[21] **Companies like Missoni, Fendi, Salvatore Ferragamo, and Ermenegildo Zegna have successfully transferred ownership and management from one generation to the next.** Olsen, Kerry. "The Italian Fashion Family Diaspora Increasingly the children of the most famous brands are going their own ways." The New York Times. 2022.
[22] **Duignan, Brian.Varna:** Hinduism. Britannica. 2024. https://www.britannica.com/topic/varna-Hinduism.
[23] **Class Entitlement. Adapted from several sources:**
Global Caste: "IV. Background: "Untouchability" and Segregation." Human Rights Watch.
https://www.hrw.org/reports/2001/globalcaste/caste0801-03.htm
"What is India's caste system?." BBC News. 2019. https://www.bbc.com/

news/world-asia-india-35650616. 19

Szczepanski, Kallie. "History of India's Caste System." ThoughtCo. 2020. https://www.thoughtco.com/history-of-indias-caste-system-195496

[24] **Indian Constitution:** Law Notes. "Article 17 of the Indian Constitution: Abolition of Untouchability – LAW Notes." https://lawnotes.co/article-17-of-the-indian-constitution-abolition-of-untouchability/

[25] In 2022, Iceland ranked first in the World Economic Forum's Global Gender Gap Report:, achieving a 90.8% score, and placed third on the Women, Peace, and Security Index (WPS). World Economic Forum. 2021 with a near-perfect score of 0.907.

"Gender gap: These are the world's most gender-equal countries." 2022. World Economic Forum. 2022.

https://www.weforum.org/agenda/2022/07/gender-equal-countries-gender-gap/.

[26] **Gender Gaps:** Adapted from: Finnbogadóttir, Vigdís. Henshall, Angela. "What Iceland can teach the world about gender pay gaps." BBC News. 2018. https://www.bbc.com/worklife/article/20180209-what-iceland-can-teach-the-world-about-gender-pay-gaps.

[27] "Politically, Iceland. Global Gender Gap Report." World Economic Forum. 2022.

https://www.weforum.org/publications/global-gender-gap-report-2022/in-full/1-benchmarking-gender-gaps-2022/.

[28] Wagner, Ines. "How Iceland Is Closing the Gender Wage Gap." Harvard Business Review. 2021.

https://hbr.org/2021/01/how-iceland-is-closing-the-gender-wage-gap.

[29] "The labor force participation rate of women has never been higher." Statistic Iceland. 2017.https://statice.is/publications/news-archive/social-affairs/key-figures-on-women-and-men/#:~:text=The%20labour%20force%20participation%20rate%20of%20women%20in,gap%20was%2014%25%20for%20full-time%20employees%20in%202015.

[30] ACT on Equal Status and Equal Rights Irrespective of Gender. Government of Iceland. https://www.government.is/library/04-Legislation/Act%20on%20Equal%20Status%20and%20Equal%20Rights%20Irrespective%20of%20Gender.pdf

[31] "ACT on Equal Status and Equal Rights Irrespective of Gender. Chapter II Rights and Obligations." Government of Iceland.

https://www.government.is/library/04-Legislation/Act%20on%20Equal%20Status%20and%20Equal%20Rights%20Irrespective%20of%20

Gender.pdf.

[32] **Gender gap:** "Gender Gap: These are the world's most gender-equal countries." World Economic Forum. 2022. https://www.weforum.org/agenda/2022/07/gender-equal-countries-gender-gap/.

[33] "2024 Global Peace Index" Vision of Humanity. 2024. https://www.visionofhumanity.org/maps/#/

[34] **Safest place in the world to live:** "Safest Place in the World to Live" SurfSide. https://surfsidesafe.com/safest-place-in-the-world-to-live

[35] **Maternal Mortality:** "Maternal Mortality: Levels and Trends 2000 to 2017". World Health Organization. 2019. https://www.who.int/publications/i/item/9789241516488.

36 MoLSAMD, and UNICEF. "Child marriage in Afghanistan: Changing the narrative" UNICEF. 2018.
https://www.unicef.org/afghanistan/reports/child-marriage-afghanistan

[37] Fore, Henrietta. "Afghanistan: Girls at increasing risk of child marriage." United Nations. 2021.
https://news.un.org/en/story/2021/11/1105662.

[38] Moylan, Danielle. "Afghanistan is Failing to Help Abused Women." The South Asia Channel. 2015.
https://foreignpolicy.com/2015/05/01/afghanistan-is-failing-to-help-abused-women/.

[39] "Afghanistan: Girls Struggle for an Education
Insecurity, Government Inaction, and Donor Disengagement Reversing Vital Gains." Human Rights Watch. 2017. https://www.hrw.org/news/2017/10/17/afghanistan-girls-struggle-education.
https://www.bing.com/search?q=average%20temperature%20in%20afghanistan&qs=n&form=QBRE&=%25eManage%20Your%20Search%20History%25E&sp=-1&pq=average%20temperature%20in%20afghanistan&sc=3-33&sk=&cvid=774BECB1910D4F04B8164970DAEBA9BB&ghsh=0&ghacc=0&ghpl=

[40] **Afghanistan's climate can be harsh, with summer temperatures averaging between 28 and 32 degrees Celsius (84-90°F) and sometimes soaring to 43 degrees Celsius (109°F):** Webster, Lexi. "Afghanistan's Scorching Summers

[41] History Editors. "Enlightenment" History.com. Updated: 2020.
"https://www.history.com/topics/european-history/enlightenment

[42] **Power Distance:** Hofstede, Geert. *Cultures and Organizations – Sof-*

tware of the Mind. McGraw-Hill. Chapter 7. 2010.

Chapter 6

[43] Scholars across psychology, sociology, and anthropology have studied the concepts of collectivism and individualism. I have gathered insights from the following books and tailored them to my observations and experiences:

Hofstede, Geert. *Cultures and Organizations – Software of the Mind.* Pages 89-102. McGraw-Hill. 2010.

Triandis, Harry C. *Individualism and Collectivism.* Routledge; 1st edition. 2019.

Trompenaars, Fons. Hampden-Turner, Charles. *Riding the Waves of Culture: Understanding Diversity in Global Business.* Nicholas Brealey Publishing. 2020.

Hall, Edward T. The Dance of Life: *The Other Dimension of Time.* Knopf Doubleday Publishing Group. 1984.

[44] **Filial Piety:** Smith, Tyler. "Filial piety and Individualism: Cultural Differences in Parental Care." Williams. 2021. https://sites.williams. edu/chin427-springgrass/spring-2021/filial-piety-and-individualism-cultural-differences-in-parental-care/

Mack, Lauren. "Filial Piety: An Important Chinese Cultural Value." ThouhgtCo. 2019. https://www.thoughtco.com/filial-piety-in-chinese-688386.

[45] **"Every person who is not a minor has an obligation, to the extent that the person is capable of doing so, to maintain the person's parents and grandparents who need such maintenance because of age, physical or mental infirmity or disability.":** "Common Wealth of Dominica.". 2017.

https://dominicanewsonline.com/news/wp-content/uploads/2017/06/Maintenance-Act-2017-Revised-and-Final1.pdf.

[46] **2018 survey by Statista, around 6% of undergraduate students in the United States reported living with their parents:** Korhonen, Veera. "Living arrangements for undergraduate students in the U.S. in 2018". Statista. 2024.

https://www.statista.com/statistics/914589/us-college-living-arrangements-undergraduate-students/

[47] **70% of young adults in Croatia, Greece, Portugal, Serbia, and Italy live with their parents. In contrast, in Scandinavian countries such as Finland, Sweden, and Denmark, the percentage is much lower, with**

fewer than 20% of young adults living with their parents: Hatfield, Jenn. "Young adults in the U.S. are less likely than those in most of Europe to live in their parents' home." Pew Research Center. 2023. https://www.pewresearch.org/short-reads/2023/05/03/in-the-u-s-and-abroad-more-young-adults-are-living-with-their-parents/

"Young people living with their parents" Eurostat. 2018. https://ec.europa.eu/eurostat/web/products-eurostat-news/-/DDN-20181214-1

"In the US, that percentage is 32%, varying significantly between those with and without a college degree.": Vespa, Jonathan. " Jobs, Marriage and Kids Come Later in Life". United States Census Report. 2017. https://www.census.gov/library/stories/2017/08/young-adults.html

Fry, Richard. "Young adults in U.S. are much more likely than 50 years ago to be living in a multigenerational household." Pew Research Center. 2022. https://www.pewresearch.org/short-reads/2022/07/20/young-adults-in-u-s-are-much-more-likely-than-50-years-ago-to-be-living-in-a-multigeneratio-nal-household/

[48] 'Exploring the Rich Tapestry of Wedding Traditions in Different Cultures." The West Venue. 2023. https://www.thewestvenue.com/post/exploring-the-rich-tapestry-of-wed-ding-traditions-in-different-cultures

[49] Hofstede, Geert. Hofstede, Gert Jan. Minkov, Michael., *Cultures and Organizations. Software of the Mind.* Chapter 4. McGraw Hill. 3rd Edition, 2010.

[50] Lassen, Madison. "Human Connection in a Virtual World." Patterson Consulting Group. 2021. https://www.pattersonconsultinggroup.com/post/human-connection-in-a-virtual-world

Chapter 7

[51] Wobblehead in India: Cook, Sharell. The Indian Head Wobble or Shake: What Does It Mean?. Trip Savvy. 2022. https://www.tripsavvy.com/meaning-of-the-indian-head-shake-1539322

[52] Hall, Edward T. The Hidden Dimension. Chapter X. Distances in Man 113-125. Anchor; Edition Unstated. 1990.

[53] Kreuz, Roger & Roberts, Richard. "Proxemics 101: Understanding Personal Space Across Cultures." The MIT Press Reader. 2017. https://thereader.mitpress.mit.edu/understanding-personal-space-proxemics/

[54] "Personal Space by Country 2024". World Population Review, 2024.

https://worldpopulationreview.com/country-rankings/personal-space-by-country.

55 Personal Distance: "Personal Space by Country 2024." World Population Review, 2024. https://worldpopulationreview.com/country-rankings/personal-space-by-country
Miller, Christina. "Ranked: Countries with the most (and least) personal space, 2024". CEO World Magazine. 2024. https://ceoworld.biz/2024/02/02/ranked-countries-with-the-most-and-least-personal-space-2024/#google_vignette

56 Hall, Edward T. The Hidden Dimension. Chapter X. Distances in Man 113-125. Anchor; Edition Unstated. 1990.

57 Shiina, Minoru. "Understanding Japanese Social Norms: A Glimpse into Cultural Etiquette." Dorado Group. 2023. https://dorado-group.jp/blog/japanese-social-norms-a-window-into-cultural-etiquette

58 Pandey, Vaishali . " 15 Different Countries And How People Greet Each Other Around The World." Postoast. 2022. https://www.postoast.com/how-people-greet-each-other-around-the-world/
Diri, Berkir. "Beyond "Hello": Exploring Different Greetings Around the World." Atlas Localization. 2023. https://atlaslocalization.com/beyond-hello-exploring-different-greetings-around-the-world/

59 Keltner, Dacher. "Hands-On Research: The Science of Touch." Greater Good Magazine. Berkeley. 2010. https://greatergood.berkeley.edu/article/item/hands_on_research

60 Global Sustainable Development Goals. Take Action for the Sustainable Development Goals - United Nations Sustainable Development

Chapter 8
61 Global Citizen Rights. Universal Declaration of Human Rights | United Nations

Chapter 9
62 "International migration." United Nations. https://www.un.org/en/global-issues/migration?utm_source=chatgpt.com

[63] **Self-Discovery:** Adam, Hajo. Obodaru, Otilia. Lu, Jackson G. Maddux, William. Galinsky, Adam D.   Living abroad often leads to greater self-awareness and clarity about your values and goals. . Lu, William Maddux, and Adam D. Galinsky. "How Living Abroad Helps You Develop a Clearer Sense of Self." Harvard Business Review. 2018. https://hbr.org/2018/05/how-living-abroad-helps-you-develop-a-clearer-sense-of-self

[64] **Healthcare:** Several Sources:
"Countries with Universal Healthcare 2024." World Population Review. 2024.
https://worldpopulationreview.com/country-rankings/countries-with-universal-healthcare%5C
Cacace, Mirella. ResearchGate. https://www.researchgate.net/figure/1-Types-of-health-care-systems-with-respect-to-the-role-of-the-state_tbl1_4732027
"World Health Statistics 2024: Monitoring Health for the SDGs, Sustainable Development goals." World Health Organization. 2024. https://www.who.int/publications/i/item/9789240094703
Health care systems by country – Wikipedia. https://en.wikipedia.org/wiki/Health_care_systems_by_country
Vankar, Preeti. "Health and health systems ranking of countries worldwide in 2023, by health index score." Statista. 2023.
https://www.statista.com/statistics/1290168/health-index-of-countries-worldwide-by-health-index-score/.

[65] "Global Health Expenditure Database." World Health Organization. %GDP 2021.
https://apps.who.int/nha/database/country_profile/Index/en. 2021
"Countries with Universal Healthcare 2024" World Population Review. 2024.
https://worldpopulationreview.com/country-rankings/countries-with-universal-healthcare%5C

Chapter 10

[66] Oberg, Kalervo. *Practical Anthropology* (PDF). 1960.

[67] **Guilt, a moral emotion, arises when someone believes they have compromised their standards or violated moral norms, taking significant responsibility.** "*Guilt: Encyclopedia of Psychology*". Archived. 2008.
https://web.archive.org/web/20080502063427/ http:/www.enotes.com/ga-

le-psychology-encyclopedia/guilt
"In psychology, what is "guilt," and what are the stages of guilt development?." 2007: 'Let's begin with a working definition of guilt. Guilt is "an emotional state produced by thoughts that we have not lived up to our ideal self and could have done otherwise." 2017.

[68] **Guilt is both a cognitive and an emotional experience that occurs when a person realizes that he or she has violated a moral standard and is responsible for that violation. A guilty conscience results from thoughts that we have not lived up to our ideal self. "Guilt, Stages of Guilt Developme." JR Rank Psychology.**
https://psychology.jrank.org/pages/285/Guilt.html#ixzz8iEyGKYya

[69] **Emotional projection in psychology, where individuals attribute their unacceptable feelings or impulses to someone else to avoid confronting them. "Projection" Psychology Today.** https://www.psychologytoday.com/us/basics/projection

[70] Personal experiences and information for several sources:
"Everything You Need To Know About Expat Guilt." Expat Network.
https://expatnetwork.com/everything-you-need-to-know-about-expat-guilt/
"Guilt, Stages of Guilt Development." Psychology. JRank.
https://psychology.jrank.org/pages/285/Guilt.html#:~:text=An%20emotional%20state%20produced%20by%20thoughts%20that%20we,moral%20standard%20and%20is%20responsible%20for%20that%20violation.
"Projection. Psychology Today." Psychology Today. https://www.psychologytoday.com/us/basics/projection
Scott-Reid, Jessica. *Expat Guilt: When You Really 'Should' Go Home But Don't.* *The Wall Street Journal.* 2015. https://www.wsj.com/articles/BL-272B-1275
"Expat Guilt: Breaking Down This Common Phenomenon." ASI Movers.
https://www.asimovers.com/blog/articles-4/expat-guilt-breaking-down-this-common-phenomenon-83#:~:text=The%20expat%20guilt%20is%20protean%20and%20easily%20triggered,what%20an%20expat%20should%20and%20should%20not%20do.

[71] **Is this thought based on emotion or facts? What's the worst that could happen?:** Dr. Amen. Instagram Posts

[72] **"Guilt is a disguise for love."** -Mel Robbins. Watch this to never feel guilty again | Mel Robbins - YouTube

[73] Mel Robbins. "Watch this to never feel guilty again." YouTube. 2019. https://www.youtube.com/watch?v=Jh6EeA9d1ko

[74] **How to set boundaries and why it matters for your mental heal-**

th." UC Davids Health. 2024. https://health.ucdavis.edu/blog/cultivating-health/how-to-set-boundaries-and-why-it-matters-for-your-mental-health/2024/03

[75] How to set boundaries and why it matters for your mental health." UC Davids Health. 2024. https://health.ucdavis.edu/blog/cultivating-health/how-to-set-boundaries-and-why-it-matters-for-your-mental-health/2024/03

[76] Dr. Delony, John. "How to Set Boundaries 7 Simple Steps." Ramsey. 2024.

[77] **"5 Keys to Letting Go Recognizing pathological needs is hard, but it is the first step toward relief"** Brenner, Grant Hilary." "5 Keys to Letting Go. Phycology. 2020. https://www.psychologytoday.com/intl/blog/experimentations/202007/5-keys-to-letting-go?msockid=3ba2ef-50d6ab66872361fad3d7036720

Chapter 12

[78] Narang, Kapil. "The Essence of Collaboration: Ratan Tata's Wisdom on Walking Together." 2023.

[79] **"If the mountain will not come to Mohammed, Mohammed must go to the mountain"** Bacon, Francis "Essayes: Religious Meditations. Places of Perswasion and Disswasion. Seen and Allowed" chapter 12. 1597.

[80] I have drawn insights from the following books, adapted to my observations and experiences:
Carnegie, Dale. *How to Win Friends & Influence People (Revised)*. Simon & Schuster. 1936.
Lowndes, Leil. *How to Be a People Magnet : Finding Friends--and Lovers--and Keeping Them for Life.* 26-29. McGraw Hill; 1st edition. 2002.
Smith, Marcus. *How to Talk to Anyone: Master Small Talk, Improve your Social Skills, and Build Meaningful Relationships.*80-117. 2022. Lowndes, Leil. *How to Talk to Anyone: 92 Little Tricks for Big Success in Relationships.* 27-30, 204-207. McGraw Hill. 2003.

[81] Carnegie, Dale. *How to Win Friends & Influence People (Revised)*. Simon & Schuster. 1936.

Chapter 13

[82] **Spaced Repetition:** "Spaced Repetition System: Learn Vocabulary and Never Forget It! Fluent in 3 Months."
https://www.fluentin3months.com/spaced-repetition/
[83] Sagar-Fenton, Beth & McNeill, Lizzy. BBC. "How many words do you need to speak a language?." BBC. 2018.
https://www.bbc.com/news/world-44569277
[84] **Wanderlust:** "Wanderlust: The Psychology Behind Our Insatiable Desire to Travel." Neuro Launch. 2024.
https://neurolaunch.com/wanderlust-definition-psychology/
[85] *Zimmern, Andrew. Andrew Zimmern's Bizarre World of Food: Brains, Bugs, and Blood Sausage.* Ember. 2011.

Chapter 15

[86] **"Comparison is the thief of joy."** Roosevelt, Theodore. Powell, John. *Happiness Is an Inside Job, where he states.* 1989. "Comparison is the death of true self-contentment." The exact origin of the phrase remains unclear.
[87] Niebuhr, Reinhold. *Serenity Prayer.* 1930.
[88] Linehan, Marsha. *Building a Life Worth Living: A Memoir.* Random House. Chapter 28. 2021.
[89] Doran, George T. "There's a S.M.A.R.T. Way to Write Management's Goals and Objectives." 1981.
[90] Clear, James. *Atomic Habits.* 101-112. Penguin Random House. 2018.
[91] **"The purpose of a goal is not to achieve it but to become the person you grow into along the way.".** Robbins, Tony.
[92] **Staying True to Your Values:** I have drawn insights from the following books, adapted to my observations and experiences:
  Brown, Brene. *The Gifts of Imperfection: Let Go of Who You Think You're Supposed to Be and Embrace Who You Are.* Hazelden Publishing. 2010.
Covey, Stefen R. The 7 *Habits of Highly Effective People: Powerful Lessons in Personal Change.* Simon & Schuster. 1989.
Rogers, Carl. R. On *Becoming a Person: A Therapist's View of Psychotherapy.* Houghton Mifflin Harcourt. 1961.
Goleman, Daniel. *Emotional Intelligence: Why It Can Matter More Than IQ.* Bantam Books. 1995
Pink, Daniel. H. (2009). Drive: *The Surprising Truth About What Motivates*

Us. Riverhead Books. 2009.

[93] "True belonging doesn't require you to change who you are; it requires you to be who you are." Brown, Brené. *Braving the Wilderness.* Random House Trade Paperbacks; Reprint edition 2019.

ABOUT THE AUTHOR

Toyi Rodríguez is an intercultural consultant with extensive experience collaborating with *Fortune 500* companies and guiding families from over 28 nationalities through cultural transitions and navigating life abroad.

She is also a successful entrepreneur, an advocate for diversity and inclusion, and a passionate world traveler. Toyi has explored 47 countries across four continents, interacting with people from over 100 nationalities. Her firsthand experiences shape her mission to encourage people to celebrate authenticity while fostering respect and understanding for diverse cultures and perspectives, building bridges of empathy and connection worldwide.

ToyiRodriguez.com
@toyi.rodriguez

Global Citizen:
A Cultural and Transformative Journey
by Toyi Rodriguez

Format editor: Ariadna Fergadis
Picture by: Karina Roe

Contributor editors: William Johnson,
Francisco Olguin Uribe, María Castañeda,
Jorge Díaz Barajas